MY

MOURNING
YEAR

MY MOURNING YEAR

*A Memoir of Bereavement,
Discovery and Hope*

ANDREW MARSHALL

RedDoor

Published by RedDoor
www.reddoorpublishing.com

© 2017 Andrew Marshall

The right of Andrew Marshall to be identified as author of
this Work has been asserted by him in accordance with sections
77 and 78 of the Copyright, Designs and Patents Act 1988

ISBN 978-1-910453-31-5

A CIP catalogue record for this book is available
from the British Library

Cover design: Liron Gilenberg
www.ironicitalics.com

Typesetting: Tutis Innovative E-Solutions Pte. Ltd

Printed and bound by Nørhaven, Denmark

This book is dedicated to the memory of
Thom Hartwig

29 September 1953
to
9 March 1997

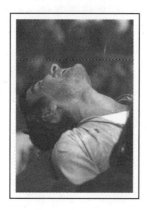

'The black bin bags piled up at the back door are not proof that my grief is settling, and I'm moving on, but testimony that he is gone for good.'

BEFORE

His name was Thom, he was thirty-six and I was thirty. He was German, I was English and we met on a beach in Spain. His English was patchy and I'd forgotten nearly all my schoolboy German, but from this unpromising beginning burst a relationship that spanned almost two hundred flights, one time zone, eighty-seven packing cases and seven and a half years.

Meeting Thom, loving Thom and losing Thom completely changed my life but to understand the journey, I need to start twelve months before we met…

Summer 1988: Settling into a New House

While the decorators were inside, I attacked the weeds in the front garden and swept dead leaves out of the garage. I remember being surprised by its emptiness. When I was a child, our garage housed not only my parents' cars but a bale of hay for the guinea pigs, our bikes, a canoe strung between two rafters, pallets of apples from the garden laid out for the winter, empty plant pots and my father's tools. This new garage had a cable run from the house and a lamp strung up across the back wall. The patterns of accumulated grime suggested a workbench. I swept the dust and the last of the leaves into the centre of the concrete floor and bagged everything up.

Even when I moved into the house, the garage remained bare. Just the car, a foot pump and a green plastic petrol can. Of course, I filled most of the house with furniture, books, my record collection and other accumulated flotsam, but I spent most of my time at work: a local radio station, twenty minutes up the road. There was always another book to read before I interviewed the author or music to be chosen for a Bank Holiday Special. When I finally got home, I'd throw a chop under the grill and watch TV. On Wednesday evenings, ironically, I worked as a relationship counsellor. At the weekend, a friend might come to stay or I'd take a walk across the fields. I had a fixed address but I didn't really belong there.

September 1989: Meeting Thom

It is amazing how one small turn can change the whole pattern of your life. I needed a holiday but couldn't decide where. One day, the guest on my radio show was Joan Le Mesurier – who was promoting her memoirs of life with her husband, *Dad's Army's* Sergeant Arthur Wilson, and her lover, comedian Tony Hancock. I still have the copy signed: 'To Andrew. Lovely talking to you. August 1989.' After the interview, we talked about her home in Sitges, Spain, famous for its beaches, film festival, historic buildings and cool courtyards. It sounded the perfect destination, but I expected nothing more than two weeks of sunshine. I was sort of seeing someone. I was happy with my life. It was just a holiday.

Sitges was particularly beautiful at the end of the season. The hazy autumn rays made the seventeenth-century seaside church of Sant Bartomeu look even pinker and the pots of geraniums on the balconies even redder. A long white stretch of sand was framed by palm trees, hotels and green distant hills. On the first day of the holiday, I chose a sunlounger, unpacked my towel, book and suncream, and took a sharp lungful of sea air. I pretended to stretch and take in the view but I was more interested in a short handsome man with twinkling eyes, a lazy moustache and a body that demonstrated the benefits of hours in the gym. By his side was a novel: *Die Geheimnisse von Pittsburgh* by Michael Chabon. My German was good enough to recognise the language and guess at the title. I'd read the book, *Mysteries of Pittsburgh*, in English the previous summer. We had something in common! I spent the morning trying not to watch him but we would occasionally exchange shy smiles.

Around midday people started to pack up and leave the beach for lunch, but I wasn't hungry – at least for food. The handsome man turned on to his back, shaded his eyes and looked out to sea.

I had learned a bit of German on a previous holiday in Spain. The most gorgeous men were German, so I'd persuaded one of them to teach me a chat-up line. 'Hello big boy' would sound stupid in English but I was willing to give it a try in a foreign language. I sauntered past my target's sunlounger, making certain that he was watching, and delivered my line:

'Wie geht's, mein kleiner Muskelprotz?'

He snorted with laughter. Fifteen minutes later, I decided to freshen my sun protection. There is a small area of the back, which is extremely difficult to reach yourself – at least that's my excuse. What I hoped was the seductiveness of Cleopatra bathing in asses' milk became the hopeless cavorting of a pantomime dame as I tried to cover this final spot. He should have shouted 'it's behind you' but instead I was rewarded with firm hands massaging my back, the hottest way possible of breaking the ice.

We introduced ourselves and I invited him for a cup of coffee at the beach café. The conversation soon moved on from basic autobiography and exchanging tourist tips. Breaking all the rules, I told Thom information that I had scarcely even confessed to myself: how I kept people at arm's length, my mother's forceful personality and how it made me fear anyone who got close would take over. As we toyed with our cups, I knew our romance would linger longer than the bitter Spanish coffee. Perhaps Thom deserved a look at my owner's manual.

'This conversation is getting too serious,' he said softly and touched the back of my hand.

Working out in the gym together, dancing in the discos, exploring Barcelona, everything – according to Thom – was *so great*. Finally, everything I'd learned about love from my counselling training as theory was making sense in practice. But, we couldn't be on holiday for ever.

Autumn 1989: Courtship

If I'd been truly honest with Thom, I'd have admitted in that first conversation that I had a weakness for holiday romances and had only just recovered from falling for a New Yorker. So I was tempted to refuse Thom my home address. However, my favourite song of 1989 was 'This Time I Know It's For Real', by Donna Summer. Thom's favourite was Sonia's number one: 'You'll Never Stop Me Loving You'. I still have the sheet torn out of a notebook with his address and telephone number on it. Thom kept not only all my letters, but every one of the flight tickets between his home town of Dortmund and Gatwick.

'I'm back home again and it's cold and rainy so that I spent my whole first day in bed sleeping and dreaming,' Thom wrote after that first holiday in Spain. *'It was very strange waking up this morning without you by my side. No you to cuddle up to, no armpits to lay my head into and nobody asking: "Wie geht's, mein kleiner Muskelprotz?"'* Thom had left Sitges before me. *'I really would*

have liked to give you a big hug and kiss you goodbye but I would never have been able to stop crying. And I promised myself not to. I did it anyway. That poor old man that was sitting in front of me in the train really was confused. Maybe he had never seen a man cry for so far.' He finished on an upbeat note. *'You are the first guy for a long time that I am curious about and who I would really like to see, hear, feel, smell and taste again.'*

Receiving that letter, I felt Thom had caught exactly the right mood. He certainly succeeded in blowing away the last of my reservations. I wrote back: *'The magic went out of Sitges after you left. The sun came out but it didn't lift my clouds. I wandered around and ended up in a chocolate shop and bought the most fattening thing I could find and tried to use chocolate to lift my mood.'* I still had another week's holiday. *'The next day I played Patsy Cline on the beach, she seemed to know how I felt. When I finally left Sitges by taxi, the sun was beginning to fall into the sea and a sad Spanish song was playing on the radio. It seemed like the end of a movie and I expected to roll the credits. Except this is real life and it's now up to us to write the next chapter.'* I was not as confident as Thom. *'I would love to see you again. I find it difficult to write down my thoughts, I hope I haven't said too much and I hope I have said enough.'*

After lots of phone calls and a few weeks, Thom decided it was time to visit me. Our first weekend together in England was a whirl of West End theatre, Bonfire Night parties and the London to Brighton Vintage Car Rally. Thom's next letter made his position clear: *'You really are the first guy in years who had such an impact on me, that I would like to continue what we have already started. Am I wrong when I say that you gave me the same impression and that we both quite feel the same? Sure, I'm anxious. Sure, distance makes it more difficult but as well means a chance, a chance that Mr "I'm afraid it could happen again" and Mr "I'm nobody to marry" could achieve something really great.'*

My passions were running so high that in my reply only the language of a romantic novelist seemed appropriate. I replied: *'There was something so poetical about the moment we were finally naked together and your bare skin touched mine for the first time. You felt so vulnerable in my arms and I felt so strong and protective towards you – while opening myself up more than I have in a long time. After leaving you at the airport I went to visit Elaine* [a friend] *it was something about not wanting to return to an empty house, a house that two hours before had been full of you. Although you left quite a few of your possessions behind, your Reebok joggers, skin cream and hairdryer…to paraphrase the words of the Patsy Cline song: "I've got these little things, Germany's got you."'*

Nobody wants to risk being the first to say the most dangerous three words in the English language. If the confession is met with horror, how do you take the sentiments back? It was not until freak spring storms caught Thom's plane as it tried to land at Gatwick and he was diverted to Brussels, that I plucked up enough courage. I anxiously scanned arrivals at Gatwick, but he was flying into Heathrow. Twelve hours after his original arrival time, we were finally reunited. Later, I wrote to him: *'I don't think that rational Andrew has experienced so many emotions in such a short amount of time. Fear that something had happened to you during your flight, worry about where you were, a feeling of stupidity that I hadn't been able to tell you earlier how I felt and then relief when you finally phoned. Next there was the rush of emotion as I finally told you I loved you. It's amazing how this wasn't as difficult as I imagined.'* At the end of the weekend, I took Thom to the airport. *'I drove home as if I was suspended in time, reliving that glorious moment at the airport when you hugged me and told me that you loved me – but then the joy turned to pain and with a wave you were gone.'*

Thom was headmaster of a school that taught German to *Gastarbeiter* (foreign workers) and people who had the right to

– 6 –

residency but could not speak the language. He could largely choose his hours and began taking long weekends in England. Radio Mercury where I worked was in Crawley close to Gatwick airport and once a month, I would finish my Friday lunchtime show and catch a plane to Germany. In between trips, Thom would leave German lessons on my answering machine:

'Imagine that it's morning and we're in bed together. You say: *"Machts du das Früstück oder ich?"* (Who's making breakfast?) I mumble something under the blanket and you say: *"OK. Ich gehe und mache das Früstück."* (OK, I'll get up and make breakfast.)'

March 1992: Talks About Moving to England

Our courtship moved slowly, with so much time apart, and it was not until my Grandmother's death that living together was firmly on the agenda. I wrote: *'Going to her deathbed made me think of our own mortality and although it sounds morbid it made me realise that I wanted you to be there when I die. The truth is I love you so much that I want to spend as much time with you as possible, sharing the burdens and joys of my life and the burdens and joys of yours. Snatched weekends, however pleasurable, are just not enough.'*

Plans are easy to make but harder to turn into reality. I took out a subscription to the *Times Educational Supplement* (TES) and ringed jobs in the language departments of nearby schools, but Thom was fed up with teaching. Perhaps he could follow his dream of becoming an interior designer in England. I had gone freelance; could I keep us both, and pay for his various German insurance policies, while he found his feet in the UK? We were both nervous about living with someone full-time and our love affair was working well. We met up every other weekend and talked for half an hour on the phone every evening. There was no need to hurry.

Spring 1995: Finally Living Together

Thom arrived with a removal lorry packed with furniture, pot plants and eighty-seven packing cases. He demoted a chest of drawers from the bedroom to the garage and filled it with all his uncle's carpentry tools. He also converted a dressing table into a work bench. From that moment onwards, there was no room for the car.

Living together proved easier and even better than we'd imagined. My parents were not particularly supportive, but my love for Thom and his love for me papered over any cracks that English middle-class politeness didn't fill. Anyway, we had lots of friends and were far too busy to care: throwing dinner parties, shouting questions to each other as we worked in adjoining offices, going to the cinema and having picnics on the beach. But however full you stuff your garage and your home with possessions, laughter and life you cannot insulate yourself completely from reality.

Six months after moving to the UK, Thom fell ill and had to be admitted to hospital. His plans to open an interior design business were put on hold, first temporarily and then indefinitely.

It doesn't seem possible…but after eighteen months of up-and-down health, Thom died on 9 March 1997. He was only forty-three.

March 2017: Going Public

Twenty years after Thom's death, I have given his tools to my neighbour, thrown away the German two prong plugs and I have cleared away the last of those eighty-seven packing cases from the garage. By all outward signs, I have moved on. So why do I feel the need to not only return to my diary but publish it?

My cousin's husband collapsed and died of a heart attack during a Saturday afternoon football match, leaving a widow and three boys under fourteen. I wanted to offer more than a letter of condolence and a brief hug at the funeral. One of my best friends lost his partner after a long illness. They had been together for twenty-seven years. I wanted to help beyond the usual invitations to the cinema or dinner. But how?

When I write about relationships, I can draw on my training and years of counselling couples. I have no qualifications to write about bereavement – beyond my personal experience. So I shared my diary with first my cousin and then my friend and later when another friend's father died, I gave it to her to read and after that a work colleague's wife died… The feedback from these readers was positive. It was comforting and validating to know they weren't the only ones unhinged by grief.

So I have edited out the worst examples of self-pity, and added more description and explanation where necessary, but basically it remains the same. To help keep track of my various friends and family members, there is a dramatis personae at the back of the book.

Andrew Marshall

PART ONE

Terminally Ill

Thursday 30 January 1997

Our GP agreed to call round. This was not a good sign. OK, when I was a kid and sick in bed with a bottle of Lucozade, a box of fruit gums and Mummy suggesting that I might like to listen to *Desert Island Discs*, the doctor would make house calls, take my temperature and say: 'Keep him warm and give him plenty of fluids.' Times might have changed and Thom's stomach might have swelled up but he is still fit enough to be in charge of the laundry, still fixing his own low-fat meals and still getting out of bed most days.

This morning, he put on tracksuit bottoms and a sweat shirt, and came down to the living room. Rather than lying down on the sofa, he opted for the Corbusier chaise longue – that he'd once given me for Christmas – as it was easier to roll on and off. He looked really bloated, like he was six months pregnant. I wondered if it was wind. Maybe that's what Thom thought. I had a quick look round, cleared away a couple of newspapers. The place looked presentable. The doorbell rang and I showed the doctor through but cannot fill in the next bit. I remember he did not take off his coat and I don't think Thom got up. It would have been too awkward. Did the doctor examine him? He must have done. His diagnosis was bleak.

– 10 –

'I'm afraid that you have only weeks to live.'

I waited for Thom to react. He didn't.

'Your liver has failed and the ascitic fluid has leaked into the abdominal cavity.' He tapped Thom's stomach. 'You can hear the fluid move.'

Thom appeared mildly interested. I was still trying to process the first statement. I had to concentrate.

'What's ascitic fluid?'

'A clear liquid.'

I felt like a first year medical student.

Dr Toynbee's eyes were sad. Thom's were unreadable. I can't understand why I didn't ask if there was any treatment. What about draining off the fluid? Could they give him a diuretic? The next bit is blank too. But I remember talking to Dr Toynbee in the hall. For some reason, I didn't want Thom to hear. Dr Toynbee was already making polite goodbye noises. I had questions. His hand was on the front door. It was now or never.

'When you say weeks, do you mean weeks adding up to months? After all, we've all just weeks to live…' I wanted to start running on the spot or fall to the ground and do twenty push-ups.

'About a month.'

'Will it hurt?'

'There are worse ways of going.'

'Will I be able to take care of him at home? He wants to stay here.'

Dr Toynbee looked at the track lighting in the hall.

I let him escape. There's only so much honesty I can swallow.

I found Thom in the kitchen. We must have exchanged a look but here again is another blank. Later, I remember him standing in the living room, by my grandmother's bureau, when he asked:

'So where would you like to take one last holiday?' He tried to make it a joke.

For a second, I imagined renting one of those weatherboarded cottages in Maine, New England – nothing between us and the North Atlantic beyond miles of sand dunes and reeds. I'd take long walks along the beach and Thom would learn to paint watercolours. However, I could also picture cylinders of oxygen on the veranda and bags of clear liquid that needed emptying and tubes everywhere.

I shrugged and Thom looked embarrassed. Who were we fooling?

'I suppose we'll have to tell people the truth,' I finally said.

'I want a second opinion.'

Suddenly, I could breathe again.

I had a magazine article to finish. So I escaped upstairs and closed my office door. Downstairs, Thom switched on the TV and had breakfast.

There is an abyss between us far greater than up stairs and down stairs. It opened up sometime towards the end of last summer, although it's hard to be precise because terminal illness creeps up on you. We'd driven out of Brighton on the cliff road, past Telscombe where last year Thom had spent his summer sabbatical – between finishing work in Germany and starting a business or finding a job in the UK. It was a beautiful day and we could have parked the car and climbed down the steps, negotiated the wall by the pumping station and trekked across the rocks to the gay beach. However, Thom would have been exhausted just by the stairs. We were a team, in this together, so I told him to drive on. But I think we both realised the difference: I could choose whether I went to the beach or not…but Thom had no choice.

So why didn't I go downstairs and talk about the doctor's diagnosis. Why didn't I ask: 'How do you feel about the news?'

Perhaps I dare not stretch out my hand, in case Thom pulls me down into the darkness too.

He might be going to die but I want to live.

Wednesday 4 February

Thom has phoned Herdecke hospital in Germany and asked to be admitted as soon as possible. While we wait for this second opinion, everything continues as normal. The bloating is not too bad and although Thom's spending longer in bed, he seems reasonably cheerful.

So far this week, I've been up to London to schedule more music for the bar at the Café de Paris and yesterday did an interview with BBC Radio Suffolk. I'm not certain where I found the energy. I saw my private counselling client, and fortunately she has decided that she does not need any more help. I wish I felt the same.

Thom's been talking to Walter (his best friend) on the phone in Germany. I'm telling nobody about the diagnosis until we know for sure. Last night, he banged on the bedroom floor. I was watching *Coronation Street*, so I went up reluctantly. I offered to read another story from *Winnie-the-Pooh* or perhaps we could discuss what I've started to think about as 'the situation'. Thom shook his head; he wanted me to sit with him.

I cannot just sit.

This morning, I caught the 8.40 train to London for my weekly recordings of *Agony* for the cable channel Live TV. The scenarios that the production assistant faxed were as outlandish as ever: 'My teacher says he'll give me good grades if I go out with him'; 'My girlfriend's pussy gets in the way of our loving' and 'My boyfriend wants me to dress up like Geri Haliwell from the Spice

Girls'. We had recorded two shows when the producer came striding on to the hot set:

'Nice outfit Andrew.' I was wearing an orange jacket and a saffron shirt. 'Except, can you stop recommending counselling all the time. It's so downbeat.'

'Right, Pearl,' I nodded enthusiastically. I might be on the bottom rung of show business, but I am determined to cling on. She gave the thumbs up sign and retreated back to her control box.

I turned round and looked up the set with its large sixties pop art heads of beautifully made-up girls with diamond-shaped tears rolling down perfect cheeks. It was my way of reminding myself that this show was all about appearances.

'Only three more,' said Kate. (Agony aunt to my agony uncle.)

I sat bolt upright on the red sofa, held my stomach in and hoped the lights did not shine off my bald spot.

Monday 10 February

I had lunch with my old boss at Radio Mercury on Friday. He has bought one local radio station and plans to build a network. I told him to keep me posted. In some parallel universe, it sounded like a good idea. I even attended a training day on Saturday at Relate on brief focus counselling. It seemed rather appropriate as I cannot think further than a couple of days ahead. Line dancing on Sunday evening, I took my mobile in case Thom needed me. Otherwise the weekend was full of blanks.

Thom's body is creaking under the strain. It's like watching him age with a finger on the fast forward button but I don't say anything. He has always been so body conscious.

There is some good news. They've finally got him a bed in Germany. But being selfish, I fear everything will be harder for me – away from my support systems and in a foreign language.

'Do you really think this is such a good idea?'

One look into his tired eyes and I capitulated and booked two tickets for Thursday. His German health insurance provides him with a private room. The alternative is the Royal Sussex County Hospital in Brighton where I once came across an elderly man left alone on a trolley in a dirty corridor.

So I phoned my mother and told her I won't be able to meet up with her, my sister and nephew and niece on Thursday to see the Tower of London and the Crown Jewels. I explained that Thom was ill again and that we were flying to Germany that lunchtime. I didn't explain how ill and she didn't ask any questions but that's normal; my family does not do difficult conversations.

To my eternal shame, I didn't come out until I was almost thirty. With nobody ever discussing anything personal, I never had to deal with 'are you seeing anybody?' or 'when are you going to bring home a nice young girl?' They must have suspected long before I came out, but it would have been embarrassing to ask and being both English and middle class my family goes to great lengths to avoid anything like that – thank you. The day after I finally 'confessed', I asked my mother how my father had reacted. Her reply was that they needed more time to talk. About six weeks later, I asked again – only to be told that two retired people were 'too busy'. She has never told me if they did talk and I have followed the unspoken family rules and let the topic drop.

I was equally evasive when Thom's mother phoned. He was asleep, so I followed his instructions and told her he was at the supermarket. I could tell she was suspicious but I hid behind my limited German vocabulary.

I understand his reluctance to worry her but his insistence on not dwelling on 'sickness and disease' shuts me out too. When Dr Toynbee sent a counsellor round to the house, Thom was charming but politely refused the offer to talk. Afterwards, I asked why.

'I can always talk to you.'

Except, two years after a life changing fight at Projekt Deutsch Lernen (German Language School where Thom was headmaster), I still didn't know what happened and why he decided to quit and come to England. I might be trained to ask questions – both as a journalist and a counsellor – but I can never pierce Thom's armour and trying just puts his back up. To paraphrase his favourite German saying about cooking:

'A man can taste everything, he just can't know everything.'

Wednesday 12 February

I had a meeting yesterday with a radio production company about the possibility of a programme from the Café de Paris and went back up to London today for Live TV. It seems impossible but it's all down here in my appointments diary.

I returned home with the latest from the outside world; Thom had the latest from the front line. The ascitic fluid has broken through his abdominal cavity, swelling his penis to what he called 'porn star proportions'. He had phoned the doctor who suggested trying to push the fluid back up again. Thom pulled back the bedclothes and I had a quick look at his penis. A very quick look. He had been partially successful. I felt helpless and hopeless.

I have been telling myself that I have to keep Thom's illness secret or potential employers will go elsewhere. To someone who is not likely to miss deadlines for magazine articles; to someone who is not going to cancel and disappear off to Germany. And then how will I pay for the plane tickets and keep up the mortgage? And would everyone knowing actually change anything? And what's so wrong with feeling blank?

Thursday 13 February

Thom's body was so swollen that the only trousers which fitted were a pair of dungarees and then only by leaving the buttons down the side undone. I lent him a pair of my shoes – two sizes bigger – and went outside to see to the car. I drove it a couple of times round the close to allow the heater to take the edge off the cold morning. When I returned, he'd packed a duffel bag with essentials for the journey, his CD Walkman and somehow had chosen just half a dozen CDs from his collection.

Wrapped inside his largest duffel coat, Thom looked both shorter than usual and younger. He climbed inside the car and, pleasantly surprised by the warmth, pulled down his hood. I felt a surge of pride that I might be bad at distended penises and I might have questioned going to Germany, but I'd got this right. I looked at my watch. It was later than I thought. It had taken longer to get Thom ready than I'd expected. My mind was full of calculations about how long it would take to get to the airport, park and check-in, so I didn't notice if he looked back as I drove off.

I stuck to the speed limit and tried to avoid the bumps in the road because even the slightest jerk etched pain across Thom's face. He tried to find a posture that cushioned the blows and I slowed down to a crawl. Did he have any regrets? What was he thinking? I don't know because he didn't say anything and I was busy micro-managing the journey from our arrival at the airport to boarding the plane.

Although I'd booked 'special assistance', I knew from bitter experience that it only starts after boarding formalities have completed. (Previously, I'd been forced to leave Thom at the entrance because there was nobody to greet him. When someone was eventually found he didn't have a wheelchair, he was not sure where he'd find one and check-in was about to close. Fortunately, Thom saved the day by volunteering to sit on a trolley and I pushed him to the check-in desk – with seconds to spare.) This time I'd borrowed a wheelchair from the Red Cross, so there would be no mistakes. For once, Thom arrived in good time with his dignity intact.

At the desk, he stood up, smiled at the check-in lady and handed over his passport. For one glorious moment, he was just another customer. But, of course, he had to sit back down again and be wheeled over to the special assistance lounge. I rushed back to the short stay car park – pushing the empty wheelchair in front of me. It took longer than expected to fold it into the boot and move the car to long-term car parking. Fearful of missing boarding, I sprinted from the courtesy bus drop-off point up the ramp and into the terminal. The adrenaline pumping. I rejoiced in my speed and moved up another notch. For a few moments, I was liberated from Thom's weary pace. The faster I ran, the lighter I felt until I reached that blissful moment of abandonment that top athletes talk about. My body no longer felt pain and I seemed to be floating down the corridor. Freedom. But all too soon, I was back. Thom was already sitting on one of those battery-operated cars that goes beep, beep. He looked so frail and vulnerable that I felt guilty I could still reach nirvana; guilty I was so powerless to change anything; guilty that my love could not save him.

I have never considered Gatwick airport exposed but the February winds were cutting. Waiting on the tarmac for the 'all clear' signal so that our buggy could approach the aircraft, Thom was shivering and trying to retreat further into his duffel coat. I asked the driver if he could reverse back under the terminal and give us some protection from the elements. How could he fail to notice Thom's suffering? I would have to be more vigilant.

There are three categories of disabled passenger: those who need assistance through the long corridors, those who need to be taken to the steps and finally those who have to be carried on board. Thom proudly walked up the eight steps, grateful that he had not sunk into the third category. However, his pride cost him dearly and he slumped grey, cold and exhausted into his seat. If there had been room, I am sure he would have curled up in the foetal position.

'Am I doing the right thing?' he asked.

It was warmer in the aircraft than on the tarmac but the staff had left the rear door open for deliveries and in preparation for the arrival of the other passengers.

'It's not too late to turn around,' I replied hopefully.

Thom shook his head. There was no alternative.

'You need to concentrate on the pleasure of sinking into bed in Germany,' I suggested. 'Imagine freshly starched linen. Focus on that, and you'll make it through the discomfort of the journey.'

He smiled. His resolve strengthened.

I asked the hostess for a coffee to warm Thom.

He squeezed my hand.

I looked away and opened my *Vanity Fair* at a spread about Cool Britannia and how London was swinging again. If I concentrated hard enough, I could still pretend that this was just a normal flight to Germany.

'Thank you. Fresh linen. It's a lovely thought,' Thom murmured.

The rest of the passengers arrived, giving us enquiring looks: how did you get here first? The doors were sealed and we left England behind.

I was worried about the next leg of our journey. We would have to change planes at Münster. In addition, the hospital would not be ready to admit Thom until the next day. I wondered whether my German would be up to making the necessary hotel arrangements. Fortunately, the transfer went smoothly. Special assistance was waiting at the steps of the plane and understood that sick and disabled people felt the cold. Whenever

Thom's energy flagged, he remembered our linen goal and found the energy to press on.

On arrival at Dortmund (Wickede) airport, I pushed Thom to the information desk and he slowly stood up and took charge. He negotiated a hotel and a room close to the lifts. I could only admire his resolve. I pushed him to the taxi rank, where he briefed the driver. He also dealt with the check-in staff at the hotel and I followed on behind. However, once in our hotel room, and linen heaven, Thom crumpled back into a small tired old man.

Friday 14 February – Germany

Despite being a four-star hotel, there was no room service. So I went down to the breakfast room and asked the staff to make up a tray. I returned with coffee and freshly baked bread, plus Thom's favourite: unsalted German butter. Everything was beautifully presented with silver pots, starched napkins and a small white vase with a single bloom. Thom had shaved and showered and was sitting at the table. I was thrilled to watch his face light up in wonder at the treasures I'd liberated from downstairs. He had often complained that nothing tasted as good as German bread, so each mouthful was pure pleasure.

I'd often wished that I'd ignored our financial worries and, while Thom's health still held up, booked plane tickets to the most exotic destinations in the world. Yet, even if I'd taken him everywhere from Antigua through to Zanzibar, I doubt that I could have matched the perfection of that breakfast. For fifteen minutes, we had not a care in the world. It might even have been better than flying over the Grand Canyon for his fortieth birthday or the ecstasy of making love. I suddenly remembered the date. Happy Valentine's Day, Thom.

Before Thom could be admitted to Gemeinschaft Krankenhaus Herdecke (hospital), he had to collect all the necessary paperwork from his doctor. Germans love their bureaucracy. With Thom not feeling strong enough to leave the taxi, I marched up the stairs clutching my *Collins Pocket German Dictionary*. At first, the receptionist looked blank. But once I made myself understood, everyone could not have been more helpful. I was touched by the genuine affection of the doctor and the nurses for Thom. The receptionist leaned out of the window and waved down to the taxi. The forms were signed and I was instructed to pass on everybody's wishes. I must remember to have the dictionary ready at all times.

At the hospital, I completed all the admission formalities on Thom's behalf and wheeled him on to his ward. Although I had visited Thom here when he'd been undergoing various tests and treatments, over the past year and a half, it was the first time I'd really seen the place through his eyes. Beside the nurses' station, there was a communal area where patients were encouraged to eat together, talk and play the boxed games stacked in the corner. We had arrived at lunchtime and the surrogate family were very welcoming. I was even asked to join them for something to eat.

The hospital practises anthroposophical medicine – quite popular in Switzerland and Germany but almost unknown in the UK. Rudolph Steiner, the father of Anthroposophy, is best known here for his schools and for Eurythmics – not just an eighties pop band with Annie Lennox and Dave Stewart but a system of body movements designed by Steiner. Anthroposophical medicine considers itself an extension of orthodox medical practice rather than an alternative. It does not see illness merely as an unfortunate accident or mechanical breakdown but intimately connected to the whole person and an opportunity to get the mind and body back in balance.

While we ate, Thom supplemented my meagre knowledge of anthroposophical medicine with all sorts of fascinating titbits;

for example, the nurse whose husband creates anthroposophical kitchens. Apparently there are no corners in these kitchens, because corners trap energy! Although sniggering at some of these ideas, I was very impressed by the hospital's atmosphere. In the corridors were showcases full of interesting rocks and minerals and paintings and sculptures from the art therapy classes contributed to a homely feel. Vases of flowers were lovingly arranged around the communal areas and there was a balcony where patients could take the air and look at the mountains. Time and thought had been given to feeding the soul as well as healing the body. I finally began to understand why Thom wanted to return.

Once lunch was over, a nurse showed Thom into room 44c. The walls had been rag-rolled in pale blue paint, which reminded me of an upmarket Soho coffee shop. To further the illusion, there were easy chairs and by the window, which overlooked the gardens, a small table and a hard chair. Thom unpacked his overnight bag into a generous wardrobe and put his CD Walkman on a bedside cabinet. I walked round the room – no corners! I opened the fridge; examined the private shower/toilet and looked at a reproduction of a bland inoffensive impressionist painting hanging on the wall. No television. Anthroposophical medicine believes patients are better contemplating good health in silence.

Thom climbed into bed and within half an hour fell asleep. He felt safe, so I put down my book and wandered down to the lobby and my favourite facility – the coffee shop. While most hospitals I know have a small refreshment stand, run by volunteers, which sells instant coffee and maybe an iced bun, the Gemeinshaft Krankenhaus Herdecke offers freshly ground coffee and fifteen different cakes and pastries.

On previous stays I would wheel Thom down for a moment of normality. A cup of black filter coffee can divide up the long afternoon and provide a rhythm to a day otherwise measured by the doctor's rounds, watching, waiting – and more waiting. On this occasion, rather than sit alone watching the water sculpture in the foyer, I decided to take my coffee and chocolate cake up to Thom's room on a tray. He had woken up.

'Would you like some *kaffe* and *kuchen* too,' I asked.

He waved his hand away.

I sat down by the bed and slid my fork through the perfectly moist cake, delighting in how the chocolate crumbled.

'Could you sit over by the window, darling? The smell of coffee is turning my stomach.'

I picked up my bounty and retreated.

'I think it would be better in future if you didn't bring that up here,' he whispered.

A coffee had been the first thing we had shared together in Spain. Thom's first present was a cafetiere, after being appalled that I only served instant. Our home now boasts one filter and one espresso machine, plus two cafetieres. Coffee can no longer be a shared daily ritual; it will have to be my secret vice.

The doctor arrived to examine Thom and as the ascitic fluid had flooded his penis again, planned to make a small incision and drain it off. He returned with a scalpel. I knew that Thom wanted me to stay but I couldn't bear to watch. I sat outside the room, contemplating what a crap partner I had turned out to be.

Monday 17 February – Germany

After Thom's consultation with the doctor, he was in a much brighter mood.

'They think they can give me six months.' He beamed.

'That's wonderful.' Up to that moment, I hadn't realised I had been living holding my breath. Six months felt like for ever. Almost immediately, a small nagging voice inside asked: 'But at what cost?' I pushed it down and smiled.

Although Thom's health has stabilised, mine has taken a turn for the worse. Perhaps it is the relief of handing him over to the care of others, but I have relaxed my body's defences enough to let in the most aggressive cold with terrible coughing fits. Last night, I hardly slept for coughing up huge wads of phlegm. The looks from my hostess at breakfast suggested that she had heard every convulsion. At the hospital, I did my best to hide my illness but Thom, worried about catching germs, banished me back to England. I have more editions of *Agony* to record, so decided to bow to his wishes and recover at home.

Before heading to the airport, I trudged down the street to the chemist's for effervescent vitamin C tablets. I felt exhausted and unreachable:

'But what right have you to be miserable? Your problems are nothing in comparison with Thom's!' I told myself.

Struggling with my inner demons, I forgot to look in the right direction crossing the road, and was almost knocked over by a car. The driver honked, and dazed, I jumped back on to the pavement. What if I'd been killed and it was Thom rather than me who had to attend a funeral? I have to be more careful. I am just skin and bones and flesh.

Thursday 20 February

Back in Sussex, everything says, 'Thom': the light in the shape of a half-heart, the white square lamp that when switched on reveals a salamander climbing inside, the Bauhaus chair and the shallow black matte shoe cupboards that house his CD collection. Beyond the pile of unopened mail, there is nothing to suggest that I've been away or that anything has changed.

I drifted through daily events but my imagination skulked the corridors of Herdecke hospital. Previously when Thom was in hospital, I would call his bedside phone several times a day. But this lifeline has become a curse. I seldom get an answer and when I do – the tiniest voice whispers: 'Can you call back later, I'm sleeping.'

Before Thom moved to England, half our courtship was conducted on the telephone. Sometimes it even seemed easier to gossip with the receiver to our ears rather than face to face. But now Thom sounds like he has slipped into another dimension. I long to hold him in my arms, but there is not much chance of that. Even if I did defy him and returned to Germany, he would no longer snuggle into my armpit as any contact hurts his bloated body. All he will allow me is stroking the back of his hands. The no-go zones are increasing. I feel that I am losing him, inch by inch.

Emotional sightseers have become another burden. They feel they have the right to intrude, to know all the details and 'share' in our pain. They compose their face into what they imagine is a caring expression, but I know that they have children to pick up, aquariums to clean out and normal lives to lead. 'How's things?' they ask.

Yesterday, I bumped into such a friend in the supermarket. She was so sympathetic and supportive that I could feel the emotions building up inside me; if I didn't escape I'd be standing by the cold meats counter with tears streaming down my face. I smiled weakly, made my excuses and headed towards the check out. Keeping my emotions under control takes up so much energy, energy that I need to support Thom and to keep going through a million household tasks. In the end I felt angry rather than grateful for her concern. Anyway we have so many problems, how could anybody possibly help us?

Unable to deal with further enquiries about Thom's health, I phoned our friend Maureen (who works on the switchboard at Radio Mercury). Could she be my central contact point? We agreed that I will provide regular health bulletins and anyone interested could call her. It will be especially useful when I return to Germany as I have neither the one mark coins nor the desire to make many calls – and Thom's parents must be my number one priority.

Later, I went up to the village to buy the things that I'd forgotten in the supermarket. Valerie, my next-door neighbour, called out. I felt rude giving out Maureen's number – especially as Valerie has been very supportive and sent 'get well' cards over to Germany, but at least I made it back inside in one piece.

Friday 21 February

While I have been behaving like a hedgehog in a ball, Thom is harder than ever to reach. When we hadn't spoken for twenty-four hours, in despair, I called my friend Nancy Roberts, a radio agony aunt. She had some blindingly obvious advice:

'If you're so worried, speak to his doctors.'

Why didn't I think of that? Connecting with the sane part of my personality is becoming increasingly difficult. Thank goodness for friends! Nancy offered her husband, who is German, if I felt my vocabulary was not up to the task. Reassured by having something to do, I phoned the nurses' station and booked a conversation with Thom's doctor.

Unfortunately, the news was far from reassuring. Thom has not responded well to the treatment and the doctor doubted Thom would make it to Thursday and our planned reunion. I was ready to start calling all the airlines but the doctor told me that I was overreacting. We should speak again after the weekend.

Monday 24 February

I am living under water. I can glimpse normal life carrying on above me but all I can do is watch the waves of despondency.

Depression is woven into every fibre of my body. My cold has got worse, my sleep even more interrupted and everything is an effort.

After a long weekend, I was almost trembling as I punched in the numbers for the hospital. My breath came as short spurts while I waited for the doctor to be fetched.

'Nothing to worry about. Come on Thursday as planned.'

Wednesday 26 February

Back up to Canary Wharf so I could record five more editions of *Agony*. The platform at London Bridge underground station was packed and I had to fight to get on a train to Bank. There was something comforting about the anonymity of a crowd, all the bodies pressing against yours. None of them knowing anything about you. Nobody wanting to know anything.

Later Patricia, the hostess of *Agony*, asked:

'How's Thom?'

'I know this sounds strange but you can get the latest by phoning…'

Startled, she replied: 'Never mind, I wasn't really interested. Just asking to be polite!'

Thursday 27 February – Germany

My anxiety levels reached fever pitch as my plane touched down; the closer to the hospital, the more vivid my imagination about the state of Thom's health.

Herdecke is an awkward trip by public transport from Dortmund, where I have been staying with friends. Needing maximum flexibility and minimum stress, I asked my travel agent to pre-book a hire car at the airport. I have to confess that

I was nervous about driving on the right-hand side of the road, partly because Thom had always driven in Germany and partly because my brain can slip into autopilot in cars. (I have suddenly found myself several miles further down the A23 in Sussex than I expected, with no memory of driving there.)

Unfortunately, there had been a mix-up and Hertz produced a manual car – despite very clear instructions that I needed an automatic. I was under enough pressure without adding a gear stick, so I refused it. None of the other airport car-hire companies had an automatic. I went back to Hertz. Their best offer was to return tomorrow. The assistant explained that the problem had been spotted this morning but five hours later nothing had been done. Her explanation did not help. Where was a senior staff member so I could make an official complaint? No idea. It was amazing how many angry German words I knew. The assistant looked down at her paperwork. The steam started building behind by ears, my face turning puce. What had Thom done to deserve being so ill? Why was this happening to us? Frustration coursed through my veins; bile replaced my blood. The car-hire receptionist's professional politeness was slipping; the volume on my anger turned up another notch. I pictured myself leaning over that counter, grabbing her by the throat and spitting in her eye. It would have felt so sweet, so cathartic. Startled by the force of my anger, I tried to mentally step back. Who was this monster waving the keys to a manual car? Fortunately, I managed to rein myself in – and narrowly avoid arrest – by stomping off to the taxi rank. They can put a man on the moon but they cannot put me into an automatic car!

Arriving at the hospital exhausted by travel, worry and anger, I discovered one final barrier to my reunion with Thom: a notice, in German, pinned to the door of his room. I thought it instructed visitors to report to the nurses' station before entering, but had I translated it correctly? For once there was no nurse around, so I spoke to an orderly who told me to wait while he fetched the chief nurse. I sat outside Thom's room on a soft chair while hard thoughts raced through my mind: had Thom died and the notice was there to prevent visitors walking in on a corpse?

Rather than hyperventilating, I started pacing the corridor until the nurse finally arrived. Thankfully her face was not composed into the 'solemn but comforting' expression medical staff reserve for bad news. Relief flooded through me.

She explained that the notice was to ensure everybody washed their hands in a special liquid to avoid spreading bacteria into Thom's room. In his private bathroom, I found a dispenser of thick red gel. After washing and drying my hands on paper towels, I walked out of the bathroom and into Thom's room. His greeting was so simple but so pure:

'Hello,' his grey face tried to look animated but it was as if he had run out of smiles.

I pulled up a chair and tried to tell him about my terrible journey and the conversation with the doctor, but all my pent-up emotions came rolling out as tears. I sobbed into his bedclothes. Thom stroked my hair:

'You don't have to be brave for me, it's all right to cry,' he told me.

I marvelled at how even at this stage he could be so unselfish. What right do I have to weep? He was still looking after me even now. How will I ever cope without him?

'Go on – cry some more,' Thom added. 'I no longer seem to be able to, but don't let that stop you.'

Perhaps as we reach the end of our life, first we lose the ability to run, skip and jump; then to walk unaided; finally all our emotions wear down to nothing as we retreat back into ourselves. I prayed Thom had lost the capacity to be afraid. While we were being so candid, I longed to ask him. But I didn't.

Imminent death doesn't change us, Thom remains forever private. I knew that any questions would only be greeted with an exasperated shrug and eyes shooting up to the ceiling. So I sat quietly at his beside. Half an hour later, my patience was rewarded:

'I'm not frightened of dying,' he confessed.

I have to be grateful for that, because I am.

Friday 28 February – Germany

Returning the next morning, I was jealous of how the nurses effortlessly moved Thom, without hurting his swollen stomach, and coped with all the squeamish side of his decay. I might pretend to have come a long way in the past thirty years. But it's just a small step from being a child – watching *Dr Who* through my fingers – to being a man who looks away while the sores on my lover's arse are bathed. Despite all my best efforts I remain stubbornly the same. The nursing staff glide quietly and economically round, instinctively knowing his requirements, while I clutter the room with newspapers, books and CDs – an endless source of annoyance and a trial for Thom's dwindling resources. All his life force is focused on feeling comfortable. While I'm too clumsy for anything more than checking whether his bedcover is tucked under his chin. Even these attempts at helping are exhausting him:

'Would you like your back rest position changed?' I'd ask.

'Just give me a break for a few seconds.'

Thom's command of English has started to slip. Feelings and words are things he no longer needs, but they remain my only hope of connecting. On Thom's bedside table, there was a pen and notepad. It would be better to scribble a million rhetorical thoughts than keep asking one more overanxious, too ready to please question. I picked up the pad and wrote:

For the first time in our relationship, I feel on the outside looking in.

I turned over the page and ran the tips of my fingers across the bumps raised by pressing too hard. It was comforting. I looked over at Thom, he had fallen asleep again. His bedcover had slipped down again and I gently pulled it under his chin. I kissed his forehead. I looked back over all my words. They felt cleansing.

My ambition has always been to move from cable to mainstream TV. My newspaper and magazine articles are simply a means to an end: profile and money. Yet suddenly I have this need, this compulsion to write. I even took the notebook with me when I left Thom's room. Instead of reading a book over lunch, I started to write:

I enjoy lunch in the staff canteen: schnitzel with bacon, pineapple and melted cheese, along with cauliflower and a perfect sauce. All around me, nurses and other medical staff are joking and gossiping. When I've finished eating, it seems strange to dig into my pocket for money. I stare at the coins in my hand as if they are from an alien world – they have no value upstairs in Thom's sickroom.

Later, I write still more:

Back on the ward, life is very different. Thom has managed just a few bites of his meal, which he struggled out of bed to eat at the table in the corner of his room. His reward is spewing up gallons of green liquid, like a scene from the movie The Exorcist *– only far more frightening because this is real life. I try to cover my fear with a quip: 'Linda Blair eat your heart out,' but neither of us laugh. Somehow I know he's thinking the same thoughts as me – we both fear this will be his last meal. He's already lost control of his bowels and now suffers the indignity of rubber pants. He has been transformed from a handsome athlete to an old man with an aching body, from in-line skater to nappies lining his underwear. Now something that we all take for granted – digesting food – is denied.*

A few hours later, Thom beckoned. I leaned forward and he whispered into my ear:

'If anybody had told me the hardest part of living was dying...' The effort to finish the sentence was too much. Like many long-term couples, I could complete it: 'I wouldn't have believed them.'

He nodded.

When the sun dropped below the mountains outside the hospital, I asked if I could have the light on. Thom knew that it was to read and made a tired gesture of resignation. He particularly hated the tall standard lamp by the bed because the shade, made out of beige carpet, offended against his sense of style. My defence mechanism delved into a book by Terry McMillan (*How Stella Got Her Groove Back*) finding love with a twenty-year-old Jamaican boy rather than my terrible present – losing it with a forty-something man in Germany.

I read a couple of pages but every time I looked up the walls seemed to move an inch closer; the last hour of winter sunshine was now only an impression on drawn curtains. I opened a packet of salty pretzels. Thom and I had words about the noise I made eating them: this was another example of my selfishness. I felt chastised and ashamed. Far too much energy has been going into tracking down doors in my pain, fumbling in the blackness for a secret button, a hidden passageway and escape into a bright airy world where Thom wasn't dying. I should have been cherishing every moment together and storing up the feelings of love for the empty days ahead.

I sat watching Thom, scribbling in my notepad, hoping that he will wake up again and I won't have to live with our last words being the petulant bickering of a long married couple:

There is a symmetry to all long-term relationships, at the beginning and the end you find yourself tiptoeing round any conflict. When you first meet you are afraid to have cross words in case the argument heralds the end. Now I fear the end will be an argument.

His eyes opened:

'I love you, darling.'

'I love you more than you love me,' I replied and he managed a shadow of a smile at our long-standing private joke. This shared history will always be stronger than the kind professionalism of the nurses. I wrote on my pad:

Am I being jealous to divert myself from the immense loss?

Saturday 1 March – Germany

I'd left Thom's room for another coughing fit. On my return, I washed my hands in the red gel in his bathroom. Even though I doused my hands in eau de cologne, the smell of stale soap lingered.

I found Thom's favourite nurse, Martina, sitting on his bed. He was chatting away happily and making no attempt to move her. I have been banned from even perching there – in case I pass on germs. I couldn't have been angrier if they had been making wild passionate love. Of course, I didn't say anything. I just picked up my book in a way that hopefully made my displeasure clear.

After she had gone, I told Thom:

'She doesn't like me.'

'She doesn't think you realise how serious the situation is,' he said.

I wanted to reply 'Don't you think I've done my best to shut it out', or maybe kiss him, only lightly on the lips, but that's been banned too. So I just smiled and patted his hand instead.

Thom settled down for a nap and the missing kiss hung in the air.

I remembered the first morning after Thom moved to England, he had just stepped out of the shower. I needed to brush my teeth and he was towelling himself down. The mirror was all steamed up. I reached round him – the bathroom was too small for two people – our bodies touched accidentally, on purpose.

'I'd like to kiss you, but I've just washed my hair.' Thom did his impersonation of Bette Davis in *The Cabin in the Cotton*.

He smelt fresh and clean, and he did kiss me.

Next, I pictured Thom on our first full holiday together. We'd brought along his friend Heidi and returned to Sitges. For some reason, he'd borrowed her underwear for a photo shoot in our bedroom. We were all laughing. I clicked away and Thom posed. He looked surprisingly vulnerable, despite his velvety muscles, in a lacy black bra and panties. Afterwards, Heidi fixed spaghetti puttanesca on the apartment stove. We found a tablecloth for the kitchen table in the cupboard. I opened a second bottle of red wine, we drank to each other's health and Thom kissed me. He tasted of garlic.

That night, my heart pumping, I took Thom back to the same beach where we'd met nine months previously. The sunloungers looked ghostly white in the starlight.

'Will you be with me…?' I wanted to say 'for ever', but that sounded too long, too intimidating. I was standing behind him; my arms around his shoulders. He snuggled against me for warmth and protection from the blackness.

'I want us to belong together.' I didn't have the words and the law didn't allow us anything beyond a private arrangement.

Thom turned and looked up at me:

'We'll promise on the moon and the stars that we'll be together for…twenty-five years,' he said.

I held him tighter.

'On that anniversary, we'll get roaringly drunk and decide what comes next.'

I kissed him and he tasted of hope and the promise of all those years together.

When I brought my focus back to the hospital, the memories of Thom seemed more real than the motionless shape in the bed in front of me. I read silently for a while before Thom's father Erwin arrived. He had been to visit Thom's mother Ursula who, by a strange coincidence, was undergoing treatment for a degenerative bone condition in a nearby hospital. Erwin is a proud self-reliant man of almost eighty years old and so like his son. I will never see Thom reach this age and I thought: 'Yes, I would still have fancied him as an octogenarian.' But this comforting thought was soon replaced by the awareness that Thom and his father could have been brothers. Illness had aged Thom at such a rate that Erwin Hartwig could now be Thom's older brother, almost forty years age difference winnowed down to forty months.

I slept at the hospital that night. Martina arranged for an extra bed to be wheeled into Thom's room. So I only left to return to our friend's apartment for a shower and to change clothes. Twenty-two hours out of twenty-four spent in hospital but then time stands still in a sickroom. In the waiting, you can live for ever.

Tuesday 4 March – Germany

I was only thinking of myself when I decided to return home to England. My excuse was my television programme – other people were counting on me. I didn't even fool myself. I needed to breathe some fresh air and the prospect of speaking English again was very appealing! After five days in Germany, constantly adapting to the demands of dying, I was increasingly aware of my own mortality – as if death were catching. My hacking cough was worse, my left eye had developed a nervous twitch. I had diarrhoea. Even crunching Imodium tablets only slowed it down. Either I had psychic bowels or my body was telling me something my brain chose to ignore; poised somewhere between hope and denial, my bowels were telling me to let go.

I quote from my notepad:

Death is not a spectator sport. OK I want to be there as another experience – which makes it sound like a trip to Euro Disney. I would like to witness the spirit leaving the body and the sky opening to reveal St Peter and the heavenly choir – the full renaissance painting. But all I can do is watch, I feel unable to offer any succour to the man I love – there can be no more succinct definition of helplessness.

Before I flew back to England, I arranged for a new private number on the telephone beside Thom's bed. Thom was detaching himself from friends with their selfish requests to go on living. He was trying to find enough energy to die.

On the plane, there were complementary copies of *The Independent* newspaper. They had published my article giving advice on 'Illness Etiquette'. I sounded so knowledgeable, so together and such a fraud.

Wednesday 5 March

Back home, I had one day without sickness and disease. With full make-up for the bright lights of a television studio, I looked reasonably normal. However my make-up girl, worried about the poor condition of my skin, asked if anything was the matter. I might have replied truthfully but a researcher barged in:

'You live in the country, don't you Andrew?'

'I suppose Hurstpierpoint is the countryside.'

'Do you know any farms where we could film *Topless Darts*?'

In the evening, Thom phoned. His parents had finally asked to see his doctor. Thom had shielded them for so long, it was hard to stop pretending. His mother's excitement whenever he managed a few mouthfuls of broccoli was increasingly hard to bear. So Thom asked me to call his parents and find out what the doctor told them and how they received the news. It was a bizarre conversation – once again in German – because Ursula, Thom's mother, jumped to the wrong conclusion and thought I was in the dark too.

I called Thom to report back. The doctor had confirmed what their hearts and eyes must have already told them. However, I was able to reassure him that his brother, Jürgen, had already started to support them. How will Erwin and Ursula ever cope with the knowledge that they will outlive their youngest son?

Thursday 6 March

While I was packing to return to Germany, the phone rang. It was Thom.

'Hi, how are you? I'm looking forward to seeing you,' I told him. 'I should arrive about five. I've double-checked the car this time. The only automatic is a BMW. So I'll be arriving in style.'

'Could you clear all the papers off my desk and bring them with you?'

'Anything else?'

'Bye.'

With not a single word more than was necessary, he was gone.

When I arrived at Herdecke, I tried to interest Thom in all the latest trivia from home: both the washing and drying machine had broken down that morning. I thought it might have been a blown fuse or even a wiring problem in the utility room. What did Thom think?

In happier times he would have enjoyed getting out his toolbox and sorting out the problem. Instead, he shrugged:

'You'll find someone else to fix them.'

Thom seemed calmer. Before when he complained about not wanting to go on living there was an energy, a restless impatience in his voice.

'As requested, I cleared your desk at home this morning.'

Thom pointed to the small table by the window. There would have been a pleasant view but the curtains were drawn.

Later Walter, his best friend, arrived and sorted through the mound of letters, muttering. He had volunteered to unravel Thom's complicated financial affairs, but previously Thom had been too proud. The three of us chatted while Walter opened unpaid bills; another mortal problem surrendered to someone else. The atmosphere was very peaceful: Walter smoothing out the folded papers; Thom alert and full of jokes; while I was pleased to enjoy a moment of semi-normality.

Afterwards, Walter and I went to find somewhere to eat in the town but I can remember neither the food nor our conversation. Later, when I returned to the hospital, Thom and I talked about our future together. It is impossible to believe our love could ever end. I was almost too embarrassed to share my thoughts. They sounded like those of a small child:

'I believe that you're going to be my Guardian angel,' I told him, 'your body has worn out but soon you'll be free to watch over me – not held back by sickness and disease.'

'You'll need someone to take care of you,' he replied, 'that way we can be together for ever.' He seemed pleased that our love could survive. 'Let me die,' he said quietly.

'You're free to go.'

'You're the best man I ever knew.'

'Have I ever told you what beautiful eyelashes you have?' I replied. 'Strong and ever so long. I'd never noticed before.'

Thom squeezed my hand and let me lean over and kiss him on the cheek; it was strangely warm, not so waxy and more alive.

Friday 7 March – Germany

After my first decent night's sleep in ages, at our friend Martin's flat in Dortmund, I returned just in time for the doctor's daily rounds. A nurse tried to move Thom into a chair but he kept slumping face down. I helped her make him comfortable in bed again.

The doctor's visit was a farce:

'It's time you decide where you want to live. Germany or England?' he told Thom. 'Travelling backwards and forwards is not good for you.'

Thom said nothing, just another shrug.

I'd been beamed down to a parallel universe! Did the doctor not have eyes in his head? I was no expert, but I knew that Thom had just one destination and it was neither Germany nor England.

The doctor bustled out, full of his own importance, but I could tell the nurse wanted to talk. I followed her out in the corridor.

'You have to prepare yourself for the end,' she quietly explained.

At a time like this, men know what they are supposed to do – and English middle-class men in particular: we swallow hard, thank the staff for all their hard work and find something practical to do. Not just a stiff upper lip, but a whole body rigid with suppression. But I needed help and I needed it now.

'Can you hold me, I need to be held,' I told the slightly startled nurse.

She opened her arms. I clasped her tightly to me and cried and cried and cried. I had hardly talked to this woman, just nodded as we passed on the corridor and three weeks earlier did not have even that acquaintance.

I must have been about nine, the last time I cried in public. Of course, Thom and I had cried together once or twice during his illness, but in my defence exceptional circumstances gave me 'a get out of jail free' card. We had shared so much together, why not a few tears? No, this moment with the nurse was entirely different, I had crossed two taboos at once – I had asked for help *and* cried in public. And I didn't care any more!

Not surprisingly, the nurse started crying too. She broke away and escaped to the nurses' station but I felt much stronger. I was ready to make the necessary telephone calls to Thom's father, brother and Walter – the small circle that Thom still wanted to see. They agreed to change their plans and come to the hospital. Returning from the public phone kiosk, I was stopped by the nurse who was rather ashamed that her professional distance had been compromised. I thanked her and told her not to worry.

Back at the bedside, Thom had his eyes closed. Sleeping or unconscious? I was angry with fate for bringing him so low and still offering no release. I picked up my notebook:

I gently stroked the back of his wrist. Waxy skin stretched over luminescent bones, he felt only half alive under my fingertips. I could sense the rotting beneath. Thom no longer has control over his bowels, seldom eats anything and even apple fruit juice is too acidic for his stomach. Is it a miracle and a curse that the human body can put up with so much and still function?

The last threads attaching Thom to the world were microscopic but strong – bonds of cotton rather than iron girders tying him down. I imagined him floating above the bed. I longed to grab on to his heels; pull him back to earth; gather him in my arms and soothe all his problems away. But what right did I have to cling on when all he wanted was to leave? I just stroked his wrist again with every ounce of love in my body.

On one of my more frequent visits to the toilet, to cough without worrying Thom, I found Erwin, Thom's father, sitting alone in the corridor.

'Why are you waiting outside?' I asked in German.

'I thought it better not to disturb you.'

The world was ending but we were tiptoeing round for fear of upsetting each other.

I brought Erwin back into room 44c.

'Hello,' said Thom quietly.

'Hello,' replied his father. Having fought in France, during the Second World War, he must have seen more than his fair share of death but he remained extremely uncomfortable.

I waited but father and son had nothing more to say to each other.

No, 'I love you.' No, 'Goodbye.'

How much traditional manhood stunts us! If I'd had enough energy, I would have been angry. Nothing more than 'Hello.' Surely Thom wanted to say something more?

But then I guiltily remembered: I hadn't told him that the nurse thinks this is the end nor that I'd arranged for a final file past.

I just smiled and kept my counsel.

So Erwin and I stood there, and Thom lay there, the three of us looking at each other. Three men trapped with nothing but empty gestures and the faint glimmer of another way of being in the corner of our eyes.

Erwin retreated to the door; opened his wallet and started giving me money for the previous day's flight to Germany. My first instinct was to refuse but I guessed this was his way of showing he cared. So I accepted. When we stepped back to the bed, Thom's eyes were closed again. Gut instinct told me he was giving his father the excuse to leave, rather than sleeping. Even now, the closest Erwin had come to his dying son was the corner of the bed nearest to the door. I suggested retreating downstairs.

Over *kaffe* and *kuchen* – caffeine and sugar, best friends through my zombie days – Erwin did his best to bridge the silence.

'What did your father do in the war?'

I wanted to hug him, it was one of the most beautiful things he has ever said to me! His generation of Germans seldom talk about the war, even to their children. Erwin and Ursula had always made me welcome, but at that moment I knew I was fully accepted as part of the family.

'I'm afraid that he was too young to fight,' I replied sadly, unable to match his intimacy. The conversation dwindled into silence. We said our goodbyes in the lobby and separated, as always, with a handshake.

Jürgen, Thom's brother, had cancelled his business meetings in Frankfurt and come straight to the hospital. However, at Thom's bedside, he had nothing more profound to say either. During the afternoon, Thom rallied slightly. I felt guilty about everybody rushing to the bedside: was I the little boy that cried wolf?

While Thom was asleep, I suggested that Jürgen and I went down to the coffee shop and discuss whether we should comply with Thom's wishes and fly him back to England. (Jürgen works as a senior lawyer for the German airport authorities and has been looking into the practicalities and has even offered to pay.) It would mean a long journey by road from Herdecke hospital to Frankfurt airport and then another from Stansted to the hospice in Sussex. Thom was no longer capable of crossing his hospital room, let alone travelling halfway across Europe. But he felt that England was now his home and where he wanted to die. How could we refuse his last wishes?

We sipped our coffee and spread whipped cream over our apple pie. When was the last time I'd eaten a proper meal? I pushed my plate away. Perhaps it was all the practicalities that needed to be discussed, perhaps the enormity of the pain, or maybe reaching out to the nurse had unlocked something inside, but I wept and Jürgen wept with me. It was one of the most liberating moments of my life. Suddenly I realised that I was not alone with this decision. Jürgen and I could make it together.

In the early evening we finally managed to grab Thom's doctor for a consultation. He confirmed that Thom was not strong enough to be moved. However, I was not prepared for the doctor's next statement:

'Sometimes when we stop treating people they get better,' he claimed.

After the honesty of the nurse, Erwin and Jürgen, it seemed like the doctor lived on another planet.

'How?' I wanted to ask. 'Please, don't build up my hopes,' I wanted to say. However, from somewhere on the ceiling, I watched myself sit there nodding blankly.

The doctor stood up. The consultation was over. We all trooped back into the sickroom and the doctor told Thom that he would not sanction a flight home but would review the situation in a few days. He bustled out.

It was left to me to ask him the obvious question:

'How do you feel about that?'

'It was the only thing I had left to live for,' Thom whispered back.

I tried to push back my feelings of guilt. I was saving him needless suffering. It was not easy, but today I had become Thom's parent. Daddy knew best.

Thom wanted me to stay the night, so the nurses rolled a spare bed into the room. I would much rather have returned to our friend's apartment and coughed without worrying about Thom. A hot shower and half an hour's release watching his collection of *I Love Lucy* videos had become my idea of heaven. Of course, I agreed to sleep at the hospital.

In the middle of the night, I was woken by a crash, looked up and realised that Thom had knocked over his glass of water. I was so exhausted, I could hardly mumble: 'Press your call button for the nurses.'

No sooner were the words out of my mouth, before I'd tumbled back into my nightmares.

Saturday 8 March – Germany

Early morning and the cleaner arrived. She picked up a plastic beaker, mopped up some liquid beside Thom's bed and gave me a dirty look. He had obviously not called the nurses during the night. I kicked myself for being selfish and when the cleaner had gone I threw on yesterday's clothes. The morning routine was about to start: Thom's bedlinen would be changed and tests done. I would definitely be in the nurses' way.

I told Thom that I was leaving for a shower and a change of clothes.

He did not answer.

Back at the flat, there was nobody to talk to – at least in English. Fortunately Kate, my fellow Live TV agony aunt, was already up when I phoned. Although not much more than a month had passed since I'd confided about Thom's health, we had already grown close. I felt I could talk without feeling judged:

'I don't know how much longer I can cope,' I told her. 'He wants to die, he's told me, but he just can't!'

I expected only sympathy, but Kate had a practical suggestion:

'Light a candle, it can sometimes help a spirit pass over,' she advised.

It did not make a lot of sense but why not? It would provide an excuse for delaying my return. I would indulge in some retail therapy.

After the overheated corridors of Herdecke hospital, the streets of Dortmund were cold and crisp. I headed straight for Karstadt – the large department store in the city centre where Thom and I had often shopped together. I wanted flowers to brighten his room but found it impossible to choose. They were all beautiful but they were also dead. There was enough of that in Thom's room without importing more. So instead of cut flowers, I bought a small pot of daffodil bulbs with four golden crowns. Next, I looked for the candles and was pleased to find that Karstadt stocked a wide choice. Thom had loved vanilla-scented ones and after a slightly panicky search, I found one. At the till, my purchases seemed deeply contradictory. I wanted his suffering to be over, so planned to light the candle and help him die, yet at the same time I'd bought spring flowers: a symbol of renewal, hope and my desire for Thom to live for ever! It made no sense.

Thom loved flowers, and shopping come to that, so I was looking forward to giving him his presents. On my return to his darkened room, I was full of renewed energy.

'Look, what I've bought you.'

I laid out my gifts but Thom hardly noticed.

He mumbled a few incoherent words and tried to reach for his drink, but his hands just flailed helplessly in the general direction of the bedside table. I lifted up his head and helped him take a few sips.

My presents were no comfort any more.

All I could offer was my undivided attention.

Feeling guilty, for not spotting how fast he had deteriorated during the night, I vowed never to leave him alone again.

Thom beckoned. I leaned forward.

'Yes?'

He answered in strange hybrid language – part German, part English, part something else. He pointed wildly at the ceiling. He became impatient with my stupidity.

I leaned closer still.

'What darling? I can't understand.'

Thom pointed again; this time at the window.

So he wanted the window open, but it already was open. I tried pushing it wider, but he shook his head and exhausted, he slipped off to sleep.

I picked up my notepad:

I must try to cast off all my own concerns and concentrate 100 per cent on Thom, learn to read his mind and make him as comfortable as possible. No more personal survival tactics, I must subsume myself into Thom – dangerous and potentially painful but I'll get over it. Giving too much never feels as bad as giving too little.

I stopped writing and just sat watching Thom's blanket rise and fall until we were breathing in tandem.

The minutes turn to hours. In the silence, I can feel both the happy memories from our past together and a gaping empty future without him pressing hard on either side of me, until there is no room for the present at all.

Jürgen, Thom's brother, arrived. I was relieved to have some company and a chance to quit the room for some food and another chance to cough up more phlegm. My resolution had not lasted long.

On my return, I called the nurse to check whether Thom had soiled the bed. She pulled down his sheets and his legs were so swollen he no longer had any ankles. The nurse retreated and came back with a male colleague. Although they lifted him very gently, Thom started whimpering. Each and every one of my nerve endings went into shock, we had become so closely linked in the last few hours that my senses were playing a countermelody.

I wanted to crumble into a ball in the corner of the room and howl. I couldn't maintain the facade of being a responsible adult any longer, but while Thom was paralysed by his useless body and his scrambled brain, I was still a walking talking person. I had responsibilities:

'Can't you see how distressed he is? DO SOMETHING AND QUICKLY.'

Thom moaned, obviously still in agony.

'We could try morphine,' one nurse suggested to another.

'GET A MOVE ON THEN.'

If they had been any slower, I would have ordered a shot for me, and Jürgen too.

When they reappeared with a syringe and needle, I left. Jürgen remained with Thom. I paced up and down the corridor, unable to cope with witnessing any more suffering and trying to clear my head. When I came back, Thom was sleeping peacefully. I prayed the morphine was giving him beautiful dreams.

By the evening, the drugs had worn off and Thom started slipping in and out of consciousness. I suggested that Jürgen went home but turned down a telephone offer from Walter to join me for the night shift. I knew I had very little time left with Thom and although it sounds selfish I wanted him all to myself.

I picked up my notebook and started writing:

It is very quiet at the weekend in a hospital and at night, with even fewer people around, it becomes increasingly difficult to believe that there is another world out there. I stand at the window but all I can see is my worried reflection looking back. It further reinforces my sense of dislocation. Although rationally I know that Thom has completed his preparations to leave this earth, I cannot really believe it is going to happen. How can someone you love so intensely die on you? If only there was something I could do. But the truth is Thom's hospital bed has turned into a deathbed and there is nothing left but guard what remains of his dignity.

A nurse arrived with a wet spatula and wanted to roll it round his mouth. She said it was to stop him drying up and feeling uncomfortable, but I could tell from his protestations the last time that he hated someone, without permission, shoving something in his mouth. So I told her firmly that it would not be necessary. She looked a bit huffy but retreated.

Ever since Thom first became ill, our loving bond has become even tighter. But today I can only reach him by opening up all my senses and beyond. If I strain at every inch of my intuition I can still just touch his shadow as it slips away for ever.

Although Martina, Thom's favourite nurse, had a day off, she came into work to say goodnight to Thom. As she stood by his side and stroked his forehead, he seemed to turn his head and look at her. His sad eyes were trying to say something. I wish I could have read them. Was he saying: 'thank you for coming', or 'how could I have sunk this low' or just 'help'? She caressed his face and once again I felt jealous that Thom had registered her arrival while I remained, along with the chairs and the French Impressionist painting, a fixture in the room. Yet mingled with these dark emotions was an overwhelming gratitude that she cared enough to come. Martina said goodbye and once again I was alone.

This time round, I was determined to sleep at the hospital again. The nurses explained that I could stay for only one night without paying. I just shrugged. What did I care about money? They wheeled another bed into Thom's room. Before getting undressed, I lit the vanilla-scented candle and prayed that when the flame burned itself out Thom's suffering would finally be over. I tried to read a biography of Barbra Streisand but despite staring at the same words over and over, nothing made any sense. So I put on the earphones for Thom's Walkman and flicked through the CDs he had chosen all those weeks ago when he packed for his final journey. In the end I settled on Mary Chapin Carpenter, we'd shared a wonderful night at one of her concerts, and her album *Stones in the Road*. The wistful purity of her voice was very calming. The title track seemed to sum up my mood the best; it made my small coda in a neverending opera a little more bearable.

The room was full of perfume from the candle and I wondered if it was anything like the crepe jasmine that Mary sings about, blooming on St Charles Avenue in New Orleans. It was somewhere Thom had always wanted to visit but he will never hear the bells of the streetcars, nor the jazz from the bars, and he will never taste the Creole cooking.

I drifted off for a couple hours of restless sleep but although my body desperately needed refreshing, my brain was working overtime. Thom's breathing was getting louder and louder as he fought for every lungful. I put the earphones back on, but even Mary's sweet voice could no longer cover up the horror. The liquid had finally reached his lungs. Thom was being drowned by his own body. I dressed and sat listening to his struggle – a worse torture than anything the Chinese could have dreamed up. I looked at my watch, three o'clock in the morning. The vanilla candle had gone out while I tried to sleep, the wax almost completely exhausted, so I re-lit it.

Suddenly I felt more alone than I had in my whole life. I didn't want to be alone. The night nurse popped in to check on Thom and told me that Martina was willing to be woken and return. I accepted, not that it made any difference to Thom. We might be born into a room full of midwives, mothers and fathers but we make that first journey alone and however many people sit round our deathbed they are just witnesses – we are, once again, all alone.

Martina and I sat together for about twenty minutes just watching and listening to Thom's struggle. We could no longer reach him; we could not help him. My face was blank but I jotted down my thoughts in my notebook:

I think I have some idea what it must be like to discover your partner is having an affair. At the very beginning of a terminal illness, you know something is wrong but just can't put your finger on it. When the evidence starts to build up – just like a wronged spouse who's ignored all the late nights at the office and the bizarre items on the credit card statement, you excuse any health upset as tiredness or stress. As Thom has been seduced by illness, there's been less and less time for me. Occasionally like a repentant lover torn, he has returned for one last look into my distraught eyes. No matter how loudly or passionately I plead, he is deaf to my promises that it will be better next time, we can start again, life will be better. Death is now truly Thom's lover and it is pulling him tighter and tighter into a dark all-enveloping embrace.

It is difficult to imagine the end of anything. The universe is infinite. Even if there is a brick wall somewhere after Pluto, there has to be something on the other side. Watching somebody die – however much you are prepared and long for the end – it is impossible to believe that there is not another breath, and yet another, into infinity. But, on Sunday 9 March 1997 at 03.55, I discovered just how short our time on earth is. Thom's chest heaved for a last time and I looked at Martina:

'Is that the end?'

She nodded and Thom made one last gurgle. He was dead.

Finally, I symbolically blew out the vanilla candle, tried to close his eyes, close his mouth but failed. Then for the last time ever I did something I'd been forbidden to do while he still lived: I kissed his forehead.

He still seemed alive to my lips but I knew it was just an illusion.

Thom did not live there any more.

A doctor was called and Thomas Holger Erwin Hartwig was officially declared dead. Over the past eighteen months my emotions have been on such a rollercoaster but now at the end of the ride, I dug down and come up with – nothing. I just felt nothing.

Nothing, nothing, nothing.

The love of my life, the scaffolding of my soul, the person who made my life make sense had died and I felt nothing.

Nothing.

PART TWO

Bereavement

Sunday 9 March – Germany

As I drove home from the hospital, listening to the radio for company, I remember being surprised at how much of the German DJ chatter I understood. When a British pop star was interviewed, I initially didn't spot the change of languages. The nurses had been worried about me driving, but I was fine. Honest. My rented BMW automatic 3.1 floated through the dark streets. With power-assisted steering, it responded to my slightest touch. I was back in control again; away from that bloody hospital. Hallelujah. I was also driving on the opposite side of the road from normal and in shock, but I was all right. Really. I'd made it through the worst.

On the outskirts of Dortmund, there is a large and confusing junction. Somehow I started down the left-hand side. Another car beeped me and I quickly swerved over. By now I must have been half a mile from the flat, but it seemed like for ever. The cars parked on the kerbside seemed to hold a strange fascination.

I became preoccupied with beautiful fantasies of crashing into them; longing to crumple metal, leap out of my BMW and run my fingers over flaking paintwork. It took all my concentration to keep on the road. I prayed that the car would be easy to park. I didn't trust myself not to slam into the back of another car and feel the release of breaking glass. Somebody must have been looking out for me, because there was a large space almost opposite the flat. I could drive straight into it.

I tiptoed into the flat; suppressed a coughing fit and remembered Walter's promise to visit Thom early that morning. Suddenly it was of tantamount importance that I should stop him arriving to find his best friend dead. The bad news would be much better coming from me. But it was half past four in the morning, no need to spoil Walter's sleep, I'd do it later. I searched for, but couldn't find, the walk-about phone. It would be in the bedroom, where my friends were sleeping, I tried to sneak in but woke them.

'Thom is dead. I need the phone,' I whispered, in the same way that you'd announce using up the last of the milk.

'Oh,' murmured a shape half in and half out of the bed.

No discussion.

I found the walk-about, closed the door and we all went to sleep.

I must have slept for about an hour and a half. After that I lay in bed watching the hands of my wristwatch reach seven o'clock. For some reason I thought that it would be inconsiderate to phone any earlier. Walter answered after about two rings. I didn't really need to say anything, he must have automatically known. Why else would anybody ring at seven on a Sunday morning?

But I said it anyway:

'Unsere Thom ist tod.' Suddenly the truth sunk in. Thom was dead. Yet at the same time, speaking a foreign language made the information less real. I cannot be talking about anything that affected me: I'm English.

Walter wanted to help, what could he do? I hadn't thought any further than stopping him arriving at Herdecke. There was no future beyond that point.

What was I supposed to do next?

I took a second to think.

In my haste to escape, I'd forgotten all Thom's possessions. The Walkman, the Mary Chapin Carpenter CD, my Barbra Streisand biography and he even had some money in his bedside drawer. I couldn't return alone, would Walter come too?

We arranged to meet at the hospital.

Next I phoned Jürgen and told him it was over. He agreed to phone his mother in hospital and his father too. He also suggested driving over to Dortmund and taking me back to Frankfurt. What? I'd planned going to Herdecke, but what next? All these decisions! I told Jürgen I'd think about it.

Getting out of bed, slipping on some jeans and walking to the kitchen proved to be so exhausting that I had to sit down before switching on the kettle.

I needed another rest between throwing a teabag in the mug and adding milk.

Once the kettle boiled, I sat looking at it.

Finally, with a supreme effort, I poured on the hot water and disposed of the teabag. Another rest, shorter this time, and I was ready to take my first sip. It tasted good. I should eat something. After a while, I found some bread and made toast. There was no sign of the friends who were letting me stay on their sofa bed. Were they still sleeping or lying low, embarrassed about what to say?

Since returning to Germany, Thom had asked everybody except his family and Walter to stop visiting. With the exception of Maureen (who is manning the Thom information line) and Kate (the agony aunt to my agony uncle), I've cut myself off from everybody outside that circle too. No wonder my hosts stayed in bed.

After finishing breakfast, it took me about fifteen minutes to feel ready to walk to the bathroom – not very far in a one-bedroom flat. Once there, I cancelled the idea of a shower; drying

myself off would have been too exhausting. I should accept
Jürgen's offer and allow myself to be folded into the embrace of
Thom's family. I made the call, sat on the bed for a while and
finally returned to the bathroom for a shave.

Still no sign of my hosts.

I'd just finished dressing when the doorbell rang, so I buzzed
down.

It was Walter. He'd come to drive me to the hospital.

For a second, I was annoyed. 'I've hired this wonderful BMW
to provide some pleasure on this visit to Germany and everybody's trying to stop me driving it.' However, in my zombie
state, I was even less capable than last night so I agreed. It was
probably dangerous for me to cross the road alone. Walter waited
while I looked for some plastic bags to pack away Thom's things.

I left without saying goodbye to my hosts or explaining what
I was doing.

At the hospital, Walter accepted an offer to view the body. I preferred to wait outside the nurses' station until Thom's room was
unlocked. I spotted Thom's doctor, who tried to avoid eye contact with me. He could have walked up the corridor and mumbled something or put a silent hand on my shoulder, but with
a sideways glance he disappeared round the corner. My widow-
hood must have made me untouchable. I was one of his failures.

Finally, someone arrived with the key and let me re-enter room
44c. I was struck by how bright and empty the room looked. The
curtains had been drawn back and light streamed through the
open window. The bed had been removed and the floor had been
freshly disinfected. Thom's possessions were stacked into neat
piles and his clothes folded on the table. Yet despite the staff's
efforts, I could still hear echoes of Thom's death rattle and de-
tect traces of the struggle between cells programmed to replicate,
divide and survive and an illness bent on destruction. The smell

of decay clogged my nostrils. I reeled back into his bathroom and started sorting through the half-used bottles of shampoo, body wash gel and Juvena Men's Division skincare products. Perhaps, it would be easier if I just concentrated on the practicalities. I fingered his bottle of 1881 cologne and sprayed some on my wrists. Immediately, the smell conjured up a memory of Thom freshly washed on a Sunday morning ready for the languid pleasures of no particular place to go. I felt strangely comforted and strong enough to return to the empty room.

Although there were only a couple of sports bags' worth of items, it took ages to sort through everything. As it was cold outside, I decided to wear one of Thom's quilted jackets. I reached down into the pocket and found a till receipt from Tesco. It was brightly coloured with Christmas decorations and I lovingly ran my eye down the column of purchases: oranges, shelled walnuts, mincemeat 600g, kitchen roll x 4. Physical proof that we had a life together.

I was loved and I did love, but now all I had was this debris.

For a second, I considered keeping the receipt but common sense told me there were a million more personal possessions and memories to treasure. The loneliness rose up around me. I remembered our first German Christmas together, the crowded Weihnachts Markt stalls, the bananas on a stick covered in thick dark chocolate and the kitsch Christmas tree balls with a manger scene in the middle that Thom insisted on buying. Reluctantly, I screwed up the scrap of paper and threw it away.

Next, I picked up Thom's Filofax and immediately felt like an intruder. I would never have opened it before, but now I needed the addresses of all his German friends. Flicking through his notes and a diagram for a new bathroom for the house, I realised that this was the closest thing I would ever come to being intimate with Thom – ever again. I sat down and got my breath back.

Something was missing: the pot of daffodils I'd brought yesterday. I checked the windowsill. I lifted Thom's pile of possessions in the vain hope that they were hidden by them. I scanned the corridor and the patient dinning area. Nothing. I tracked down a nurse:

'Have you seen a small pot of flowers? They were in room 44c. They're mine,' I asked in my haltering German.

I must have been agitated because she replied slowly, very slowly.

'We used them for an art installation. Over there. Beside the sun balcony.'

We walked down the corridor and my daffodils were the centre of a spring display with some driftwood and stones. It looked like something a primary school teacher would arrange in a corner of her classroom.

'They're mine.' I seized the pot. 'You do understand.'

She seemed slightly annoyed that I wanted to ruin their handiwork and I hesitated for a moment. But it was incredibly important to take something living out of that house of death.

Despite promising Thom that I would eat healthily, nowhere beyond McDonald's was open for Sunday lunch in central Dortmund. To ease my conscience, I calculated that a fillet-o-fish was better than a beef burger and ordered one. I changed my mind and then changed it back again. I couldn't even work out what to put in my mouth. How will I deal with difficult decisions – about funeral services, coffins and priests? Picking at my pre-packaged salad, I tried to remember when Jürgen was picking me up. Stupidly, I had not written down the time and had left his mobile number back in the flat. Did we have time for a leisurely lunch or just a snack? Walter tried to make small talk but I hadn't the energy. I just sat and stared at the bland paintings on the wall. I had not realised that Thom's dying would be an anticlimax or how blank I would feel.

Gradually it was filtering through: today was when my suffering would really begin. All the angst started to float up to the surface. Nasty tangled selfish feelings, so different from the pure love of the last twenty-four hours. Previously, Thom could always take the edge off my pain. He would suggest looking in his bedside fridge where he stored a little treat: a bottle of beer or a fruit yoghurt. If that failed, one look at his ravished body, and I no longer worried about my needs. Except Thom was no longer here and the fridge had been emptied.

A McDonald's employee cleared away our trays of half-eaten food and packaging, his activity further seemed to underline my aimlessness. I did not even have the diversion that most newly bereaved people have – that of arranging the funeral as everywhere would be closed on Sunday. Perhaps we could sit in McDonald's a bit longer and have another cup of coffee? All the clean surfaces and the staff in uniform reminded me of the hospital.

'Walter, I think we should leave?'

'Where do you want to go?'

'Anywhere.' I was beginning to be haunted by stillness; and stillness is one step removed from death.

By some miracle, Walter, Jürgen and I met up at the flat. While we'd been away, my hosts had gone out. I lay down on the sofa for half an hour in the living room and Jürgen and Walter tried to pick their way through Thom's complicated legal affairs in the kitchen. I closed my eyes, but sleep was elusive. So I decided to phone England and let our friends there know. It had been hard enough in German, how would Maureen react? Strangely detached, I watched myself pick up the phone, and talk into it. Thom had always been the witness for my life – forever interested in all the details – so had I taken over that role? Or maybe without a witness I felt that I had ceased to exist? Certainly, the man on the phone had nothing to do with me. I listened as he tried to soften the news. How would I play this scene differently? Would I have managed something more than the bald facts?

Maureen sounded resigned. Somehow that brought me back into my body again. She didn't say much. Thank goodness. I didn't need a feeble attempt to console me. I asked her to phone my parents and tell them about Thom's death. Why didn't I call them myself? I was tired, in shock and didn't want to abuse my hosts' hospitality with too many international phone calls but if I'm being truthful: it seemed too intimate.

Falling in love with Thom broke the 'don't ask, don't tell' truce over my sexuality. I wanted my mother and father to feel the same excitement I did about finding a wonderful man to share my life with. *High Noon* was over Sunday lunch at my parents' house. Roast beef, roast potatoes with gravy, cauliflower, peas and carrots – followed by my mother's home-made meringues and a raspberry trifle. It was not a success. The conversation was sparse and stilted. After clearing the table my parents buried themselves behind the Sunday papers, and I found myself slipping back into old family patterns and opened up a section too. Afterwards in the car, Thom and I had a terrible row.

My mother's comment to my sister, in her weekly telephone conversation, spoke volumes. When asked what she thought of Thom, her reply was: 'I could find nothing wrong with him.'

So I gave Maureen my parents' phone number and silently wished her luck. She told me she was about to go off to church and she would pray for Thom. I was both grateful for her prayers and envious of her belief. I tried not to cry until I put the receiver down. I don't know why because saltwater was etched round every syllable. In the kitchen, I found Walter and Jürgen both crying. It was strangely comforting that this time someone else was in tears.

I had a strong urge to visit Ursula, Thom's mother who had only been to her son's sick bed once because she was ill herself.

So Jürgen drove me to her hospital. She looked very white, but I doubt I'd win any prizes for most healthy thirty-seven-year old. Erwin wheeled her into the day room and she clasped my hands tightly. I returned the pressure. She had been there when Thom arrived in the world; I had been there at the end. We looked deeply into each other's eyes, both trying to communicate, both trying not to cry and further burden the other.

Ursula broke the silence:

'Did he suffer?' she implored.

I lied.

Since retrieving the pot of daffodils, I had scarcely let them out of my sight. However, I handed them to Ursula; if anybody needed this gift of life from Thom's room it was her. She looked a bit surprised, living flowers were considered a health risk at that hospital, until I explained their significance. To complete this improvised ceremony, I broke off one of the blooms for myself. For the first time ever, I kissed her on the cheek and left.

Then we drove back to Frankfurt where Jürgen's younger son was about to celebrate his birthday with a meal out. I hoped his special day would not forever be linked with his uncle dying. After putting my overnight bag up in the spare room, I asked to look through Jürgen's photo album. I had a desperate need to erase my final picture of Thom. Hoping to superimpose a healthy face over the sunken cheeks and grey skin of yesterday. While Jürgen found it, his wife pressed my daffodil between the pages of a German art book. I skimmed through their photo album of recent family gatherings. Confirmations, Christmas and other social occasions were all full of Thom's smiling face. Unlike my photos, many of which have been posed, Jürgen snaps away when people are not looking and achieves a wonderfully natural expression. I sat for what must be five minutes just drinking in one shot of Thom from last year where he is listening to his mother. One second frozen in time, I wished I could go back there again. Thom's smile is easy and relaxed; his skin glows and his eyes are so full of love.

'Would you like to have the photograph?' Jürgen took it out of his album.

I reached for the travel tissues.

After a bath I retreated to the spare bedroom and phoned my friend Kate. I briefly told her that it was all over.

'Thank for letting me know but being a bit of a witch, I already knew.'

I put down the receiver and considered: who next? I automatically thought of calling Thom. Whenever we were apart we called each other early evening and shared our days. I almost pressed the first digit before it hit me: I can no longer phone him. OK, my brain knew I'd never see him again but somehow this still had not travelled down to my fingers. They itched to call his bedside phone. I opened my notepad again:

Before, I found the idea of widows laying an extra place at the table strange, now I understand. Thom is such a part of the fabric of my life even looking at the corpse is not enough. I think he's away on some business trip. I can understand the concept but not the reality that death is final.

Monday 10 March – Germany

I'd brought Thom's will and funeral instructions over to Germany. I sat in Jürgen's living room – full of the same designer furniture that Thom loved – and opened the envelope that I'd hoped would always remain sealed. Although I knew the contents, it was shocking to read Thom's bold, confident handwriting again. Some of his requests were not difficult: he wanted to be cremated and for us to choose the cheapest coffin available. Other wishes, I knew, would be cruel for his parents. Thom had written: *'I do*

*not want any sad faces, because I had a good life and **no** religion.'*
His parents, both in their late seventies, had a strong faith and
'seeing their child off properly' could be a great comfort. How
could I reconcile these two sets of wishes? Worse still, Thom
wanted the funeral in England. When he'd written the letter this
seemed perfectly reasonable – after all he didn't expect to die in
Germany. But could I really take the corpse back to England?
His mother was still in hospital and I doubted whether his father
would want to travel to England alone.

I had tried to discuss my dilemma with Thom during the last
week of his life.

'I know you don't want to talk about sickness and disease but
we need to talk about your funeral.'

'Did I tell you that I read this article about a British family
who'd been on holiday in France with their Granny when she had
died suddenly.'

I should have expected something like this.

'They propped the corpse up on the back seat of the car and
headed home,' he continued. 'At the border, they tried to persuade a suspicious immigration officer that she was asleep.'

'I don't think so,' I told him.

'Just cover me with a blanket and drive fast, I won't mind.'
Thom smiled but his face was grim.

Once again, he had charmed his way out of a tight corner so I
let the subject drop. But I had lots of unresolved questions: what
kind of service? Who would conduct it? The closer to death, the
less energy Thom had to answer. Finally, he told me:

'Do what you feel is best.'

My return ticket was for the day after next. I was due in London
to record special editions of *Agony* for ratings week. I could have
cancelled but I needed my old routine back. I wanted to go home.
So in effect, I had just one day to make all the arrangements.

What should I do? Thom had told his parents about his wishes. If they had demanded a funeral, I might have found the energy to fight but they were quietly resigned. How could I torture them more?

I shared my dilemma with Jürgen. He was prepared to follow Thom's letter of instructions but I could tell he was also worried about the impact of his brother's death on his parents – especially his mother.

I looked Jürgen straight in the eye and told him:

'Funerals are for the living too.'

So I suggested a compromise: a conventional funeral in Germany and a memorial service back in Sussex.

First stop of the day was the hospital where I learned the German for death certificate: *Totenschien*. Next, we went to Thom's bank in Dortmund and closed his account. With those formalities over, Jürgen suggested some lunch. Did I know somewhere close by to eat? Of course, I'd been coming to Dortmund for the past seven and a half years.

It was only when we sat down in the traditional German café that I remembered Thom had brought me here on my very first visit to the city. Over the following years, we would regularly drop in for a hot chocolate after shopping and read the inner sleeves of the CDs Thom had just bought. I could feel the tide of loneliness rising higher and higher. I would have to be more careful or risk being drowned altogether.

After eating but not really tasting my food, we went to the undertaker's and I had to master yet more new German vocabulary. It was a small shop in a small parade in a suburb I had never visited before. Thom would have been horrified. He believed that everything, no matter how simple, should be beautiful as well as functional. So among the eighty-seven boxes that he brought over from Germany were Alessi corkscrews, Philippe Starck kettles and Eileen Gray tables; none of these designers made funeral urns and neither did Calvin Klein, Ungaro or Gucci.

'Don't be a style fascist,' I told myself, 'just choose something plain.'

But the first urn had an angel flying up to heaven and the second a pair of hands clasped in prayer. It was my first clue that funerals had probably not changed much since my grandmother buried my grandfather nearly forty years ago. So I suggested popping round to the nearest designer kitchen shop and buying a simple steel biscuit tin. The undertaker looked over his half-rimmed glasses, left a pause and said:

'It's against the law in Germany.'

'Why?' I asked.

'On health grounds,' he replied.

Next he took me through a heavy curtain at the back of the shop and into his coffin showroom.

'It's OK,' I told him. 'I just want the cheapest.'

'That's the one the state buries paupers or bodies nobody claims.' He gave a dismissive wave towards the darkest corner of his dark showroom.

I backed down and allowed myself to be shown the solid walnut and cherry wood veneered caskets, the purple crushed velvet and blue crêpe interiors and finished with electro-plated brass handles. I had stepped into a Hammer Horror movie.

'Just give me the second cheapest,' I told him. It was the second of Thom's dying wishes that I had disregarded within the space of five hours.

We returned to the undertaker's desk.

'Where would you like us to scatter the ashes,' he asked.

'Beachy Head. It's an English beauty spot. But it's OK, I can do that for myself.'

The glasses went down the nose again.

'Let me guess. It's against the law,' I said.

'Human remains can only be scattered in designated gardens of rest and then only by someone with the approved qualifications.'

'Why?' I was getting truculent.

'Public safety.'

Jürgen took over and put up a stout case that because I was English different rules applied. Eventually, we won the undertaker round. Finally, we had finished and could leave, but there was just the matter of the wording for the formal announcement of Thom's death. By the time we debated which local newspapers it should appear in, I had run out of opinions. So Jürgen and the undertaker discussed which papers Thom's friends were most likely to read, while I studied the blotter on the desk and let my numbness spread. A few calls were made and the funeral was set for Friday.

'Would that be OK?'

I nodded.

One of Thom's friends, Andreas, was a minister. He had been a guest at Thom's farewell to Germany dinner party, a little over two years ago. If anybody could walk the tightrope between beginning the healing process for Thom's parents and respecting their son's non-religious wishes, it would be him. The night before, I had found his number in Thom's Filofax and made an appointment. The last one of the day. I introduced Andreas to Jürgen and vice versa. Then Andreas drew our attention to a student who had been sitting in the corner.

'He's doing work experience with me,' he explained. 'I hope you don't mind him sitting in on our meeting?'

'Yes, I do.'

Andreas looked surprised. His question had been phrased to almost eliminate any chance of objecting, but something inside me snapped. Being looked at was just too draining. I felt enough like a zombie without a stranger staring at me. There was an awkward silence. Andreas nodded to the student and he shuffled out.

Overcome with tiredness, my German started to disintegrate and, for the first time in days, I spoke English. Jürgen and Andreas managed surprisingly well arranging the service in a foreign language. I listened but offered little.

My flight was from Dortmund airport. So Jürgen dropped me back at my friends' place, I gave him a hug and thanked him for everything. The flat was empty. I spent the evening alone and watched more *I Love Lucy*.

Although exhausted, sleep was difficult. The coughing attacks were getting worse, and I was plagued by nightmares. I found myself wishing I'd left the hospital earlier and avoided Thom's lingering death. I should have said goodbye before he became unconscious, and then walked out; a proper ending rather than the long miserable fade out. By the early hours, I was coughing harder and more painfully than ever before – almost to the point of throwing up.

Over this rumpus, I heard a match being struck in the next room; a flare of sulphur and the soothing aroma of a vanilla candle seeping under the door. I got out of bed to check – despite knowing nobody else was in the flat. I slowly opened the door. The bedroom was empty. My friends had not sneaked back during the night, but I definitely smelt vanilla. In fact, I was completely enveloped in vanilla. It was bizarre but rather comforting. Returning to bed, I finally remembered something Thom had said a few weeks earlier:

'If it is possible, I will find some way of coming back and telling you that everything is all right.'

I couldn't ignore the evidence. I had smelt a vanilla candle, even though there were none in the apartment. Amazing. Perhaps while Thom's essence left his body, it became wrapped in this aroma. Now rested, on the third day after the battle of death, he really was free: reborn with a cloak of vanilla to fill the empty miles between us. I stopped coughing and let a golden calm slowly spread through my body. Perhaps there is life after death.

Tuesday 11 March – Germany

The next morning, I wondered if I'd dreamed last night's experience. I must have done. Either that or grief had turned me temporarily mad. No. It had seemed so real. I lay in bed and listened to the traffic outside. Perhaps, I had been tricked by some dark corner of my own imagination. I should get up and pack. I pulled myself up and sat on the bed. I had a full day ahead and no time to worry about what was real and what was not. But then, I was followed into the kitchen by the smell of vanilla. It was not as strong as last night but still unmistakably milky, sweet and warm.

Dortmund airport was fogbound and passengers to other destinations were being sent off in buses to unaffected airports. Worn down by the shock of bereavement, the prospect of many extras hours' travelling was profoundly upsetting. Except, just as I began to despair, I smelt the vanilla candle again. It had the same effect as Thom patting my hand and telling me to calm down. How weird was that? Surely, I'd been mistaken. Fifteen minutes later, even though the fog had not seemed to clear, my flight was announced. Puzzled, I boarded the plane and the journey continued without further incident.

When I returned home, Valerie, my next-door neighbour, came running out.

'I wondered if you needed change for the taxi.'

'No. I'm fine.'

'If there's anything I can do.' She had obviously heard the news from Maureen.

I had a quick think. I had to keep moving forward but I also had to step round any Thom-shaped black holes.

'Could you tell the butcher?' Thom had been a good customer. 'It would avoid...' I couldn't name my fears. Maybe I was worried that he'd ask after Thom and I'd be pulled out of the 'normal' world (where I was just another customer ordering a chop for the weekend) into the 'real' world (where I was in danger of constantly crying). Maybe I felt that he should know. Maybe I was just being English and wanted to avoid any embarrassment. Maybe if someone else told him, Thom would be a little less dead. Valerie readily agreed. I thanked her and let myself in.

The mat was flooded with letters. Maureen, on my behalf, had asked for written condolences. I wanted to keep the phone lines open for business calls. The answering machine was flashing and, without thinking, I pressed the play button:

'Hello darling.'

It was Thom's weak voice.

I had obviously not picked up quickly enough last Thursday when he phoned to ask for his paperwork and the answering machine had kicked in. He sounded so ill. I'd forgotten how ill. I sounded so worried. I'd forgotten how worried. I shuddered and tried to step over this black hole by hitting 'delete'.

On the next message, *She* magazine wanted to know if I could write an article. I jotted down the details. The next two were from my mother. She wanted to come and visit. My TV producer needed to go through the scenarios for tomorrow and brief me on *Royal Agony*. Maureen had questions about the memorial service and an offer from my friend John to accompany me back to Germany for the funeral. Overwhelmed, I drifted into the kitchen and put the kettle on. The dishcloths hanging on the rail were the same as they always were. The view from the window of the garden and small copse beyond hadn't changed. The track lighting that Thom strung over the sink and hob was still there. I made myself a cup of instant coffee, rather than grind fresh beans and find the filter papers. I took the mug through to the living room and lay down on the sofa, Thom's sofa, and the source of many arguments about what was most important: comfort or style.

Until three days ago, my life had shrunk down to a pinpoint: watching Thom lie in bed in a room with the curtains drawn. Now, I was back blinking in the daylight. All these questions needed answering but I didn't have any answers. I almost wished that I could be back at the hospital again, my time filled with waiting and the rhythm of caring. Three days ago, every moment, every breath had a sharpened sense of relevance. No phone messages, no babbling about the inconsequential, just one bed and one chair. It might sound perverse, but with all the heightened emotions it was a very living time. But what next?

Faced with vast fields of emptiness, I chose 'normal' over 'real' life and decided to get a haircut for tomorrow's TV show. I drove to Brighton and after visiting our usual barber's, remembered there was nothing in the house to eat. I would treat myself and get a ready-meal from Marks & Spencer. The slight hill up to the Clock Tower felt like the north face of the Eiger. I stopped for a rest and leaned against Waterstones' window. How would I make it up to London and a full day's filming? I dug into my depleted energy reserves and pushed on. Suddenly I found myself carried up the hill on a cloud of vanilla. I didn't care whether I was going crazy, whether my mind was playing tricks. I would believe. Thank you, Thom.

Wednesday 12 March

I had been tempted to cancel Live TV, but we were in the annual ratings sweep and special programmes were planned. The production team had worked extra hard, how could I let them down? Kate, my witchy friend and work colleague, had already explained about Thom, somehow I would make it through the day. After all, I just had to sit on a sofa – exactly what I would have done at home. At least this way, I'd be paid for it!

Unable to deal with being jostled at London Bridge, I decided on a taxi instead. Luckily there was no queue, but deadened with grief I was too slow and another commuter grabbed my ride. I stood for a second on the pavement, unable to believe the unfairness and screamed at him, apoplectic with rage. He gave me a look normally reserved for someone holding a gun to your head and stepped back. Somehow I had crossed from 'normal' to 'berserk' without even stopping at 'real'.

Live TV was home to a dwarf weatherman who needed a trampoline to reach Scotland on his forecast map and where every time a stock price went up the pin-up female presenter took off another item of clothing. The management liked everything bright and breezy – just the place to go four days after your partner dies.

The day started well enough, with laughter, as we watched premade mini films where actors recreated royal problems. The producer had spent half the annual prop budget on a cheap fake crown and was determined it should receive maximum exposure, so the actress playing the Queen even wore it during breakfast with 'Prince Edward'.

While we were in make-up Kate calmly told me *The People* (Sunday newspaper) wanted us to write a guide to more fulfilling sex. We had been trying to persuade them to give us a joint agony column; this could be an important opportunity. Great news, except Kate had no idea how many words they wanted, no idea of the deadline or the rate they were paying. I stormed off and phoned the editor:

'No problem, of course we can write 2,000 words,' I told him.

'Could we have it tomorrow? Oh, one more thing… Make it funny.'

From this article, to a regular column, to TV stardom – it was just three steps to heaven. I gritted my teeth. Kate would provide the inspiration, I'd write the piece in the morning before flying back to Germany for the funeral.

'Sure no problem.'

Afterwards, I changed into a blue suit and tried to relax while the make-up lady prepared me for the first of our five shows. She was trying to tone down the two large black rings under my eyes, when the director popped her head round the corner:

'I'd like to introduce everybody to the Live TV lawyer,' she said too brightly. 'She'll be sitting with me in the control room and making certain nothing libellous is broadcast.'

'I am a journalist. I do know the laws of libel,' I snapped.

'Just to be on the safe side, remember we're not advising the real royal family but people who have problems like theirs.'

'So we're dropping: "My mother refuses to abdicate"?'

The *Agony* programme was recorded 'as live'. Any problems and we had to go right back to the beginning and start again. My false smile was soon stretched so tightly I'd lost all feeling in the lower half of my face. When the lawyer's constant interference prevented us from taking lunch at the normal time, my temper became so frayed it was only Kate's calming influence that stopped me storming off.

After lunch in the canteen, Kate needed a cigarette and we adjourned to the smoking room. I wanted to thank her for the suggestion of the vanilla candle and how it seemed that Thom was using it to communicate with me.

'It's really strange, because smell has always been the weakest of my senses.'

'It's the last thing to go when someone dies.' Kate smiled.

I suddenly felt very guilty about drinking black coffee in Thom's room.

'There's something else that I should tell you. I went to see a medium for advice about my divorce and she had a message for you.' Kate took a drag on her cigarette. 'Thom wants you to know that there will be someone else.'

The smell of stale tobacco had become overpowering. I wanted to be sick.

At the end of the recordings, I needed a glass of wine. I'd never really been a drinker but over the past few days had craved the release of alcohol. I should have gone straight home but there was still that article to write. Kate and I found an empty wine bar and tried to be witty about sex.

'I've always thought the only place for butter in the bedroom is round the door handle – to stop children's little fingers opening it,' she said.

As the bar filled up with young men and women in expensive suits, I began to find the crowd oppressive. I wanted to curl up and sob. My notepad had only a few mad ramblings and Kate's weird one-liners. How on earth could these be turned into an informative article?

Back home, I tried to start writing but I was exhausted. The phone rang. I guessed it would be my mother. I had meant to call my parents yesterday, but changed my mind after reading a letter of condolence from my father (on both of their behalf):

What can we say which will be of any comfort to you? We were so distressed to hear from Maureen that Tom [sic] had died this morning in Germany. You have obviously been very concerned about his health for a long time but we had no idea that it was so serious. Even so, we know that however much such things might have been expected it is always such a dreadful shock when it does happen. It also seems much harder to accept with one who was so relatively young. You are very much in our thoughts. Please let us know if there is anything we can do. If you would like, Mummy could come down and see you on Wednesday or Thursday. It is most unfortunate that we are going to be away from the end of the week and won't be around to support you at the funeral or the memorial service. All our love.

The phone call was indeed from my mother:

'Thank goodness, I've reached you…'

I was too angry to listen to the rest. They had shown no interest in Thom's illness. They had not even sent him a 'get well soon' card. Their twice yearly timeshare in Portugal clashed with the date for Thom's memorial service in England. I could not play happy families.

'Leave me alone.'

There was an embarrassed silence on the other end.

'You're hounding me.'

'I want to help.'

Without knowing how, I'd slipped from 'berserk' into 'mad'. I swore once, maybe twice, and slammed down the receiver. I regretted the swear words but the energy felt good.

Thursday 13 March

Although my home office is smaller, and the computer older, I did not feel comfortable moving into Thom's office in the spare bedroom. Maybe after the funeral. Somehow, I managed to access 'normal' life and spent the morning writing the 'funny' article about sex. When I read it back, my words seemed wooden. I couldn't imagine anyone reading it and having joyful lovemaking, but I'd run out of time. So I sighed and faxed it to the features editor.

Fortunately, flights to Frankfurt are from Gatwick's North Terminal (Dortmund is from the South Terminal) so there were no memories to flip me off-course. For some reason, I met my friend John at a café on the other side of passport control.

We had some lunch, although I still could not taste anything. Our flight left at 13.45 p.m. and we landed in Germany at 16.20. I managed to remember the complex instructions on how to find Jürgen's driver, where to turn right, which sign to ignore and his description. He took us to Jürgen's office, large and very impressive, and Jürgen drove us back to his house.

John is comfortable in any surroundings and can talk to anybody. So I let him fill the silences. It all went rather smoothly with only one slip into real life:

'What about the boys and the funeral tomorrow?' Jürgen asked.

'They're teenagers. They're old enough to choose.' I was puzzled. Surely, Jürgen didn't think their sons should be shielded from their uncle's funeral?

'Then they don't want to go.'

Why not? I wanted to ask. I thought they loved Thom too?

'You don't mind?' Gabi, his wife, asked.

By this time, I was back in normal life and feeling no pain. I nodded.

After supper, we drank grappa and I retired early up to bed. I'd packed a stuffed toy that I'd bought Thom when he was first ill and went to sleep clutching it like I was a small child.

Friday 14 March – Germany

Funerals are supposed to be a comfort, and indeed I found my grandmother's service healing. However, I just floated through this day. It was not what Thom wanted. The slight differences between German and English funerals further added to my sense of unreality. There were no black cars and the coffin was waiting for us in the crematorium chapel. It was completely covered in white lilies, his favourite flower, and I wished I hadn't ignored his wishes and bought the more expensive coffin. The turnout was impressive, especially as Thom had not lived in Germany for quite some time. As I met each of his closest friends, I hugged them tightly – almost as if a small residue of his personality clung to them. If I squeezed hard enough, would he return to me?

All the seats in the crematorium chapel were soon full and a few dozen people were standing at the back. Among the mourners were so many teachers from Projekt Deutsch Lernen (the language school where Thom had been headmaster) that the school was closed for the day. I did not understand one word of the service. Like an actor in a long running play, I knew my part but could not connect with the emotions. My tissues were occasionally of use pressed to damp eyes, but there were no sobs, no weeping, just horrible nothingness. I expect people thought me brave, but it was just something I had to get through.

Although there was a mechanism to lower the casket down into a basement, I'd vetoed this idea. I didn't want Thom descending down into the earth like a pantomime demon. Worse still, I was told the machinery made a lot of undignified noise. Instead, Andreas, Thom's priest friend, had suggested a bowl of sand by the coffin. As each of us left we would light a candle, think of Thom and place it in the bowl.

After a funeral lasting thirty minutes, Andreas looked up at me expectantly. I took this as the signal and stood up, took a candle, lit it and pushed it into the sand. I silently promised Thom his memorial service would be better and walked out of the chapel. The grey stone corridor was empty. Thom's mother, who was still in a wheelchair, would light the next candle, and then Erwin who was pushing her. They seemed to take an age. The only sound was the echo of my footsteps as I paced up and down outside the chapel. I had never felt so achingly lonely. I kicked myself for not thinking through the candle ceremony. After an eternity, everybody filed out. Martina gave me a quick hug but had to return to the hospital and finish her shift. I shook hands with as many mourners as possible and invited them for refreshments. The Germans, being forever practical, build a café beside each crematorium. Unlike an English funeral nobody has to butter bridge rolls and there are no worries about over- or under-catering.

The café staff were all wearing black but somebody had tried to cheer the place up with plastic flowers. We were shown to a long table covered in white linen with posies of fresh flowers at regular intervals. I should have been thinking about Thom and trying to remember the good times. Instead, I wondered what it would be like to work in such a place. Serving nobody but the recently bereaved cannot be a particularly pleasant job, but at least it is steady.

After hot soup and rolls, I felt a little more human and began to look around. There was another group of mourners in the café. Looking at the average age, I guessed the departed must have been at least in their seventies. With the exception of Thom's parents and aunt and uncle, my guests were all in their thirties and forties. We should have been attending weddings and christenings, not funerals. It must have been particularly bitter for Thom's parents. His father, Erwin, stoically wheeled his mother, Ursula, everywhere and later returned her to hospital for more treatment.

Saturday 15 March – Germany

Not wanting to spend longer in Germany than strictly necessary, we flew back from Frankfurt on Saturday morning. On the flight, I tried to make a list of all the places I'd been with Thom: Berlin (twice), France (twice possibly thrice, I cannot be sure), Sitges in Spain (twice), Portugal, Italy and America (once each). It seemed a short list until I remembered that we'd once driven back from Herdecke, so Belgium too and definitely France (again).

After we landed, I dropped John in Crawley and went straight round to Maureen's for a memorial service planning meeting. We sat in her living room, I had a cup of coffee and she had a list of questions.

She'd already phoned all the local theatres to hire a studio space – we'd decided Saturday afternoon would be the time most friends could attend. Unfortunately she had drawn a blank and I immediately started to panic. I didn't want the memorial service in a church. This time I was determined to follow Thom's instruction to the letter. Luckily a friend had offered his large home, which along with ten bedrooms boasted a ballroom. I agreed it would be perfect. There was more good news. Maureen had found the number for the jazz singer, Stacey Kent, who had performed at my cousin Sue's wedding. Thom had been so impressed by Stacey Kent that he had joined her mailing list and every month a letter would arrive at my house, addressed to him, with details of her forthcoming gigs. Unfortunately, her local dates had never coincided with Thom's weekends in England, so he had never seen her perform again. It would be brilliant if she would sing at his memorial service. Live music would make it more of an occasion. Maureen agreed to call her. However, there was one big problem: the date. We probably needed two weeks to arrange everything, except that would take us to Easter weekend and lots of people would be away. I could scarcely think of more than forty-eight hours into the future. A delay of three weeks seemed like three years. Worse still, I'd decided the memorial service should mark the end of my voluntary exile and I would start returning calls and accepting invitations again. Would this coming Saturday be OK? Maureen winced, but agreed.

I began to get an insight into just how much I owed Maureen. I'd given her the names and phone numbers and she'd worked through the list, phoning and informing everybody about Thom's death.

'The hardest call was speaking to your parents,' said Maureen. 'I got your father and explained I was a friend of yours and that Thom had just died. His reply: "Hang on, I'll go and get Jill."'

Because Thom had kept the gravity of his illness secret, Maureen had been the bearer, over and over again, of shocking news. She had had to support our friends and deal with her own grief. How could I ever thank her enough?

When I returned home, there was a letter from my parents. It was in my mother's handwriting but signed Tony and Jill:

Andrew Darling,
It is important that you know how distressed and saddened we have felt for you during these last few weeks. You have been constantly in our thoughts – you may well be right – perhaps I should have sent some messages to Thom – and looking back, I understand what you say – and I can only tell you that my oversight was so unintended.

When Thom first fell ill, my parents showed little interest. I was too preoccupied to worry. However, after Thom had been in hospital several times, and they had never even sent a 'get well soon' card, I began to become irritated. Especially as over the same period my mother had a double knee operation and my father a successful triple heart bypass operation. Their hospital rooms were overflowing with cards. It was obviously the 'done thing' in their circle, but they never thought of posting one to Thom. I kept my mouth shut and just let it ride. I was tired of fighting and Thom certainly did not mind. We had had far greater problems than worrying about two stubborn old people.

No way did we even intend to reject him – for we were happy that you had found a kind and gentle companion. You see while being thankful and grateful for just that reason, it has been a difficult time for your father, who loves you dearly and I have tried so hard to act as a bridge to help both of you.

My father's problems with my sexuality was news to me. And rather than a bridge, I would have said an uneasy truce. They did their best to forget Thom and from time to time, when it annoyed me, I would get angry and something would change. Slowly but surely, I won Thom the right to be seen as my 'significant other' but it felt like a hundred year war with two armies gaining a few feet of ground and then retreating.

It was so good to be able to talk to Maureen at this dreadful time – for I wanted her to tell you how worried I was. I feel your father and I owe her so much for all her support for you, at what must be probably the worst time of your life. This comes with our love always.

I put the letter back in the envelope. I was too tired to write a reply and too angry to risk phoning. For the first time since Thom died, I was not rushing in – throwing dirty clothes in the washing machine – and rushing out. I switched the central heating back on and, with my coat still on, wandered round the house. On the bedside table, Thom's side, there were over thirty bottles of medicines and countless creams. By the bathroom sink was the kitchen stool where, in the last weeks, he would rest while brushing his teeth or halfway through shaving. By the toilet, I found the box of moist tissues he used when even the softest paper was too harsh. Downstairs, the kitchen cabinets were crammed with out-of-date food products claiming to offer all the nutrition of a meal-in-one convenient drink. Among the supposedly healing herbal teas on the windowsill, was just enough room for the small cactus that Thom had bought from a local garden centre. It had finally started blooming and was bent under the weight of two large red flowers.

I retreated into my office. Surely, I'd be safe here? I felt better surrounded by all my books and papers, until from the window, I caught sight of Thom's German VW car with the Red Cross wheelchair still in the boot. Thom had loved to drive, the radio turned up and singing along as he sped across Germany to the beaches of Northern France. He had hated to be reduced to using the wheelchair when I took him to Brighton to go to his barber's. There were too many painful memories here too.

My best friend Gary was coming for the weekend, which seemed appropriate as he'd known Thom only a few hours less than me. (We'd been on holiday in Sitges together when Thom and I met.) I didn't have to collect Gary from the station until the evening, so plenty of time to blitz the place. I returned to the kitchen and sat down; perhaps a cup of coffee would be a better idea. I took the coffee through to the living room; covered myself with the blanket Thom used to keep warm and lay on the sofa. How could I ever cope with a Thom-free life? Perhaps I'd be better waiting for Gary to help with any clear-out. His mother had once worked in a chemist's, so he would know which of Thom's medicines to keep and which to throw away – or at least, that's the excuse I used for doing nothing.

Gary arrived empty-handed at Hassocks railway station. I thought Maureen had asked him to bring food. Somehow the message had got scrambled, so we went to the supermarket. Pushing a trolley up and down the aisles, I was completely overwhelmed by rows and rows of choice. Gary was getting impatient. I forced myself to concentrate. What should I prepare for supper? Chicken? Pasta? Pizza?

My mind was a total blank.

Finally, I gave him the trolley:

'You decide. I'll pay. It's just that I can't make another decision today.'

So Gary filled the trolley while I wandered aimlessly behind him.

After supper, he made me sort through the bottles of medicine on the bedside table. I kept the sleeping tablets – maybe I could use them. Next, we blitzed all the herbs that were supposed to save Thom and amazingly filled six black plastic bin bags. I breathed a little easier.

Sunday 16 March

During the night, I had yet another coughing fit and woke Gary who is a light sleeper.

'You sound terrible.'

'I can't seem to shift this cold,' I explained.

Gary returned with an asthma inhaler.

I took a lungful and amazingly stopped coughing.

'But I've never had asthma before.'

'It's part of getting older.'

And a little closer to death, I thought.

Monday 17 March

I have put the pillow in the middle of the bed, as I sleep better with something to hold on to in the cold hours of the morning. It also makes a convenient barrier between me and the empty half.

After breakfast, I returned the wheelchair to my doctor's surgery and made an appointment to see him later in the week. With the final reminder of sickness and disease expunged, I thought I'd feel more comfortable. But just seconds after stepping through the front door, I knew it was just wishful thinking. Even the most mundane items, such as the tumble dryer, had memories attached to them.

When our old one broke down, yet again, I was desperate to replace it as quickly as possible, especially as Thom had become preoccupied with germs and I had to strip the bed without allowing either the cover or the duvet to touch the carpet. Thom believed the floor would be teeming with bugs. Perhaps there was some truth behind this mania but once, when I was struggling to slide the duvet into a clean cover and the corner slipped on to the floor, he insisted that I wash it again. I regret that this was one of the few times I lost my temper with him.

Anybody else would have visited the nearest electrical super-store. However, Thom was determined to choose our new tumble dryer; despite not being well enough to leave the house. He gave me a list of acceptable German manufacturers to call for brochures. I protested but he wore me down. The manufacturers must have suspected industrial espionage, because extracting information was almost impossible.

After Thom had studied all the data, compared prices and phoned friends in Germany, we were finally ready to order. From the bed, Thom phoned the store to check availability and delivery dates. All I had to do was turn up and sign the credit card slip. He made a great choice. The machine senses when the washing is dry and then shifts to cool air, which prevents the clothes crumpling. I could rhapsodise about its microtherm chip and special features for ever: the easy-to-use dials, the sleek white sheen of the metal door and the efficient German technology that never lets me down.

Thom's personality is stamped across everything I own.

Tuesday 18 March

I tried to write the article for *She* magazine. The brief is simple: read through the six case histories of couples with regular relationship problems and predict where they would be in five years' time. Normally, such an article would have taken about an hour. However, this time, I made notes about one couple then took half an hour off under the blanket on the sofa before I could start again.

I had thought that 'once it was all over', my energy would kick back in and I would cope in my usual wave of 'things that have to be done'. But I had been proved wrong.

The afternoon post gave me plenty of the wrong kind of energy. Up to this point, my sister Gayle has acquitted herself quite well. She had sent a card and had the grace to admit:

Although I didn't know Thom very well, I do know that you loved him and you made each other very happy.

With my parents sunning themselves in Portugal, it was important that at least one member of my family acknowledged my pain and turned up for the memorial service. However, her second card explained that she would not be able to come after all. I became so possessed with the dark forces of 'berserk' that I came close to bouncing off the walls. I switched on my computer and tried to conjure up a foul letter full of threats of Biblical proportions:

I am writing to tell you how much your card upset me. Before it arrived I was having a tolerable day but after reading it I was consumed with hurt and anger. At the very start of my relationship with Thom you snubbed him by not inviting him to your home. Something that you never apologised to him for. Since then you have done your best to ignore him. Finally, you are unable to attend his memorial service because of 'previous commitments' and 'other people are counting on us'. Did it ever occur to you that I was counting on you?

I can't understand how friends (some of whom are not particularly close) have been so supportive and yet no members of my immediate family can attend his memorial service! You are still ignoring him and my feelings.

I was very lucky to have had unconditional love from Thom, but it highlights how conditional my acceptance is in this family. I am

OK as a brother and son as long as I play the game your way – keep my mouth shut and show no emotions. Anything less and you are not interested.

Despite my initial feelings, I do not want to close the door on our relationship. Blood is thicker than water. If you still want to help me through my dark days, a visit from you and the children during their summer holidays would be appreciated.

I wanted revenge but my letter came out reasonable. I wonder if I'll get a reply.

Friday 21 March

Stacey Kent, the singer, is available for an hour on Saturday afternoon. Recently, she has become quite famous, appearing in Ian McKellen's film *Richard III*. Her price is £1,000 – more than the whole funeral in Germany. I have second thoughts, but only for a moment. The closest Thom and I came to a public declaration of our love was signing a form in a back office at the Oxford Street branch of Lloyd's Bank, which changed my personal account into our joint one. With no recognition for the beginning of our relationship, I was doubly determined that the ending would be truly meaningful. So I booked Stacey Kent.

I have also finished the article for *She*. The editor was amused that I suggested the man whose wife was much more successful than him should boost his self-esteem through voluntary work, for example going into local politics. It turns out that the editor had deliberately misled me. What I thought were the problems of ordinary couples were, in fact, famous ones. She thought that if I knew the real identities it would have coloured my advice. So I had written that Tony Blair (then leader of the opposition) should become a politician! Mortified, I went and read the brief again. Only someone very stupid, or too tired to leave the sofa, would not have spotted the ruse. Oh dear, I've suggested the Prime Minister, John Major, is likely to have an affair. I hope Norma does not read *She*.

I've hardly been out this week. I went to Live TV on Wednesday and yesterday a friend helped me pick out a bush for Maureen's garden as a thank you. Otherwise, I've been comforted by following all of Thom's house rules; even the ones which I used to bridle against. I caught myself leaving my keys on the kitchen work surface – another source of germs – I quickly scooped them up and deposited them on the hall table. For a blissful second I would pretend that Thom might walk downstairs and discover my transgression. I tried to work again but it was almost impossible.

At my doctor's appointment this morning, Dr Toynbee diagnosed stress-related asthma. However, he was more interested in discovering whether I was still eating – apparently a key indicator of depression. I reassured him that my appetite was in full working order, not that I obtain any pleasure from the food I mechanically place in my mouth – three times a day. I was about to leave the consultation room, when Dr Toynbee called me back:

'I'm very impressed by how well you looked after Thom.'

I just shrugged. If I had no choice, how could I take any credit?

Coming back from the chemist's, and collecting my prescription, I met one of the community nurses who had cared for Thom. She seemed embarrassed but we were in the twitten (Sussex word for a narrow path between two buildings) and there was no escape.

'How are you coping?' she asked.

How could I possibly answer that question? I muttered something.

'Well life has to go on, doesn't it?' she added.

I nodded glumly.

Why do people have to try and make it better? Why can't anybody just acknowledge my pain?

Saturday 22 March

The invitations to Thom's memorial service asked everybody to wear bright clothes – as Thom had requested 'no black and no sad faces'. I chose Thom's light blue jacket that he often wore to weddings. We'd been raiding each other's wardrobes since we first met, but this morning I took sharing a step further. I slipped on a pair of his underpants, which previously I'd been banned from borrowing on the grounds that I stretched them.

It was a beautiful day and sunlight streamed through the French windows at my friend's large country house. It made a wonderful contrast to the drawn curtains of Thom's sickroom and the gloomy corridors of the crematorium. John, who came with me to the funeral in Germany, had coordinated and paid for the flowers and caterers; another friend hired chairs; one of my neighbours had scanned Thom's photo on to his computer and printed off an order of service; Maureen had found a visitors' book to record who came. Co-opting friends for organising the 'big day' felt much better than handing everything over to the smooth professionalism of the German undertaker.

As each guest arrived, I greeted both the men and the women with a hug. Partly to say thank you, but also to avoid difficult conversations. I didn't want sympathy or reassurance. Who cared if I'd feel better in the future? I had no idea how to make it through the next twenty-four hours, let alone reach this mythical 'future'.

Two of the earliest guests were my mother's brother and sister: Uncle David and Aunt Nancy. We stood in the empty drawing room and discussed their journey, the map that Maureen had provided and whether it was OK to park in the road outside. We skirted round the absence of my parents and my sister.

My cousin Sue made it down from London with her husband and new baby, even though she had given birth just a few days earlier. Her husband, Derek, held up their daughter and declared: 'New Life'. I should have been comforted by the idea of one life going and another coming in, but for the first time ever I felt my love for Thom had been sterile. It was a moment of utter despair. I took a deep breath. There were over forty names signed into the visitors' book. We would need more chairs. I had a quick sob in the toilet and then found three more chairs.

The memorial service was going to be held in what my friend called the ballroom – a large room with a parquet floor where fifty to sixty seats had been set up. The double doors to the room were kept closed as Stacey Kent's three-piece band was still setting up and the guests waited outside in the drawing room. They were standing around not certain what to expect or what to say to each other; clumps of lone people with the one person who united them all for ever absent.

I kept my head down as I crossed the drawing room and added extra chairs into the back row of the ballroom, the musicians – guitar, double bass and saxophone – began to play subdued background music. I was immediately transported back to my cousin Sue's wedding and wished again that it had been possible for Thom and I to marry. A burst of confetti, families posing for photographs and a three-tiered cake – everything Thom would have hated and fought against. I threw open the doors to the ballroom and asked the guests to come through.

My friend John had been the master of ceremonies at many Royal Philharmonic Orchestra concerts, so he was the natural choice to host Thom's memorial. With just the right blend of informality and a sense of occasion, John introduced the first item. Thom was just forty-three, very much a child of the sixties with a rather wry sense of humour. So he chose to start by playing the Rolling Stones' 'You Can't Always Get What You Want'. Next, a German friend, who lives in Brighton, read a poem also used at Thom's funeral, which allowed us to hear some of his mother tongue. An English friend recited an excerpt from Kahlil Gibran's *The Prophet*, which included the line: 'The deeper that sorrow carves into your being, the more joy you can contain.' If only it could be true.

At this point in the ceremony, the guests were invited to speak. Even though they had been alerted on the invitation, British reserve meant few had the courage. However, Maureen remembered Thom's first Christmas in England, how he arrived a stranger but left a friend, and Nancy Roberts, the radio agony aunt, recalled his last Christmas: what a good host he was and how much he loved to see everybody have a good time. Slowly the outer edges of my frozen empire began to melt. John recited some lines from Gilbert and Sullivan's *The Yeomen of the Guard*, which Gilbert had also chosen for Sullivan's funeral. He also had a surprise – Bette Davis (Thom's favourite actress). Everybody laughed. A screen had been set up and we watched a set of clips from *Now Voyager*, *Dangerous*, *The Letter*, *Cabin in the Cotton* and *Jezebel* – all Bette's greatest screen moments. I just hoped Thom was watching, because I knew how much he would have enjoyed it – and there was more to come. His favourite singer was Mama Cass so naturally he would have wanted some of her music. I'd asked Stacey to sing 'Dream a Little Dream of Me'.

The music resonated through my whole body; seeking the nerves under my skin; the emotions under the shock. Her jazz voice wove round the song, matching my sense of longing. Although the tears streamed down my face, my heart was singing along. Words alone had not been strong enough to reach me but this live music was opening me back up to beauty.

I had chosen two further songs for Stacey to perform, which summed up my feelings about Thom: 'The Very Thought of You' and 'Our Love is Here to Stay'. As her voice filled the room, I finally felt able to reach out to all my supportive friends. Their love held me aloft above my pain; I felt like a rock star diving into his audience as I body surfed through the service. Video cameras were rolling to record everything, and it is thanks to the video that I can transcribe my words. I didn't want to speak, but John felt that because I asked everybody else to share I could not duck the challenge. I stood up with not one idea of what to say, but somehow I found these words:

'I've always wondered why Thom liked Bette Davis so much; I've never put my finger on the answer until I watched those clips of Bette as Jezebel determined to wear red while everybody else wore white. Thom too was always determined to do it his way, for instance today he didn't want the traditional funeral. The special thing about Thom was although it always had to be done his way, he was normally right. This is a indeed a lovely way to be remembered.'

I stopped and reached out to Maureen who was holding my box of tissues. I blew my nose.

'I was going to spend ages writing something to read out today, but never got round to it. Putting into words how I felt about Thom, and still feel about him, was just too hard. That's why I chose the song instead – "Our Love is Here to Stay". I feel lucky to have known him because he gave unconditional love. As all my counselling colleagues here today will know, very few people give unconditional love. We are all lucky to have known him. Thank you for coming.'

We finished with the song Thom wants to be played when his ashes are scattered: 'Four Strong Winds' by Judy Collins. Her still quiet voice is accompanied by just a guitar and piano; her style is so simple but, because it comes from the heart, so effective – just like the way Thom loved me, his family and all our friends.

Why can't I just be grateful for the time we shared together rather than mourning our lost future?

When the Judy Collins CD finished everybody left the ballroom, but I sat with my head in my hands for a few minutes more, trying to cling to the last echoes of music for ever. Finally, Tom Flood, friend and supporter through Thom's illness, came and sat beside me. He took my hand and I looked up. It was time to step into the drawing room where the caterers were handing round drinks and canapés. I really needed a glass of red wine. The drawing room was alive with conversation and laughter. It felt good. A perfect balance had been created between our sorrow and Thom's desire that we should enjoy ourselves.

I found that I could smile as well as cry – something that had been impossible at the crematorium. Not surprisingly it was the memorial celebration, rather than the traditional funeral, which I found the most healing. None of the guests had been to one before, but there was universal agreement: memorial services are too good to be left to just the rich and famous. I found it so beautiful, my only regret was that we couldn't do everything all over again, but that is how I feel about life with Thom too.

When everybody had gone and the chairs stacked, I wondered what happened next. Up to that moment, I hadn't given any thought to after the memorial service.

'What do we do now?' I asked Maureen. It was still only early evening.

'I thought we'd see how you felt.'

'What about a Chinese?' John suggested, helping me step over another Thom-shaped hole.

Monday 24 March

Over the years my attempts to communicate with my parents have become grander and grander. I wrote a book (that they did not read), my articles started appearing weekly in *The Independent* newspaper (but according to my mother: 'it is very hard to find *The Independent* in Bedford') and my TV show is shown up to five times a day – seven days a week on a cable channel (their street is cabled but they do not need any more television). Short of erecting a billboard outside their house saying: 'Hear me!' there was nothing left to try – except the complete opposite. So I have decided to stop speaking to my parents – at least for the time being. Our relationship does not work any more, and I need my mother and father too much to pretend that what they're currently offering is enough.

Thursday 27 March

I am exhausted, both emotionally and physically. Over the past two months I have kept a bedside vigil, made arrangements for both a funeral and a memorial service and fought with my family. But at least, it has kept me on the edges of normal life. The nights have been a different matter. I have this recurring dream where I abandon my house, a bit like people with mortgage arrears who post their keys through their building society letterbox and just disappear. It feels so sweet, so tempting, so liberating. With berserk life about to close in over my head, I decided to phone my friend Nancy Roberts:

'When I'm not certain what to do, I sometimes imagine that I'm a caller on my own radio show. What advice would I give myself?'

OK. So what would I say to someone in my situation? I thought for a second.

'You need to get away,' I told myself. 'That's it! A holiday! One week when I can close the front door and not be forced to look at all the souvenirs of life with Thom: the espresso machine, the bean grinder, the coffee filter machine, the five different coffee services, not including stainless-steel cups with in-built thermos to keep the coffee warm.'

'Steady. Steady. Focus. Where would you like to go?' I asked myself.

'Somewhere hot, somewhere I can unwind.'

I made a mug of instant coffee and settled down with my atlas. The traditional sunlounger by the sea held no appeal – far too much time for contemplation.

'What about a major city? With art galleries, historical monuments, places of interest?'

'Of course,' I replied

'So who are you going to go with?'

'That's the problem. Who would be available at short notice? Anyway, other people are exhausting. If I went on my own, nobody would know me. I wouldn't be a widower. I could be just Andrew.'

'So go on your own,' I said to myself.

I settled on southern Spain, which I imagined would be warm in April, and did not involve a long plane journey. In Hurstpierpoint library, I found a guide to Seville. The Alcazar fortress with its legendary palace gardens looked breathtaking. The city's oldest building, the Gothic cathedral, dated back to the early fifteenth century. In comparison, Thom's slow collapse was not even a blink of an eye. I had found my holiday destination.

'Hey, talking to yourself isn't such a bad idea.'

Saturday 28 March

Easter weekend and Jürgen flew over from Germany to pick up some family souvenirs for Erwin and Ursula, to sort though Thom's German paperwork and collect his car. I gave Jürgen a big hug and for the first time since Thom had died, I used his coffee grinder and percolator. We took our *kaffee* and *kuchen* through to the living room.

Jürgen gave me an update on sorting out Thom's affairs. It was fairly straightforward as he had no investments or pension. Jürgen had cancelled his American Express account and that meant that my partner card was no longer valid. No problem. I only had it for emergencies. Jürgen had a bit of cash from closing down Thom's current account, and would use that to pay his return trip through the tunnel. However, he'd discovered a savings policy that Thom had taken out in my name. I didn't understand. He had said nothing. I felt a wave of warmth. Thom was still looking after me.

After the de-brief, I took Jürgen upstairs to Thom's office. I hadn't been in there much, even though his computer has Internet access. Surprisingly, I didn't cry as we sorted through all his drawers, even when we found a box full of clippings from German magazines about his favourite rock group the Mamas and Papas that stretched back to the sixties. There is something terribly sad about the clutter we accumulate.

While Jürgen separated out-of-date guarantees for electrical appliances from letters needed to wind up the estate, I decided to make a start on the bedroom. Beyond clearing away the old medicines, Thom's bedside table was exactly as he had left it. Two minutes would probably be all that was needed, but I'd put the job off until I had emotional support. I could hear Jürgen methodically working his way through the shelves and packing away any German books or videos he fancied. Meanwhile, I achieved little more than staring and sighing. I picked up the book that Thom had been reading: *The Bette Davis Murder Case* by George Baxt. It was covered with dust.

If dust is made up of tiny particles of our dead skin, I wondered, how much of Thom I could reclaim by smearing my finger across the cover?

Under *The Bette Davis Murder Case* was A A Milne's *Winnie-the-Pooh*. We had almost reached the end. I flicked through the pictures and remembered evenings shared together with the residents of the Hundred Acre Wood. A world where all problems can be sorted by the end of the chapter.

I kept thinking about the night when I hadn't wanted to sit with Thom.

What if he'd been building up to say something important? Why did I miss out on those few extra minutes with the man I loved? I dusted the books and left them on Thom's side of the bed.

In the evening, I took Jürgen to the local Indian restaurant. These are quite rare in Germany, so I had to explain all the different strengths of curries. Of course, I remembered doing the same for Thom several years ago. It was extraordinary how everything – even eating a prawn madras – has become about loss.

Sunday 30 March

Jürgen packed Thom's car this morning and drove it back to Germany to sell. I waved him off. It should have been one less problem gone. I don't need two cars and certainly not one which is right-hand drive. Except, it is another lost link with Thom and I both want to escape those and hold on tight.

The black bin bags, piled up at the back door, are not proof that I'm moving on but testimony that Thom will not be returning. All the faith we put in those herbs and potions, creams made from ingredients picked only at first light by peasants halfway up the Himalayas, now they are just rubbish waiting to be ground up along with the neighbours' cornflake packets, tin cans and potato peelings.

If only we'd put more credence in conventional medicine and less in people with beards playing tapes of dolphins singing. If only, if only, if only. How easily I could drown myself in 'if only' but I'm not going down that route.

Last night I couldn't sleep properly and spent the early hours tortured by an urge to scratch myself all over. The heartache is trying to claw its way out of my body.

Monday 31 March

The last day of the bank holiday and I visited my friend Tom Flood at his flat in Palmeira Square (Brighton). He had just come back from a business trip to Japan as guest of the government. Despite the conservative Japanese culture, there were no raised eyebrows that Tom took a man as his official 'plus one'. With the sun streaming through the large windows on to the balcony, I felt incredibly sleepy and curled up on the sofa and slept for three quarters of an hour. I awoke refreshed. It was nice to socialise without feeling that everybody was watching and wondering how I was coping. I returned home in the early evening to pack for tomorrow's trip to Spain.

The lights were on in the living room. For a second, I could believe that Thom was waiting for me rather than the mundane truth: the lights are on a timer to deter burglars.

Still no reply from my sister to my letter.

Tuesday 1 April – Seville

For the first time since meeting Thom, I have gone on holiday alone. I stepped off the plane into an unknown world full of new adventures and new possibilities. With hardly anybody speaking English and my Spanish only stretching to asking for coffee, water, beer and my bill – everything is a surprise. At dinner, I looked at a menu full of strange words, pointed and hoped for the best. Somehow it seemed to perfectly symbolise my life, I don't understand why I have lost Thom or what will help. The best I can do is guess.

Wednesday 2 April – Seville

My first full day in Seville and I aimlessly wandered round the ancient Santa Cruz quarter; through the cool narrow streets, with buildings built so close their eves almost touch, into sun-drenched squares full of orange trees and flower-filled patios. I watched an elderly lady work her broom over what already seemed a clean doorstep, her activity further underlining how for the first time in weeks, I was busy doing nothing.

After buying a dictionary and a map of Seville, I slowly began to find my bearings. Already the city has taught me something: I can cope on my own, even if language and custom make me a stranger. Of course, I wish that I could share everything with Thom and certainly I miss his fluent Spanish to smooth the way. But sitting sipping freshly squeezed orange juice at a pavement café, I can acknowledge the truth: it might have been a better holiday with Thom but it would have been a different one and I was enjoying the moment.

Thursday 3 April – Seville

On the third day, I managed to plug myself into the healing power of beauty. Among the icons and religious paintings at the Museo de Bellas Artes there was a peace that transcends art, something almost spiritual. The gallery was empty. As I wandered from room to room, each portrait of Jesus on the cross at Calvary had the same pain etched across his face. I was irresistibly reminded of Thom's final agony. It became obvious that these artists were not painting from their imagination but from deaths they had actually witnessed. The eyes of all the Renaissance Christs started to follow me round the room. They all had the same haunted expression. I had a revelation: not only do all babies look the same but perhaps all corpses too. We might choose different paths from cradle to grave, and find different disguises along the way, but ultimately we are all the same.

Sprawled across a banquette looking up past the richly ornate columns of the main gallery to the painted domed ceiling – for an instant I actually thought the cherubim and seraphim had sprung into life and were sweeping back the bricks and mortar to reveal a glimpse of heaven. One moment, I could understand everything: the complexity of the atom, the path of the planets, the feral thrust of life, the secrets at the hearts of mankind, but the next moment, I was back in the gallery and instead of knowing all the answers, I was no longer certain that I knew the questions. My heart was beating faster, perhaps a hint of sweat on my upper lip. I ran my fingers over the velvet banquette, grounding myself, but I still had a lingering sense of having touched ecstasy.

I returned to the ground floor of the gallery again. It seemed more healing than the prescribed places of worship, such as the Catedral y Giralda where five tour guides in five different languages spout dates and facts but no understanding. I pulled my notepad out of my rucksack and appropriately enough was drawn to a painting of heaven and hell. *Juicio Final* was by Martin de Vos who lived between 1532 and 1604. It was amazing how he could reach through more than four centuries and still touch me. As good a definition of immortality as there could ever be! I wrote on my notepad:

Great creation often springs from our unconscious; many artistic geniuses claim to be just conduits for a muse perched at their shoulder. The painters whose work hangs in the Museo de Bellas Artes would certainly have believed that these muses were sent from God. I feel that by tuning into the art around me, I am one step away from understanding some greater truth.

The walls of the museum seemed to recede while the paintings moved closer, beckoning to me as if they were portals into new worlds.

The gallery had begun to fill with parties of students shuffling from room to room. Their noise and chatter became a barrier to the geniuses hanging on the walls around me. I decided to submerge myself in music. I put *Everything but the Girl* on to my CD Walkman and relaxed again into Martin de Vos's painting. Tracey Thorn's voice was even more beautiful, more angelic, more alive as it soared above the mechanical, even ugly, industrial hip hop beats. Modern music and sixteenth-century art, new and old combined. The clashing themes suggesting that I might be able to reconcile my battling emotions of sadness and my emerging sense of hope. I have left hell and even if I never reach again the heaven of my union with Thom, the worst might now be behind me.

The contrast between the bored students, here under sufferance, and my almost spiritual connections brought fresh insight: without witnessing the ugliness of Thom's decay and despair, these pictures would be just another stop on a tourist's itinerary. I remembered the reading at Thom's memorial service. Perhaps Gibran was right about the deeper the sorrow, the more joy we can contain. I have found a depth of appreciation that would be lacking if I had left early and hadn't witnessed Thom's death. Without being battered by storms, I would not be able to transcend the moment into this haven of art.

That may be, but I would have happily swapped my new knowledge for those students' innocence. Finally, I wrote in my notebook:

I have no choice but to walk my path and make the best of it.

Death is a shrinking experience with everything focusing down to one hospital, one bed, one well of pain. The visit to the Museo has been a healing, because it has allowed me to start to reconnect with the larger world.

Perhaps the central lesson for all bereaved people is to face the pain head-on. I might want the normal life but in the words of the song Thom chose for his memorial service: 'You can't always get what you want – but sometimes you get what you need.'

Friday 4 April – Seville

Spring proved to be the perfect time to visit Seville. The sun was hot enough to slow life down to a dawdle but not enough to exhaust. When I arrived, 'thinking time' was the enemy to be fought with exotic and new sights. However, with no companion and no small talk, my thoughts had room to breathe. Memories of Thom were always with me, but they no longer felt oppressive. Yes, from time to time my eyes misted over but generally I felt more grateful to have known Thom than sad to have lost him, which is a massive internal change.

Pearl, the producer of *Agony*, was born in Spain and on her recommendation I decided to see a bullfight. I found a small kiosk covered with pictures of matadors. An elderly weather-beaten man sat on a folding chair outside. He spoke no English and kept firing questions in Spanish. So I felt quite proud that I managed to work out the time, the place and the cost of a seat in the shade. He put a hand on my shoulder and pointed me in the right direction for the bullring. I nodded. It was the first time that I'd been touched in ages. I had a tinge of guilt about encouraging cruelty to animals but rather naively hoped the bulls would not be killed.

The Plaza de Toros de Sevilla was in a carnival mood, everybody was calling out to their friends or the vendors for ice creams and cold drinks. The brass band struck up a march and the toreadors entered the circular amphitheatre to applause and bouquets of flowers. The horses were so well trained that their strides were in perfect time to the music. My seat was close enough to feel the sultry air being disturbed as the toreadors thundered past and I longed to reach across, to stroke their handsome mounts and feel the muscles coiled for action. There were a few tourists in my section, marked out by our casual clothes and pale faces. The Spaniards, by contrast, were wearing their best clothes and overflowing with pride. Although I could not understand the significance of the toreadors' costumes or the protocol of bowing to the President's box, I could enjoy the sheer exuberant spectacle.

The first bull was released into the ring, a huge jet-black beast, which roared and lunged towards the toreador. He deftly spurred his horse out of the way. The bull changed direction and charged towards the section where I was sitting. Despite a hefty wooden barricade between me and the brute, some primeval fear lurched up from my stomach. Thousands of years of evolution were stripped away and I could sense my caveman ancestors fighting for survival and food.

The toreador kicked his horse into action and plunged a long dagger, decorated with bright ribbons, into the shoulder of the bull. The audience had almost stopped breathing as the toreador's horse danced out of the way of the bucking horns. The bull lowered its red eyes and charged. Adrenaline was swirling round my mouth as the toreador changed direction again and outwitted his foe again. The audience applauded and the toreador drove another dagger in at the same spot; then another; and another. There was something almost artistic about the red blood flowing down only one black leg. I shuddered at the thought of killing as entertainment. Haven't I seen enough suffering already without paying to watch proud bulls being massacred?

Yet I found myself admiring the skill and bravery of the toreador. As the bull weakened, he dismounted and with only his cloak for protection marched towards the bull. He must have perfectly judged the moment; one swirl of his cape across the bull's eyes and it collapsed stone cold dead. The audience jumped to its feet. The band struck up. The toreador bowed to the President's box and made several laps of honour. His opponent was quickly dragged out of the ring and the sand swept clean again. The refreshment sellers returned and most of the tourists disappeared. Their seats were quickly taken by locals clambering down from the cheaper seats. Everybody ordered more drinks and ice creams and I could make no sense of my competing feelings of disgust and exhilaration.

The second fight was nowhere near as skilful, there were moments when I had to peek between my fingers. Suddenly, I smelt vanilla again. I could have been deluding myself, it might have been the wind picking up the scent from the hair oil of the man sitting next to me. But it was like Thom was sitting beside me, telling when it was safe to open my eyes again – just like he did after a scary moment in a movie.

An uneasy hush hovered over the amphitheatre. The kill was not a good one; the bull had to be finished off with a short dagger. The vanilla came and went again, as if to prove that I was not mistaken. Why should this be the first time, on holiday, that I have sensed Thom's presence?

The rest of the toreadors thrilled the crowd. The carnival atmosphere returned and so did the vanilla scent. Amazingly, among all the killing, I felt closer to Thom than I had done in weeks! There was something refreshingly honest about the bullring: no euphemisms for dying, no hushed tones, no hospital games of hide the body. Having been brought up in an English town, I have seldom seen the corpse of an animal. The cows from the fields round my village are spirited away to some unknown abattoir and reappear in the butcher's cabinet chopped down into unrecognisable chunks. Personally I would never want to hunt or shoot an animal, but there is something unhealthy about the way we push the truth off-stage. Perhaps among the cheering crowds of the bullring, Thom was trying to tell me something: if we all have to die, when the death is quick, and with a dash of honour, perhaps there is something to celebrate.

Sunday 6 April – Seville

Walking back from a late supper last night, I took a shortcut through a square. Something moved in the shadows. I was not alone. I stopped. The shadow stopped. I moved. The shadow moved. I had an overwhelming need to be held, to feel the delicious closeness of skin against skin. I sauntered towards the light and looked back. A man in his early thirties emerged from the darkness, not particularly attractive. What would be the harm? I walked towards my hotel. My heart was beating faster, anticipating the release. The stranger loitered outside the hotel front doors. I beckoned, once, he shook his head. I beckoned again and he followed.

Inside my room, it was over in seconds. A lunge. An explosion. Embarrassment. He even tried to blackmail me and asked for money. I gave him a look of utter contempt. I had planned to do the using! I had wanted to take comfort, be held and give nothing back. He left empty handed and I had my worst night's sleep since Thom's death. How could I be so stupid? I only wanted to feel normal again.

If any of my counselling clients had begged to be normal, I would have murmured something faintly patronising like: 'whatever normal is'. But when your life has been thrown off course, you ache for it. When you're in pain, you long for the pain to be over – or at least forgotten during twenty minutes of good sex. Lying in the dark, I made a deal with myself.

Perhaps if I could take life in two-week blocks, I could cope. It's when I try to contemplate the future, and the agony of the empty years to come, that I do stupid things. I switched on the light and wrote on my notepad:

I must learn PATIENCE.

Monday 7 April

I've never been somebody for lists, able to organise myself without writing down: *take the car in for a service, buy a new watch battery, submit expenses.* But secretly I'd been following a Life List: leave home, buy a house, get promoted, see some of the world, launch a successful media career, find a lasting relationship and raise a dog together. I've never shared these aspirations with anybody, but mentally I'd ticked them all off, one by one. But nowhere on my list was Thom dying and leaving me behind. My list, and my future, were in pieces. Returning from Seville, I felt stronger but still had to face the cold hard facts: I was just camping out in the ruins of my old life.

What if Thom had survived and it had been me who died? His planned extension, with the glass walls to bring the garden into the kitchen and to expand the bathroom upstairs would, no doubt, be well under way. The house would certainly not be a museum to my taste – because I don't have any. So in practical ways, he would have fared better than me. He certainly would not be worrying where to put the salt to soften the water in the dishwasher – and just how much salt was the right amount. If Thom could return, he would know exactly where to find the silver-plated cutlery – because everything would be exactly where he had left it. I am not quite Miss Haversham. I have given his trousers, which did not fit me, to a charity shop, and what else? Probably nothing. Certainly the sample-sized bottles of shampoo that Thom took to the gym are still lined up on the corner of the bath. On the shelf above, there's still the machine he used to massage his feet (complete with a set of different attachments) and his electric toothbrush remains plugged in by the sink.

Thom was the homemaker. I have no energy or any idea how to re-shape the house to suit my new life, partly because it is easier to step round the past, but mostly because I cannot even picture my future.

Tuesday 8 April

John Brocks, a computer literate friend, came over from Guildford to sort out Thom's computer. It keeps giving a warning message about unfragmented files – whatever they are. I was touched that he had given up a day's work to help me out. He installed some software and explained how Thom had set up the computer, which provided a fair insight into his state of mind at the time. The 'Thom' sub-folders were labelled: Barmenia (health insurance), Dr Mohr, Health GB, Herdecke, Last Will, Misc Mail. Most of them were empty but I found a couple of business letters in German.

Next, John Brocks showed me how to switch from Thom's email account into the one he'd set up for me. As I knew nobody with an email account, John suggested sending a trial email to him. Apparently the computer uses my fax line, so I cannot fax and be online at the same time. However, John says I soon won't need a fax machine. Just as well, it keeps jamming when *Agony* sends over the scripts. I decided to keep my old office as a library and move into Thom's.

Later, I changed the duvet cover and savoured the unfamiliar pleasure of letting it brush the floor, unconcerned about the hidden germs that my shoes have brought into the bedroom. I'll never have to bundle the bedding back into the washing machine and start all over again. A small but tender mercy.

Saturday 12 April

Happy thirty-eighth birthday to me.

Even though I am refusing to talk to my parents and at war with my sister Gayle (who still hasn't replied to my letter), they have both sent parcels. Incensed, that they are carrying on as if nothing had happened, I hid the presents in a cupboard in case they polluted my birthday. My stand means there are no presents to open and only a couple of cards, but I don't feel much like celebrating.

Richard (a childhood friend) has invited me to stay for the weekend in London. I have accepted; partly because I don't want to be on my own and partly because I expect my mother will ring and I am still not strong enough to talk to her.

Sunday 13 April

I stayed over at Richard's and the next morning we walked over to the house that he is buying to measure for curtains. Talking with an old friend was comforting, although I am jealous that he has the energy to move.

Over the weekend, I was home for just an hour but my mother still managed to catch me. I listened to her wishes of happy birthday and then firmly put the phone down, without saying a word.

Monday 14 April

How can anyone who has been bereaved just take a week off work, arrange a funeral and then return to the office? All I want to do is lie on the couch. If I have any advice for the recently bereaved it would be this: invest in satellite television. After the shock of Thom's death I cannot deal with the fast pace of contemporary drama, or the struggle of meeting new characters. I much prefer *Upstairs Downstairs* where the scenes unwind so slowly that today's television directors would start twitching. Watching old *Coronation Street* episodes from the 1980s, I felt strangely powerful. As the characters struggled and worried about their future, I had the grim satisfaction of knowing exactly what fate held in store for each one of them. I have even started watching old game shows, not only can I amuse myself by guessing from clothes and haircuts when they were first transmitted, but it is easier to cope with the losers' disappointment knowing everybody has long since left the studio and returned to real life. With the same shows scheduled at the same time across the week, I can even create a rhythm and routine to my day.

Tuesday 15 April

Even though most of Thom's life was spent in Germany, there are still lots of people to inform in this country. When I asked Lloyds Bank to change our joint account, so that all my cheques no longer bear Thom's name, they sent a nice letter asking for clarification. When I explained further, they sent a second one requesting a copy of the death certificate.

Today, I went fully prepared to the supermarket to change our Tesco Loyalty Card from Thom's name into mine. I gave a full account to the woman at Customer Services and produced the death certificate. The shop assistant looked startled. All I needed to do was phone a special freephone line. I could still feel her eyes following me as I selected my fruit and vegetables.

Wednesday 16 April

I had my weekly trip to London to make *Agony*, so my relationship with the box was more interactive than just watching *Coronation Street* and shouting: 'Deirdre, if you think you've got problems now wait until you discover the heartache that's on the way!'

Recording five TV shows in one day was tiring but fortunately all the viewers' problems were totally unconnected with my life. With epics such as 'would I be happier with bigger boobs' and 'I found a vibrator in my wife's underwear drawer and now I feel redundant', there was no danger tapping into my pain. In fact, it was good to get out of the house and discover that other people are working and socialising – and oh yes, having a love life!

After the show, Kate, my co-advisor on *Agony*, wanted some advice from me, which only seemed fair. She had her car with her and suggested getting away from Canary Wharf (where the TV station was based). I had always known Kate's life was far from simple. However, I only realised how tough things had become when our conversation in the car was interrupted by honking horns. Kate was trying to cross the bridge from the wrong side.

When we'd made it safely to the pub, Kate explained that her father's cancer was no longer in remission. She was trying to be positive and look into alternative therapies but somehow we've become the experts with more problems than our viewers.

Thursday 17 April

My television viewing has taken a more sinister turn. I have started counting all the actors and actresses who are now dead but still on the box entertaining me.

Previously, freelance work had fitted perfectly round Thom's compromised health. If he was going through a bad patch, I could take on less work and be available to take him to a hospital appointment or fly with him to Germany. Although working from home could be lonely, I could break off to chat with Thom or to discuss an idea for an article with him. Now, I ache for a proper job and the safety of nine to five. In my fantasies, my new job will involve idle chats over the photocopier and perhaps shuffling bits of paper. I will have the warm support of my work colleagues and absolutely no stress whatsoever.

I read the adverts in this week's *Media Guardian* and even cut out a couple. But who am I fooling? Even a friend failing to return a message feels like an echo of death's rejection. Everybody's advice has been: 'It's far too early to make any decisions.' But it has been six weeks, I have to get back to work. I cannot risk defaulting on my satellite TV subscription.

Friday 18 April

Phobic about phoning up strangers, my only option is to speak to commissioning editors I already know. When I speak to Hilly Janes at *The Independent* she needs someone to write 'Revelations' – their celebrity profile – because the regular journalist is on holiday. With my background as a counsellor, I should be able to coax celebrities to open up about a turning point where they learned something important about themselves. I suggest rock musician Garry Christian who is about to release his first album since leaving The Christians.

Despite not being able to speak French, Garry has moved to Paris and believes this has refreshed his music: 'I believe that people would be doing far more with their lives if they had more courage to turn the corner, but fear gets in the way.'

Tuesday 22 April

I was deep into my article on Garry Christian when a Royal Mail van pulled up outside the house. Excited at the prospect of a mystery parcel, I almost jumped down the stairs. The postman handed me a heavy box – about the size of small bread bin. I read the label and realised I was holding my partner again. It was a very surreal moment.

Jürgen had been uncomfortable about flying over to England with the urn, so without giving a second thought about how it might arrive, I'd told the undertakers to send it. Signing for my special delivery, I felt like I had been beamed into a Joe Orton comedy. Should I laugh or cry?

Thom's family and Walter were not due to fly over and scatter the ashes for another fortnight, so I was faced with a dilemma: what should I do with Thom's mortal remains in the meantime? Maureen recommended asking an undertaker to store them, but that suggested Thom was not welcome in our home – a horrible thought. I wandered round the house looking for inspiration. First off, I hid the urn in a cupboard – rather than have a daily reminder of the past. However, half an hour later, this felt wrong. I took the urn out of the cupboard and put it at Thom's place at the dining room table. It felt strange to be alone in the house with his ashes, so I invited Valerie, my next-door neighbour, round for coffee. There was something very macabre about drinking out of Thom's best china while his remains watched us. When I explained the situation to Valerie, she looked round rather too quickly but on the whole took the news that she was supping with the dead quite well.

Thursday 24 April

I have decided to laugh rather than cry about Thom's ashes and have sold *The Independent* a lighthearted article about the starving leeches, live insects and pig's sperm that are also sent through the post. Apparently the ideal temperature for semen preservation is 17–20°C – the average temperature of our Victorian post office sorting depots. Even in winter, there is no danger of boar's semen freezing because the postmen are working in the vans and their body heat keeps the temperature up. Apparently, we are the envy of Europe and worldwide because they cannot believe that any-where in Britain can get semen the next day.

While writing the article, Kate, my fellow agony aunt from Live TV, phoned and admitted to participating in a 'knickers' chain letter: 'Although I don't generally approve, this one in-trigued me because I could end up getting thirty-one pairs of knickers, which is always handy, and all I had to do was put my size down,' she said. Kate had sent parcels to the two names at the top of the list: 'It was a strange experience buying underwear for other people, it was such an intimate thing to do. I knew a couple of the names, they seemed to be all sensible middle-class women who should be out walking dogs rather than falling foul of a knickers chain letter. It was exciting opening the parcels I received, although my husband thought I was completely mad. I ended up with four pairs, they were all clean, which was a relief.'

Monday 28 April

My next 'Revelations' article was actor Gary Wilmot (appearing in the West End in a musical version of Neil Simon's *The Goodbye Girl*). He chose the death of his father who was a member of a successful harmony group: 'I was only six, so I didn't attend the funeral although there was a photographer there who took a bi-zarre wedding-style photo with all the relations lined up behind the coffin. I don't even remember being told he was dead; I sup-pose I detected it from the atmosphere. I do remember a friend showing me a tiny piece in the paper. I remember the headline "*Southlander* dies at 42". I must have known because it wasn't a shock to me.'

I was interested to discover that smell was also a link between Gary and his father: 'He was always dressed smartly, meticulous about his clothing with shoes brushed until they were highly polished. To this day, whenever I smell the steam of something being pressed – it reminds me of my father.'

Meanwhile, I have begun to get used to having Thom's urn in the house and have even started kissing it goodnight.

Life might be strange but how death affects us is even stranger.

Wednesday 30 April

It is my father's birthday today. As I'm currently not speaking to my parents, I decided not to send a present or a card. I know it sounds mean and small-minded, but I'm too angry to pretend his birthday makes everything magically better between us.

Thursday 1 May – General Election Day

I have worked on every general election night since Margaret Thatcher's first victory in 1979. However, this time round, my sole contribution is a pre-recorded piece for Live TV's *Sex Show* on why politicians turn women on. I doubt many people will be switching over from the regular coverage for my insightful analysis.

As I didn't fancy watching the results come in alone, I arranged to drive over to Maureen's house. Although I enjoy the drama of election night, Thom was much more political than me. He had even been a member of Germany's socialist party.

I wished that he could have known that the Conservative Party and their Clause 28 (making it illegal to 'promote' homosexuality) and their unequal age of consent were probably on their way out. Almost immediately, my car was filled with vanilla. He did know.

I stayed up to watch Michael Portillo lose his seat to an 'out' gay man and returned home filled with hope for the future.

Saturday 3 May

Thom's funeral and memorial service had been mainly organised by other people, so I took charge of the scattering of his ashes. I booked a nearby hotel for Jürgen, his wife Gabi and Walter (Thom's best friend from Germany). Gary, who had been on holiday with me in Sitges when I first met Thom, lives in London and would stay overnight with me. I also invited our local friends Maureen, John and Elaine and booked a minibus to take everyone to Beachy Head. The cool box was packed with the best champagne and I had recorded the two songs Thom wanted played on to a cassette. I even had a dry run opening the urn and sliding out the metal container, which held Thom's last remains.

Unfortunately, the lid was tightly sealed and I used too much brute force. My hand slipped, the container tipped over and deposited a small gritty residue across the garden patio. I quickly swept it up, trying not to remember how often Thom had hosed down those same stones. I made a mental note to pack a screwdriver to prise the lid off properly. Nothing would be worse than being stuck on top of Beachy Head unable to perform the ritual. Everything has to be checked because everything has to be perfect.

This morning, the sky was blue and clear. I was relieved and even contemplated taking a picnic to Beachy Head. However,

Maureen phoned. She has eaten something that disagreed with her and was permanently closeted with her toilet bowl. It will not be the same without her.

The next call came from Germany. The plane had developed a fault, should they cancel? It had taken us weeks to fix this date. I'd told myself that this will be the turning point. I want to feel at ease in my own skin again. I take a deep breath. Fortunately, Jürgen was keen to press on and we decided that they should take a later flight into Heathrow (rather than nearby Gatwick).

By the late afternoon, when we had all gathered at my house, it had begun to drizzle and the weather had turned cold. Gary asked to borrow a coat as he'd only brought sunny weather clothing. He was shocked by how much Jürgen looks like Thom. I pretended to be surprised but the similarity has not escaped me. Although a hug of condolence from Jürgen feels nothing like having Thom in my arms, it is the nearest I will ever get.

I was never keen on Thom's choice of Beachy Head for scattering his ashes. The white cliffs and the open grassland might look picturesque but the place also holds the world record for the most suicides every year. However, Thom was adamant. The closer the minibus I'd hired got to Beachy Head, the more convinced I became that today was a mistake. Staring out of the rain-smeared windows, my sense of frustration was rising. If Jürgen, Gabi and Walter had not travelled so far, I would have suggested turning back.

A thick sea fog hung over the South Downs. I had imagined us drinking in the beautiful scenery and celebrating Thom's life, instead we could only see about ten feet in front of ourselves. My pastoral idyll has been transformed into a nightmare. I've been to hell so often I should be eligible for frequent flyer miles.

The rain had stopped by the time the driver parked the minibus. I could tell that nobody wanted to get out. The plan had been to find a particularly beautiful spot for Thom's final resting place but in the fog one tuft of grass looks much like another. It was so cold that we were all huddled into our coats, the only thought in our minds: to get it over as quickly as possible.

We followed a fence hoping that it was a barricade to stop us falling over the edge of the cliff, but after a few minutes decided to stop. With no idea where we were and at risk of not being able to find the bus again, we decided that 'here is as good as anywhere'. It was about as healing as letting down the tyres of a gang of Hells Angels' motorbikes.

We formed a small half circle, our backs to the wind. I'm mouthing words about how much I loved Thom and everybody is listening intently, so I must be making sense. But what I'm really thinking is: when does the shock of losing somebody go away? I feel numb and detached from everybody else. Jürgen, in particular, is weeping and I'm just watching with mild interest, a scientist conducting an experiment into grief.

Apparently it takes only six seconds to fall the 535 feet from the top of the cliff at Beachy Head to the beach below. So far this year the average age of all the people who have committed suicide is exactly forty-three – the same age as Thom.

Even though I'm holding his urn, which is surprisingly heavy, I do not feel really there. I reach down to press the play button on the cassette player and nothing happens. What little poetry that the moment possessed is lost as I fumble around. How could this have happened, I must have checked it a hundred times? Eventually I rewind the tape and find the first song: 'Dream a Little Dream of Me' by Mama Cass.

In my vivid imagination, the mix-up with the music has been arranged by Thom – along with the plane fault to stop us being there today. Perhaps he had read the celestial weather forecast. Misery, misery, misery. Next I play Judy Collins's 'Four Strong Winds' and start to liberate my lover. Judy sings: 'The good times are all gone and I'm bound for moving on.' I am untouched.

The wind tosses the ashes into a million different patterns, like a small child turning a toy spyglass with a kaleidoscope. I am intrigued by the shapes that the wind spells out, but I feel no connection between the man I loved and the coarse sandy substance we are casting into the fog.

Despite all the significance our culture invests in this moment, all I found inside Thom's urn was waste product. Thom is somewhere else.

Monday 5 May (Bank Holiday)

I did not feel up to socialising or pretending to work. Few people of my age have to cope with losing their partner. Fewer still have stood on these shores of hell with their eyes wide open. Strong as the temptation is to blur the senses, so far I have resisted. In an age that wants to deny our mortality and 'live for ever', this can make you feel very lonely.

I've become obsessed with the topic of death. It's a deeply unsettling preoccupation and one that is guaranteed not to make you a wow at parties. But socialising without Thom is extremely hard and I've stopped accepting those sorts of invitations anyway.

Tuesday 6 May

My cousin Sue invited me up to London because Stacey Kent was performing and launching a new CD at the Jazz Café. Before going out, we had a glass of dry white wine and she fed the baby.

'How did you cope when your father died?' I knew the basic facts but we'd never really discussed his death before. And I'd thought we were close.

Sue had the shadow of a tear in her eye.

'Please tell me about it,' I asked again.

'One of the first things I did was visit the squash club where dad had a heart attack,' Sue explained. I wanted to escape memories of Thom's death, but her instinct was to be closer. 'However macabre it might sound, I just wanted to sit there, sense the atmosphere and discover if there was any residue there. It turned out to be very peaceful. What absolutely fascinated me was the physiological things that caused the heart attack and I read lots of books to get my mind round how it could have happened; so I could understand what my father felt. My mother brought his squash clothes home from the hospital, washed and ironed them. I remember looking at that fabric and being completely fascinated, that fabric had been there and seen it all. From the objects around him I could feel the man.'

Stacey Kent was superb. Derek, Sue's husband, even bought me a copy of the CD and refused to let me pay. Thank you.

Friday 9 May

Emboldened by talking to Sue, I decided to ask other friends about their experiences of death. I had supper with Nancy Roberts – my fellow agony aunt who had spoken at Thom's memorial service.

'What particularly upsets me about my mother's death is that she died alone.'

Nancy has been a pillar of support so I felt guilty about dragging up her painful memories, but like every compulsive I could not stop. 'It can still pull me down into depression, if I allow myself to think about it, even though it was several years ago now.'

'But didn't you give up work to be with her?' I remembered.

'I was at the bedside every single day, but the night she actually died I came home to sleep at about midnight. At 4.30 a.m.,

I got a call from the nurse telling me she thought I'd better come. I went flying up the street but it was too late. I was very upset, sorry and extremely guilty that she died alone. The nurse had left the room to fetch my father and to telephone us. I know it is not rational but I can't help the way I feel.'

Hearing Nancy talk about her parents made me feel guilty about refusing to speak to mine, but I am still not strong enough for the confrontation and frightened – if it goes wrong – that I might disintegrate and, like Thom's ashes, be blown over the horizon.

Saturday 10 May

Elaine, my friend who lives up the road and I employ as a cleaner, came round this morning and together we fulfilled another of Thom's deathbed requests:

'Clean under the bed and replace the vacuum cleaner. It blows as much as it sucks.' It seemed amazing that Thom should worry about cleaning a house that he would never see again. Perhaps that's why ghosts at seances have such strange messages. Rather than great revelations about life after death, they are more likely to warn their nearest and dearest:

'Don't forget to clean the grill pan.'

Amazingly, I found carrying out Thom's final wish for a new vacuum cleaner more therapeutic than the ashes scattering. It was certainly very cleansing.

It is my mother's birthday today. I know she will be heartbroken about not receiving a phone call or even a card, but I don't care. I'm still too angry to play nice. And if I'm being honest: I want to punish my parents for never really acknowledging Thom, even though the counsellor part of my brain knows it's easier to be angry with my parents than with Thom himself.

A few days ago, I'd fancied a drink of orange squash. I shook the bottle and the top flew off. Not screwing the cap back on properly was one of Thom's tricks. Seething, I mopped up the mess and wished he were here for me to shout at. Why did he have to leave? We were supposed to be together for ever. But, try as I might, I cannot be angry with Thom for long. He was so worried about how I would cope without him – he didn't want to go.

Thom had no choice while both my parents and Gayle opted to stay away from the memorial service – no wonder I hate them. Help, I'm regressing into Adrian Mole, aged 13¾.

Sunday 11 May

This afternoon, I was working in the garden. It was a pleasure to be out in the open air but my energy levels were still poor. I stopped and looked around. The bushes needed chopping back and the flower beds were overrun with weeds. During Thom's decline, I had mowed the lawn but not much else. How would I ever catch up?

Perhaps it would be easier if I just killed myself! Shocked. I put down the shears and sat on the edge of the rockery. Even in the darkest early days, I had never considered suicide, but now the first flush of pain was receding and I felt well enough to kill myself? Perhaps blitzing the garden hadn't been such a good idea.

I cleared up the grass cuttings and put away the lawnmower. I immediately felt better. More considered thoughts replaced the suicidal ones: when Thom was worn down by illness, he would threaten to drive off Beachy Head. I knew he didn't mean it but that didn't stop me from hating him for just saying it. And how would my parents feel if I committed suicide? I might be angry with them but I loved them too.

I closed the door to the garden shed, covered my face with my hands and wept. The desire to kill myself might have lasted only a few seconds but it had been so wonderfully invigorating. So easy. So perfect.

I think it's time to get some counselling.

Tuesday 13 May

I recorded an interview for the satellite TV channel UK Living. While the director set up the shots and the floor staff made certain my microphone cable wasn't showing, the presenter Kathryn Holloway told me about her childhood nightmares:

'The teachers at my school were so graphic about hell, they handed out incredibly lurid pictures of the crucifixion with blood pouring everywhere and a blue-lipped Christ. I've always had a strong imagination and it became so bad that my doctor actually prescribed tranquillisers when I was just six years old. I would wake up convinced that I had read my own parents' gravestones or that my heart had stopped beating.'

As a child, I had a vivid imagination too and I could picture myself having similar fears.

'What made all the difference was when I was older, about twenty, and saw my grandmother die very peacefully,' Kathryn continued. 'I remember her still being warm as I placed my hand on her forehead and it resolved for me so many fears of how it could be. Although I loved her very much and felt terribly sad, I saw with my own eyes that there was nothing to fear.'

'But it's not always as beautiful,' I replied.

At that point, we were given the signal that the recording was about to begin.

Cheery music came over the loudspeakers, and on the monitors I watched bright visuals of coffee being poured into mugs.

The more I thought about it, the more I thought there was probably an article in this subject. So after the programme, I asked Kathryn for her telephone number. She also suggested phoning a friend, Patsy Tipene, an intensive care nurse, who is a Maori.

Although she left New Zealand over ten years ago, Patsy is still getting used to our approach: 'Death is almost hushed up in this country. If someone dies in our family we are with the body all the time, we will lay out and wash our loved one and put them in a shroud ourselves. We will bring them to a special ex-tended family house called a marae and everybody gathers there for three or four days before the funeral. We will even sleep there. Round the casket, there's always several people sitting sharing memories. Eight hundred people came to pay their respects to my grandmother.'

'Even children?'

'From the age of three or four I would go to funerals and just like at weddings in this country, kids are running around: playing, screaming and laughing. I'd always been used to seeing the open casket and not being afraid to look at the body. There is none of this shoving the children away in case they see something upsetting.'

'My grandfather died when I was five,' I told her.

'Did you see the body?'

'I wasn't even taken to the funeral. I stayed at home with our cleaning lady.'

'The English are strange.'

I started trawling the Internet to find how other cultures ap-proach bereavement. I particularly liked the Muslim tradition where the mourners do not cook for themselves for forty days. Instead, relatives and neighbours bring food round. In Hindu ceremonies, the family play a key role, rather than handing every-thing over to professionals – the job of lighting the cremation fire goes to the eldest son. While in Nepal, five weeks of mourning are ended by building an effigy of the deceased using their clothes to make it more realistic. Money and food are placed at its feet and children and close relatives take it in turns to make vows, giving everybody another chance to say their goodbyes. African societies are in no doubt about the importance of tears. An Igbo widow is expected to howl and wail between five and six in the morning for up to four days after the funeral. The crying is expected to be loud enough for the neighbours to hear, or everybody in the village will want to know why.

Wednesday 14 May

I interviewed Dr Tony Carr, a clinical psychologist and director of the Plymouth Bereavement Service, for an article which I sold to *She*: 'Death like living, is highly variable. Some people are blessed by fortunate and easy deaths but others are not. We tend not to talk about the unpleasant ones because they are upsetting to recall and don't make terribly good conversation. If, like me, you witness a difficult death it is a terrible shock particularly as all the terminology – passing away – encourages us to think it is a smooth affair.' Worse still, the myth of the easy death means that our culture gives virtually no long-term support to the bereaved; almost every other world culture offers more.

I concluded the article by writing:

I have decided that when my time comes I will say my goodbyes but then ask to be left alone. I do not want to have to pretend that death is anything but awful and it is certainly not a spectator sport. I don't want to worry about my final words to friends and family. When it is my turn to die, I know my mind will be on greater things than being polite.

Friday 16 May

I was anxious about going for counselling. It is normally me listening and asking questions while someone else shares the darkest corners of their heart. However, I have been 'resting' from Relate (The UK's largest couple counselling charity) since Thom's last illness. I have not returned because, to be frank, I am in no fit state to help anyone else.

Arriving too early for my appointment in Brighton, I wandered down to Brighton sea front for a short stroll. I hoped that watching the waves and the seagulls would take my mind off everything. Instead, I just remembered how much Thom loved the sea. I checked my watch: ten to four. If I walked back now, I'd only be five minutes early. Better set off back. Outside the clinic, I almost crossed over to look at the Lidl supermarket. Thom and I would often pass by on our way to the Marina cinema complex but never went inside. Three minutes to four. Maybe I should ring the clinic bell?

I was let in by a tall man with a slightly careworn expression. He turned out to be my grief counsellor. Our room had two low-slung chairs, behind them was a high bed for the alternative therapists who also practised there. I have no memories of what we talked about during our first session but complete recall of the cream eiderdown over the bed. The colour and the ridges spaced at intervals of an eighth of an inch were just like the cover over my bed from age seven to about twelve. I sat with my back to this eiderdown and faced my counsellor. I know he was tall and thin, probably in his fifties, but my mind has blanked out all his features.

This first session was supposed to allow us to get to know each other but he was surprised when I asked for a list of his qualifications. Beyond a busy private counselling practice, he explained, he was also the supervisor for a local bereavement project. It seemed that I had come to the right place. By the end of the hour, I had twelve crumpled tissues at my feet. He offered the bin and I wrote a cheque. I was in counselling.

Thursday 22 May

Bereavement's cruellest trick is to expose the fault lines in your life and blow them apart. Worse still, it happens when you have barely enough energy to microwave convenience food. Thom's death meant that I could no longer paper over the cracks in my relationship with my parents.

So what is the problem? I was brought up in a family, from a nice middle-class background, in a very nice market town in the middle of middle England. The most interesting fact about Bedford, when I was growing up, it was the only major town not to have a bypass. There were no raised voices in our house and I have never heard my parents argue. My mother is a peacemaker and if my father feels very strongly he can work himself up into a cool sulk. Kate thinks my parents sound wonderful. Her family were always screaming at one another.

My mother is adamant that she cannot remember the defining moment of my childhood. I was five years old, when she leaned over the edge of the bath and explained that my grandfather had died. I started to cry.

'Don't be so silly,' she said. 'Don't be so silly.'

I stopped and looked up at this large powerful figure bending down over my small naked body. Suddenly I realised these tears were not allowed. The kind man who had built a toy garage and carved building bricks for me was dead but I was supposed to hear the news with a shrug of my young shoulders. To fit into this family, to be acceptable, I would have to shape up and shut up. I learned my lesson very young and I tried to follow the rules, I promise, but it is just not in my nature.

Having given up work shortly before I was born, my mother turned her considerable energy into bringing up first me and then my sister. She perfected the modern science of being a housewife and the white-hot heat of new technology shone in her kitchen. Her life must have revolved around us: a cooked breakfast every morning; my father and I came home for lunch; and she made a point of being home when we arrived back from school; always willing to hear about lessons and help with homework. There was milk, never pop, to drink. It was my 'deprived' friend's house across the road where there was cola in the fridge, which rotted your teeth. Family TV viewing could be a strain especially when characters kissed, my father would shuffle his papers and my mother would look the other way. I remember Westerns like *The Virginian* not for excitement of the fist fights or shoot outs but the Marshall embarrassment of the romantic clinches. Perhaps feelings were something which only Americans from the 1890s possessed?

I certainly believe that I brought myself up emotionally, perhaps that is why I am so hopeless at DIY and anything practical. I had to channel all my energy in different directions. Looking back, I wonder why I didn't burst into the house with a gun and start shooting at everybody, but what could I do? They didn't give Uzi sub-machine guns to teenagers in the seventies.

Although Thom's arrival in my life caused family angst, it also helped ease the problems. The two of us created our own new nuclear family and I cared less how my mother and father felt. To Thom's eternal credit, he was never upset by their snubs – only mildly amused by my exasperation. At Sue's wedding, there were acquaintances my mother had not seen for twenty-five years and lots of: 'You must be Jill's son.' One particularly garrulous woman had placed all the sisters, cousins and aunts and turned to Thom to ask his connection to the family. There was a slight pause and a horrified look on my mother's face. I almost thought she was going to stage a diversion, spill her drink or throw a plate of peanuts down the woman's cleavage. Thom hesitated. What would he say? Would the horrible truth be revealed? The whole world held its breath. But Thom was far kinder than me, he replied: 'I'm a friend of Andrew's.' My mother was visibly relieved. It didn't matter that her tormentor would wonder why a grown man would bring 'a friend' to a wedding. Appearances had been kept up.

After Thom was diagnosed as terminally ill, the flight back to Germany coincided with a family day out in London to which I should have gone. I never normally cancel anything, but with Thom too ill to travel alone I made my apologies. Even these alarm bells were ignored. My mother's next call gave full details of the pleasant day out. We talked about the changes to the Tower of London since she had taken Gayle and I there as children, the conveyor belt that stops people loitering in front of the crown jewels and what her grandchildren James and Nicola had made of the ravens. She did not enquire after Thom.

Death is the polar opposite of niceness, so I did not tell her about incontinence pants and round the clock nursing. I was seldom in England by this time, so we didn't talk that often. The time between her calls to me lengthened and I never phoned because I had nothing to say that was not full of despair and pain. A good measure of the distance between us: I didn't even consider giving her my telephone number in Germany and she never asked for it.

It has been almost three months since Thom died. I've told my-self I should be ready to face my parents and attempt to cross the chasm between us. I know my mother and father would want us to make up and step back into ordinary life. I am frightened that they still can't accept I'm gay and that will tip me back into madness. I decided peace talks would be easier face to face and on home terri-tory. So I phoned and, in my most business-like tones, invited my parents down for a visit. I could tell from the edge to my mother's voice she had feared this day would never come. It will: tomorrow.

Friday 23 May

My parents stepped off the train, full of anxious-to-please smiles and a chocolate cake that my mother had baked. During the five-minute car journey from the station, she tried to make small talk but I deflected her attempt to hide in the normal life. How can I discuss the view when I'm rehearsing how to break through years of niceness? The tension rose as my mother stared out of the window searching for further topics of conversation. My father, as always, said nothing. The journey home had never seemed longer. If there were angry recriminations, I told myself I had the strength to let them walk out the door. But what if there was only the usual Marshall family damp squib?

In almost a parody of the English middle classes, I decided not to harangue my parents as soon as they crossed my threshold and instead offered a cup of tea. As I passed round the chocolate cake, my stomach began to turn in on itself and I could hardly swallow. My parents sat uneasily on Thom's German minimalist sofa, drinking out of his Rosenthal cups with their feet on his art deco rug. The silence kept on building. I was sure they must be able to hear my heart pound, but the stillness was broken only by the clink of china on china as cup was replaced on saucer. I sipped my tea and tried to buy a few more moments. Fortunately, my mother was made of sterner stuff:

'Are we not allowed to know our fate?' she asked.

My mother put up a staunch defence about their failure to attend Thom's memorial service. My father's bad back meant that he really needed that holiday; she had to put him first. No flights were available to come back early and in fact seats to Portugal are so rare that they have already booked for this autumn. My father said nothing. I was unmoved.

Next, I complained about how they treated Thom when he was alive. Apparently, I am too sensitive and too ready to take offence when none is intended. My father still said nothing.

We appeared to have reached stalemate. I took a deep breath, and was about to launch back on to the offensive when it suddenly hit me: something incredible was happening in my living room. For the first time in our family's history, everything that had been left unspoken or articulated only with a sigh, a cold shrug or walking away was being faced. The living room clock still ticked, the birds still sung in the wood at the bottom of the garden, the world had not ended.

'Have you any idea, what it is like to know that your only son is hurting and being told there is nothing you can do to help? Nothing at all,' asked my mother and she started to cry, what Thom would have described as, real tears.

Nothing I had ever done before had affected her so deeply. I felt more alive than ever before.

Except, I had really hurt her.

My father said nothing and did nothing to comfort his wife.

'My own mother once did something terrible that really hurt me,' she continued, 'but she did not realise how much. I understood and did not reproach her.'

What she meant, I thought, was: why didn't you turn the other cheek too?

I was tempted to blurt out: fool to put up with it. But I just nodded. Previously, articulating my feelings would have been labelled as 'showing weakness' and laughed at but this time I felt empowered. So I explained that when they ignored Thom or turned away when I expressed something approaching a human emotion, that I felt unloved.

For the first time my father spoke:

'But you've always been our Andrew.'

It was the first time he had ever acknowledged any kinship, any closeness to me.

'That's nice to hear, I wish you'd told me earlier.'

'We might not be very good with words, but we do love you.' His face softened.

'But for me, saying "we" distances everything,' I replied as evenly as I could manage.

When I'd 'come out' to them, it had been my mother who told me: 'We love you' and after being challenged she changed this to: 'I love you.' My father had kept his feelings firmly to himself. What would happen this time? The art deco rug between us seemed larger.

'I love you,' he said.

'Do you realise that is the first time you have ever told me that?' I choked out.

'I suppose it is.'

My heart was singing. I had achieved more than I had ever hoped.

From my experience with couple counselling, I knew that long lasting shifts are built on benefits for both sides. I consciously put away my needy inner child and tried to understand their side. Finally, we were ready for a compromise: my mother and father will try to stop pussyfooting around and be open and honest; I will try not to overreact.

For my parents, actions speak louder than words. So after lunch, I let them show their love by working in the garden. One of Thom's final projects, before illness really took a grip, was building a raised herb garden. All through that last summer, whenever he was in hospital, I had strict instructions to water everything daily. One of his favourite presents was a set of photos showing how well his tomatoes were growing. One of my happiest memories, when Thom returned home, was watching him pottering around his herb garden, pinching back, weeding and fussing. Sitting in the sunshine browsing through the Sunday papers, I could pretend that everything was normal even if Thom was still in his dressing gown.

Since Thom died, I have been incapable of looking after the herb garden. The flower bed is overgrown and full of weeds. So my mother spent the afternoon clearing dead plants, cutting back the lemongrass and pulling out the wild clematis.

Later we had tea and another slice of my mother's home baked cake on the patio. I felt more relaxed than I had in weeks, until out of the corner of my eye I saw Thom's freshly tidied herb garden. Tears filled my eyes. I was not just crying. I was overwhelmed with sadness. The full reality of death finally hit me. I was not looking after Thom's herb garden on a temporary basis, it was my responsibility for ever.

My parents had no idea how to react. My father was embarrassed; my mother was helpless. So they cleared away the table, washed up and put the cake in a tin. I sat in the garden, unable to move. The train to Bedford was due in about fifteen minutes and my parents hate being late for anything. Somehow, I drove them to the station. After a quick kiss on the cheek, they got out of the car and walked across to the 'up' platform.

My mother looked back with deep regret but what could she do? Thom was gone for ever.

Saturday 24 May

Friends can sympathise and listen. They might even give a hug, which feels good, but it is not enough. So I went to Rottingdean Gay Sauna for a little afternoon delight. After a quick dip in the pool, I sauntered down the corridor of rest cabins. A kind looking man, in his early fifties, gave me a long stare. He had a firm trim body. He was tall. And best of all, he looked nothing like Thom.

I went inside his cabin. I was immediately enveloped in hot breath, warm flesh and tingling nerve endings. My hands explored his sinewy muscles and he covered me in kisses. For the first time in months, I felt comforted, protected and more profoundly alive. Afterwards, we lay on the bed and traced patterns across each other's bodies. He introduced himself. His name was Peter. I wanted to go but he kissed me again. I explained that I had just 'finished' a long relationship. He suggested a cup of tea and a KitKat.

Later, we messed about in the sauna's pool, racing and ducking each other. Later when Peter was dressed and ready to leave, he gave me his telephone number. Could he have mine? I hesitated and then agreed. Maybe through Peter's eyes, I could become someone new.

Sunday 25 May

Peter phoned on Sunday morning and I found myself agreeing to a date. I know it is too early and conventional wisdom suggests waiting at least a year, but I'm tired of planning my social activities.

In the evening, I went to the Alternative Miss Brighton beauty pageant. Drag queens are not really my taste but a friend had suggested that we go.

When Thom was alive, everything could happen spontaneously. If there was a new movie I fancied, a quick check in the listings and we were off to the cinema. Now I have to find a friend with similar tastes, and book one of their free evenings.

If I don't keep on top of my diary, I am faced with long empty weekends.

Maybe a boyfriend will help plug the gaps? Maybe, we could stay in together from time to time. Plus, if I'm honest, I miss the sex too. So I accepted Peter's invitation. OK. What's the harm?

On several occasions during his last few months, Thom had urged me to 'find someone else after I've gone'. Naturally, I always tried to change the subject but he would insist: 'I don't want you to be alone.'

It might have been only eleven weeks and one day since Thom's death but surely seeing Peter was better than another miserable Bank Holiday Monday alone?

Monday 26 May (Bank Holiday)

Peter and I strolled across the South Downs in the sunshine towards Firle Beacon where they had lit a fire to warn of the arrival of the Spanish Armada. Peter chatted about his many brothers, cousins and other assorted relatives and, for the first time in months, I had a conversation which did not include Thom. The air was fresh and the grass springy under my feet. For a few glorious miles of open countryside, I was my own person rather than Thom's widower.

Later, over lunch at the Ram Inn at Firle village, I let drop the shocking news that Thom and I split up...because he had died on me. Once again I was crying, but at least this time I was not in hospital or a crematorium but in a pub garden with dogs running around and children hanging from a climbing frame. Peter was sympathetic but a bit surprised.

Our next stop was Berwick church. When the stained-glass windows were blown out during the war, the parish authorities asked Bloomsbury painters Vanessa Bell and Duncan Grant to paint panels to decorate the walls. The request caused controversy, after all they were living together in sin and Grant was a homosexual. As another outsider, and my bereavement had been exacerbating this feeling, I was very drawn to Bell and Grant's vibrant work. Later we went back to Peter's home and had sex.

Despite underlining how much I miss Thom's companionship and our shared history, it has been a very pleasant day out – one that I would like to repeat. Peter assured me he understands and will tread carefully.

Friday 6 June

After another counselling session, I went to the Phoenix gallery in Brighton at the recommendation of a friend to see his flatmate's exhibition. I was enraptured by the power of the huge canvases. The artist's style was ultra-realist but his subjects felt much more alive than any photograph. I was particularly drawn to one painting: a man is prostrate in front of a white figure in a hospital bed, behind are two distraught women (and a bunch of daffodils in a jar) and at the foot of the bed, unseen by anyone, two male nudes are running away trailing a red ribbon.

I asked the receptionist about the artist: 'Gary Sollars'.

He laughed because he was Gary Sollars, bartering the cost of his studio hire by working at the gallery. When his partner of thirteen years died, Gary borrowed a bed from the local Beacon hospice to recreate the death scene, set it up on the stage of a local church hall and persuaded a girl to pose as his dying partner. The women behind the bed are his mother and sister and he is kneeling on the floor with his arms outstretched. A photographer recorded everything and Gary worked from the snapshots. The two naked men trailing the ribbon symbolise Gary and his partner's relationship and the memories that live on.

It must have been so painful working on that canvas but he had created a very powerful painting.

Monday 9 June

My father and mother visited. He tackled the small odd jobs that Thom would previously have done. She helped me in the garden and I cooked lunch. A companionable day. I was grateful for their help and hope our relationship has turned a corner.

Tuesday 10 June

I did another 'Revelations' for *The Independent*. This time, it was Ian Hunter, formerly lead singer of the rock group Mott the Hoople. His turning point was the death of his friend and fellow musician Mick Ronson (once the lead guitarist for David Bowie's *Spiders from Mars*). Luckily the interview was on the phone because I almost broke down. Ultimately, the experience was uplifting. Hunter explained that rather than destroying him, the pain of the loss had helped him out of a creative dry spell:

'I believe that when people die they can leave you a little of their energy; I used mine to get me back out of the house and to make my album *The Artful Dodger* which I believe is a step in the right direction. Mick's death has also given me a sense of proportion: I think "they like it or they don't and who gives a f**k". I feel more comfortable with myself, and I don't think I'm fooling myself.'

Where is my bequest of energy from Thom?

Thursday 12 June

Engrossed in writing an article on celebrities and relationships with their dogs, I sensed something behind me. The air disturbed.

A muffled sound. A presence. An ache. Almost as if Thom was about to look over my shoulder and read my writing.

It felt so real, I longed to turn. Perhaps if I was quick, perhaps if I just – I don't know what. I stopped typing. I barely moved. My heart pounded. I swivelled round on my office chair...

But there was nothing.

Just the Turkish rug his aunt bought. The rounded door handle he brought over from Germany. The black sofabed we bought together. I returned to my article but I cannot decide:

A time slip?

A haunting?

My road to Emmaus?

Friday 13 June

My third counselling session but I was a terrible client. One half of my brain was crying out for support, the other was in counsellor mode itself and thinking 'I wouldn't have done that.'

I'd ask an agonising question and my bereavement counsellor would reply with another question:

'What do you think?'

I've used the same technique myself a million times.

And how many times have I told clients: 'You can't expect me to have all the answers?' With the shoe on the other foot, I wanted to scream: 'Why not?'

I might not be cracking up, but I feel like I'm sinking.

Saturday 14 June

Peter and I went to see a revival of *Chorus Line* at the Theatre Royal in Brighton. Adam Faith was poor as the director auditioning the hopefuls. A disappointing evening in so many ways.

Saturday 21 June

I had supper with John, who accompanied me to Germany for Thom's funeral and lead his memorial service in England, and two of his friends, Sara and Mike. They have a shaggy black dog called Tyson. He is a cross between a Parson's Jack Russell and a Labrador but looks more like Gnasher – Dennis the Menace's dog. He kept throwing himself at my feet and rolling over to have his tummy scratched. Sara and Mike jokingly suggested I should take him home. I laughed. Thom and I used to fight over what we would call our dog. I suggested 'Waldi' which is the German equivalent of 'Fido' but Thom favoured 'Ferguson', which I knew would be shortened to 'Fergie'. I had no desire to stand on the village green shouting for the Duchess of York. However, when Thom had become ill, the idea of getting a dog was quietly dropped.

If Thom had been at this dinner party, he would probably have offered to look after Tyson when Sara and Mike went on holiday, so I suggested it myself.

Tyson's owners were taken aback. He was boisterous and badly behaved.

I was still keen.

Normally, when guests came, they would lock him in the kitchen to stop him being a nuisance.

No, I was sure.

It was settled. I might not be able to share a dog with Thom but perhaps I'd like one on my own.

Sunday 22 June

My father was away playing golf and my mother came down from Bedford and stayed overnight. In the evening, I suggested going to my line-dancing club. When my mother had been a PE instructor, she had been expected to teach dance and she might find my class interesting. I explained that it was gay and lesbian but she said she did not mind. When we arrived, I introduced her to a few friends. She was slightly uncomfortable but managed to look as if she spent every Sunday with two-stepping gays and twirling lesbians. Driving home afterwards, she told me how when she left college she was offered a job in America:

'I sort of know that if I'd taken it, I would have never returned to England.' She was rather wistful.

'What stopped you?'

'It would have meant a lot of dance instruction. I preferred teaching hockey and netball.'

I'd never heard this story before. It got me thinking. Life is full of these seemingly small turning points. If she'd liked teaching dancing, my mother would not have married my father and I would not be here.

I would never have met Thom.

Friday 27 June

While interviewing celebrities is proving insightful, my formal counselling sessions have not been paying the same dividends. One afternoon, I looked up from my pile of scrunched up tissues and asked:

'How should I be feeling now? Am I doing the right thing?'

My counsellor's reply made me extremely angry: 'There are no road maps back from where you have been.'

I wanted to scream: 'WHY NOT. I'M NOT THE FIRST PERSON TO HAVE BEEN THERE.'

He smiled at me sympathetically, so instead of shouting I fumed inwardly.

Saturday 28 June

I am not certain about this dating stuff. With Peter, I'm not half a relationship but an empty space. Going out with him gives me something to look forward to, but it is also very wearing.

Last night, we went to see *The Twilight of the Golds*, a play in London with Jason Gould who is Barbra Streisand's son. It was about a family ripped apart by a new test to discover a baby's sexuality while still in the womb. Jason's character was gay and horrified by his sister's decision to abort her son because genetic indications suggested he too would be gay. One line, in particular, slays me and sums up my feelings about my parents. I paraphrase but Jason tells his mother and father:

'I love you and that's what makes me want to be part of this family. However, I love you too much to close my eyes to how I'm shut out and can never truly be let in.' Jason's character decided never to see his family again. However, he had the choice of forming a new family with his lover who, ironically enough, like Thom was ignored and shut out. It is an option closed off to me.

Walking out of the theatre with Peter, I felt isolated and alone; something exacerbated by the throngs of excited 'westenders' enjoying a balmy night out. I recovered slightly in the peace of St James' Park. Sitting on a park bench at the edge of the darkness, I tried to explain my mood. However, Peter's attempts to pacify caused even more pain:

'You'll meet someone else,' he said gently and caressed my arm.

I wanted to snap back at him: 'Stop stroking me. I'm not a fucking cat.'

Poor Peter. It must be hard dating a wounded tiger. How can I make him, or anyone else, understand: I want Thom.

I can't go forward but I can't go back either – or perhaps I'm stuck in the first line dance I learned: one step forward and two steps back.

Sunday 29 June

'What would you like me to bring?' Even as I asked the question I could feel my insides turn over. The answer is always the same. Once you have had a hit with one dish at a Relate party, you are stuck making it for ever.

Just the thought of preparing a Waldorf Salad brought back memories from last January and the post-Christmas gathering: Thom's last public appearance. The tears ran down my face as I explained, attending will be painful enough without chopping celery and apples again. In a way, I was glad to cry, hoping it would do the normal trick and lance the pain in advance. Anyway this time round it will be a garden party and therefore present fewer reminders.

Driving to the large country house of one of my fellow counsellors, I was happy and full of expectations of a great day out and catching up with friends who I've not seen for six months, as I'm still not ready to return to counselling. However, Relate gatherings are always difficult places for a heavy heart – too many people too skilled at reading beneath a fixed smile. God save me from caring and supportive people!

To start off, everything went well. I helped myself to some food from the barbecue and sat down at one of the tables that our hosts had dotted around their garden. The food was good. I had a glass of wine, but it was like immersing myself in a warm bath of caring.

To escape everybody's kindly enquiring looks I disappeared into the house to drop off my tennis shoes and racket. Unfortunately, as I crossed through the empty living room, I had a flashback.

All the ghosts of my last visit are there, standing around with glasses in their hands. It was like I'd stepped into a time machine and for a fleeting moment could re-experience that party. I watched myself find Thom a comfortable seat and the enjoyment of, for once, being able to provide just what he needed. His kind and grateful eyes looked up at me and we snatched a few seconds of normality.

The time machine froze into a New Year's toast: everybody stood with their glasses in the air. It felt so real – even though many of the same people are currently out in the garden enjoying the sunshine – I'm sure that I can step into the frame and stroke Thom's silky hair. I can hold him again and this time I'll never let him go.

Monday 30 June

I had lunch with Kate in London. Afterwards, we had coffee at a café in Leicester Square. She'd been listening to my problems about recovering from Thom's death and I'd been listening to her fears about her father's cancer. When the man at the next table left, he leaned over and said:

'You two are not supposed to get on.' Then he was gone.

We were startled for a second. Had we sounded so egotistical? Then it hit me. He must watch Live TV. After all, our programme is on five times a day, every day and on every edition Kate and I are having manufactured rows.

'I hate you,' I told Kate.

'You smell,' she replied.

'Everything's back to normal.'

It was good to laugh.

'I'll tell you what could be really helpful,' said Kate. 'Come and have a consultation with my new clairvoyant. I call her the Munchkin.'

'Do I have to dress as Dorothy and carry a basket?'

'Don't tell her that I call her that.'

'If she really has psychic powers, she already knows.'

Friday 4 July

I had another pointless counselling session. It's like watching a conjurer saw a lady in half, but knowing how he does it. My counsellor suggested going into analysis. Maury, an ex-boyfriend from New York, has had a session every weekday morning at 8.30 for the last five years. He says he's making good progress.

I thanked my counsellor but turned down the idea: nothing could be more boring than all those hours alone with my psyche.

Saturday 5 July

How should I mark this year's London's Gay Pride march and party? Originally, I decided that it would bring back too many memories and therefore was best ignored. However, Tom Flood suggested going together and meeting up with a gang of his friends. Gay Pride is one of the highlights of the year and I cannot spend the rest of my life stepping round Thom-shaped holes, so I changed my mind.

On the train up to London, I remembered the good times associated with Pride. Two years ago, the West End had been so packed with marchers that we had decided not to fight our way into Hyde Park, the setting off point for the march, but had a coffee on Piccadilly and waited. For the first time, there were floats, dancers and a tank that had been painted pink. The pavement was so packed that we had to sit on a concrete balustrade to get a good view. It was thrilling to be in the majority and we asked a heterosexual couple to take our picture. (It is one of the last photos of the two of us where Thom is in full health.

We are both holding on to a large brass ornamental post to stop ourselves from sliding off the wall.) But my memory proved too slippery, I could not keep it fixed on the positive. I wind back to last year when we had planned to still 'do' Pride, but Thom had been too tired for the march. Next we were going to drive up to Clapham Common and listen to the bands, but at the last minute he changed his mind. He had been happy for me to go for a couple of hours, but I had met up with a friend and not returned until late and he'd felt abandoned.

Worse still, I remembered Pride in 1990 or it might have been 1991. I had been torn between my conflicting loyalty to my best friend Gary, with whom I'd marched for the past few years, and Thom who was visiting the UK for a short convalescent break after several weeks in a German hospital. I had tried to please both parties by suggesting that Thom and I drove up to London and met Gary at the party in Kennington Park. Gary was still angry and Thom was annoyed. It was probably the first time I truly recognised that Thom and I were a couple and that my loyalty should lie with my partner rather than my best friend.

Fortunately, it was a glorious day and Thom always remembered how I followed him round with a fold-up chair so there was always somewhere comfortable for him to sit. That story just about sums up Thom: he always looked on the bright side.

This year, Pride was again at Clapham Common but for the first time ever, we had to pay to get into the party. We met Tom Flood's friends at the champagne tent – another innovation for this year. Unfortunately, the park was so crowded it was difficult to move around and Tom Flood did not fancy listening to the bands. So we separated and agreed to meet later. I wandered around the stalls but found nothing interesting. It was hard to see so many gay couples together. I was watching a white man kissing a black man when I remembered something Thom had said in Herdecke:

'I think your next boyfriend should be black.'

'Whatever made you think that?'

'That will upset your parents.'

'You have a wicked sense of humour.'

The couple had stopped kissing and were looking at me.

'Aren't you the one off *Agony*?' the black man asked.

'Yes.' It was difficult to know which was most embarrassing being caught staring or being recognised.

'Great programme,' he said and disappeared into the crowd.

I wanted to follow him. I wanted to kiss him. I wanted to be his boyfriend.

Depressed, I queued for something to eat. There was another mixed race couple in front of me. It further underlined my feelings of being disconnected from Peter. I bought sausage and chips and looked for somewhere to sit, except there were people standing everywhere. The only available piece of grass was by the Samaritans' tent. So I squatted down there. After I had finished eating, I got a pen and paper out of my bag and tried to make sense of my thoughts:

My heart is trapped behind barbed wire, which protects against further hurt but the hooks are so tight they cut into flesh – wounding me and making me bleed. I feel that I can never love with the same innocence and joy. In the words of Dionne Warwick's song 'I'll Never Love This Way Again'. Though I suppose I should be grateful that my theme is a classy soul ballad rather than an overblown Celine Dion number!

'Can I help you?'

I looked up.

'I saw you sitting there.'

It was someone from the Samaritans' tent. 'Would you like someone to talk to?'

'No, I was just, you see. There was nowhere…' I got up and disappeared into the crowd.

Why can't I let anyone in?

Monday 7 July

I went to the theatre with Peter to see *Martin Guerre*, the new musical from the team behind *Les Misérables* and *Miss Saigon*. I had interviewed one of the cast for *The Independent* and had been given free tickets. The score was surprisingly beautiful. During one brief passage, I felt something akin to joy.

Friday 11 July

I have been thinking a lot about Thom but hopefully in a positive rather than an obsessive way… Who am I kidding?

'Will you plant an apple tree for me?' he had asked.

I'd been sitting at his hospital bedside wrapped in my own thoughts. By this point, he spoke very seldom, normally communicating with just a gesture and leaving me to guess the rest. A complete sentence, and especially one about something beyond the room, had an electrifying effect. I put down my book and leaned closer.

'Where should I plant it?' I asked.

He shrugged. From somewhere Thom had found enough energy to ask for a living memorial, but afterwards he just wanted to be allowed to rest again.

One location for the tree was immediately ruled out: home. I am unsure whether to keep or sell the house and nothing would be worse than driving past and finding new owners had ripped out Thom's tree. Maureen suggested planting the apple tree in a container, so that it could be easily moved. I immediately had a vision of myself as a prisoner. Instead of a ball and a chain, I was dragging a tub with an apple tree. I was trapped enough by Thom's possessions without adding to my responsibilities.

Fortunately, Tom Flood is the Marketing Director of BTCV (British Trust for Conservation Volunteers) and has suggested one of their projects about twenty minutes from my home.

Today, I finally inspected the proposed site: an organic goat farm. It seems perfect. The farmer wanted to plant a small spinny to block off the road. When the trees mature, they will be coppiced and fed to the livestock. Thom's memorial will not only provide shelter for the birds but food for the goats and their kids. In some small way, Thom will be plugged into the eternal cycle.

Wednesday 16 July

With the past full of booby traps, my present freelance career precarious, the future seemed the best place to be. Unable to even imagine what it could be like, I decided to follow Kate's advice and consult her psychic.

In keeping with the Munchkin image, the woman's house was much smaller than the others in the row – as if it did not belong there but had been blown from Kansas.

A short middle-aged woman, with teeth which pointed in different directions, answered the door. Kate's description was so wickedly accurate, I almost felt I should start singing: 'We're Off to See the Wizard'.

The Munchkin led me into a very ordinary living room. The kitchen door was open and the radio was tuned to Jimmy Young on Radio 2. She sat me down at a small occasional table and asked me to shuffle some tarot cards. While my heart beat a military tattoo, she started talking about my background or as she described it: 'clearing my aura'. My rational mind alternated between deciding she was extraordinarily good at reading my subconscious and wondering if she really could unlock secrets about my future.

Often she was devastatingly accurate. In one sentence she gave me Thom's name and my father's Christian name, but she also threw out many others, which meant absolutely nothing. Some of these, she explained, were names for the future but she was probably just covering her back. However, she was in no doubt over my profession, telling me on at least three occasions that I was a writer. She decided I will only be 'friends' with Peter and predicted a job based in North London, somewhere like Camden.

If I had to divide what she told me into three categories: clear misses, correct but could possibly have been guessed and extraordinary bullseyes I would put fifteen per cent into the first, fifty per cent into the second and thirty-five per cent into the third. After forty minutes her stream of predictions dried up and she asked if I had any questions. I forgot all about career advice. Instead, clawing back the sobs, I asked:

'Why did he have to die?'

'I don't know – it was just his time,' she replied.

I had walked into her house with an open mind, but came out with more questions than answers.

Sunday 20 July

Tyson has come to stay. Within twenty minutes of bouncing into my house, he had drunk from the toilet, rushed into every room and curled up across my feet as I watched teatime TV. When I stood up to take my coffee cup to the kitchen, he stretched and followed. Somehow I doubted I would ever feel lonely with Tyson around. In the evening, Peter arrived to take me to the cinema. Tyson sniffed at him rather disapprovingly and did his best to ignore him.

Knowing that Tyson's owners locked him in the kitchen whenever they went out, I did the same. It turned out to be a long movie, so it was quite late by the time we came back.

'Your lights are on in the living room,' said Peter as he parked the car.

'They're on a timer. I hate returning to a dark empty house.'

'But your TV is on and I'm sure I can make out somebody watching it,' he said.

Maybe I'd been visited by a new breed of burglars who cannot bear to miss their favourite programmes? Instead of stealing your video, they pull up a chair and watch it on your TV. Feeling rather like Goldilocks might have done with the three bears in her cottage, I hurried up the path.

As soon as I put my key in the lock I was greeted by an exuberant bundle of black fur: Baby Bear, aka Tyson.

'We heard barking,' explained Mummy Bear, aka Valerie my next-door neighbour, 'he sounded so sad we used the emergency spare key and came round to comfort him.'

'Hello,' called Daddy Bear, aka Michael, her husband, from the comfort of my chair in the living room.

'The other neighbours thought you'd got a dog trapped in your garage and knowing we had a key, they called round,' Valerie continued.

I introduced Peter as a 'friend'. From their stares, I guessed they suspected something more.

'It seemed better to watch TV here, than leave him alone,' Valerie filled the silence.

'I suppose we should be getting home,' said Michael and they left.

Peter and I tried to kiss on the sofa, but Tyson kept on pushing his nose between us.

'I think I'd better go,' he said.

'You can sleep over,' I told him. Even after two months, we still hadn't spent the whole night together.

'I expect your neighbours are watching to see if my car leaves, I wouldn't feel comfortable.'

Secretly, I was quite glad. Having sex didn't feel like betraying Thom but allowing someone to sleep on his side of the bed did.

I let Tyson out into the garden, served his bedtime half slice of bread and settled him into his basket. Thirty seconds after completing a similar bedtime ritual myself, Tyson started barking downstairs and throwing himself against the kitchen door. Worried about disturbing my neighbours again, I let Tyson out. He galloped upstairs and with a homing device, which would have been the envy of allied soldiers during the Gulf War, ran straight to the bedroom and curled up on the floor next to my side of the bed. This seemed one liberty too many. So I leaned across the bed and banged the floor on Thom's side, after all Tyson might have snored! He reluctantly dragged himself up and slunk round. Both finally satisfied at this compromise, we drifted off to sleep.

I woke up once, and heard peaceful breathing. I inched across to peer down from Thom's side at the slumbering dog and lay there for a couple of minutes just watching Tyson's fur rise and fall. I must have fallen in sync with his breathing because before I knew it I'd been enveloped by deep refreshing sleep.

Wednesday 23 July

Life with Tyson has settled into a comfortable routine. In the morning, we walk with Valerie and her dalmation, Lily, across the fields behind our houses. On our return, Tyson lies at my feet while I type away at the computer. This is followed by a quick run in the afternoon and he goes back to sleep in my office again. In fact, I am hardly ever alone. Tyson would follow me into the toilet if he could. Even while hunting for rabbits in the hedgerows, he will bound back every five minutes to check I've not disappeared.

So far this summer, I have not been to the beach as it holds too many memories of Thom. However, this afternoon, on the spur of the moment, I drove to Telscombe Cliffs. Through Tyson's eyes, Thom's favourite beach became a source of wonder again. Within moments of arriving, he was swimming in the sea and sniffing around rock pools. When I went for a dip myself, Tyson splashed in after me – although his claws were a problem if he swam too close. While I read my book, Tyson made friends with the other dogs and in one disgraceful incident stole a sandwich from another sunbather's picnic. Despite the heat Tyson only sat down once. As I watched him rush across the shingle – so carefree, so full of life – my spirits could not help but soar.

Thursday 24 July

Although Tyson is seven years old, he has the energy of a puppy and the same ability to sniff out trouble. He never sets out to be naughty, but one thing will lead to another and before he knows it Tyson is bad, bad, bad! In fact, his owners were so certain he would play me up that they left the telephone number of the boarding kennels. This morning, they called me from a beach in Cornwall and were amazed that I hadn't sent him there already.

This afternoon, we were walking on a footpath behind the High Street and Tyson, as always, was about a hundred yards ahead. When I reached the Assembly Hall, he was nowhere to be seen. I ran up and down the full length of the path, no Tyson. I called him. Nothing. I called again. Still no sign of Tyson. I was beginning to worry, rehearsing how to start the inevitable call, when suddenly a man in a dressing gown strode out of his back door and into the lane. He looked upset:

'Your dog has been in my house,' he said.

Exhibit A, Tyson, ran up wagging his tail.

'I've been ill and I'd left the door open for the doctor. But I had the shock of my life, your dog marched into the bedroom and climbed into bed with me!' he complained

Tyson tried to lick his hand, still unable to believe that anybody would not be thrilled to meet him.

I made profuse apologies and lamely explained to the poor man that Tyson didn't behave like that at home.

Friday 25 July

Thom might have been only forty-three but in some parts of the world, even today, that's not particularly young to die. And if he'd been born into another century, forty-three would have been considered a good age. Instead of wallowing in the unfairness, I needed to remind myself that on the larger scale of human tragedy, my loss hardly rated a footnote.

So I contacted actress Ingrid Pitt – who I'd once interviewed for my radio programme – to write an article about her experiences for *The Independent*. She made her name playing vampires in seventies Hammer Horror movies but had spent her childhood in a Nazi concentration camp. She'd never spoken in detail to a newspaper journalist before, but after much persuasion Ingrid agreed to meet at Ham House in Richmond Park. I thought about taking Tyson along but decided that I would need to keep my wits about me.

Ingrid Pitt was still a most extraordinarily beautiful woman. We walked into the forest to find a quiet spot for the interview.

'Why talk about it?' she asked. 'It only gives me nightmares.'

I switched off my tape recorder. A wasted afternoon. Yet I could sense the iron strength of a survivor, someone who might understand and more importantly offer practical advice. With Ingrid unwilling to talk, I told my story instead. Thank goodness, I had become used to tears in public because I cried yet again. Finally, there was a bond between us and Ingrid opened up.

I felt guilty about using Thom's story. I felt guilty about hiding that he was German, but I switched on my tape recorder.

'*Schindler's List* tried to be honest but you can't possibly make a movie about the terror of the camps and make it look anything like it was. It was so much worse, even in your wildest dreams you cannot imagine what it was really like to be shut in a truck, to sit for hours and hours on a railway platform not knowing what was going to happen. You're eating your food and you know you mustn't because you never know if you're going to get any more. When you arrive, wherever you're going, it's totally bewildering. There are glaring lights, screaming voices, dogs barking, people being shot, so horrific, so nightmarish. These impressions come on you like a machine gun out of nowhere and for a child to live through this and think it normal is the worst.'

As I was drawn into Ingrid's story, I had the faint glimmer of an idea: perhaps interviewing people, recording their testimony could be some sort of therapy. Certainly my conventional counselling sessions, where I did the talking and someone else listened, were going nowhere. I leaned forward so I could not just hear Ingrid's words but let them enter my body.

'Somehow my mother had an antenna for trouble,' Ingrid continues. 'She would shake so I knew that something terrible was about to happen and she would hide me in the latrine to avoid a round up. It wasn't wisdom, she was a survivor with a strong will and an obsession with saving my life. What for I don't know, because everybody else died. They marched so meekly to those gas chambers. Yet I suppose looking after me made her want to survive, she wouldn't have had any compunction at all about dying once we were separated from my father. The way they took him away was terrible. They beat him over the head with their Lugers (an automatic pistol) until the blood flowed down him. I remember it so vividly.

'When our camp was being moved, or liquidated as they called it, most people were killed. We were marched into the gas chamber and I remember my mother holding me so tight. I don't know if it was luck or destiny but we survived. A Jehovah's Witness told me: "You will survive but tomorrow I will be dead" and she was right. Why didn't the gas chamber work? We must have been in there for hours, because when we went in there it was dark and when we came out it was dark again, so a whole day must have passed. It was a miracle that they opened the door because we could have just stayed there and they could have all gone.'

By this stage Ingrid was eight and she and her mother hid in the nearby forests with a band of partisans.

'Finally the Red Cross started an enormous push, finding stragglers and people left behind. We didn't know the war had been over for nine months. My mother was in a bad way when they came, she had typhus and would have popped her clogs. She was so sick and I had TB. We were taken to hospital where we stayed for months until we were both better.

'When we came out of hospital my mother put it in her bonnet that she was going to find my father. I wanted to stay where we were in Poland, I thought it was nice there but she told me that we must find my papa. So we went to all the displaced persons' camps, which was a drag, always on foot, schlepping rucksacks. God knows how many miles we walked. It was an incredible journey, it took us a year to get there. Walking and schlepping. I can remember my mother saying as we walked across Germany: "I can't stand it any more." She'd put down the rucksacks and two bags with the few possessions we'd accumulated and rest. It is terrible to have to carry things.'

Listening to Ingrid's story, in another country and another time, I still felt guilty. For my journalist's heart of ice, for not switching off the tape recorder and for surviving Thom.

'Finally, we found Father in a cellar in Berlin. I knew him as such a strong proud man. He was in the first Olympics in 1896; he rowed and was a fantastic athlete. But he'd been sent to special camp for all the intellectuals at Theresienstadt so when we found him he looked like a little old man – all thin and bent.

'Fortunately, I did have a few years with him. I always sat on his lap on the balcony and looked at all the trees. We stayed on in Berlin because my father couldn't travel. We had a house there, which we finally got back. Eventually I went to school which was a pain because I wanted to always be with my dad.'

Ingrid trained with the Berlin Ensemble, but after criticising the authorities in East Berlin the police arrived at the theatre to arrest her. They were persuaded to wait until the final curtain while she escaped to the West. Later she made the film *Where Eagles Dare*, with Clint Eastwood and Richard Burton, and our lives sort of crossed at the Bedford Odeon when my mother chose this for my ninth birthday treat.

Meeting Ingrid is a humbling and healing experience but despite her determination to forget, small everyday events can trigger terrible memories:

'Recently when it rained very heavily in London, everywhere was flooded. Our train was supposed to go through Earls Court but it didn't; it stood and it stood. I just suddenly thought of how the train to the camp just stood and stood. It was hot that day on the tube but because we were all pressed against each other like herrings and with all the waiting it brought back the cattle truck so vividly. My father had caught a fever and he laid down on the floor of the truck. The other people were annoyed because he took up too much room, making everybody even more uncomfortable. They said if he wasn't lying on the floor they would all have more space. How they bitched at my poor father. It was freezing. My mother holding me in her arms and shaking.'

While many therapists suggest that people who were abused in their childhood return to confront demons, Ingrid sees no point: 'I have never met anyone from the camps, or anyone that I knew when I was a child in Poland. I did make a film called *Hanna's War* in Hungary and I met a Polish actress who grew up outside Stutthof, the camp I was in, who used to go and pick mushrooms nearby. She had offered to take me there but I think: "Do I really want to go there?"'

I had nothing but admiration for Ingrid's strength and her resolve to march forward even when demons from the past escape and snap at her ankles. I left Richmond Park convinced that I must stop dwelling in the past. How else can I move forward?

In the evening, Peter came round and Tyson burst through the bedroom door at the crucial moment.

Saturday 26 July

Four of Thom's German friends have been competing in the Gay Games in London and asked to stay for the weekend. I was glad to have the house full again but Tyson was less keen. I had just fed him and started cooking for my other guests, when I heard a strange noise. I ran outside to look for Tyson but the garden was empty. There were some barks from Lily, next-door's dog, and a rather sheepish Tyson looked at me over the fence from their garden.

Apparently he had heard Lily's food being put down, leapt over the hedge and ran into their kitchen. Lily was so surprised that she stepped back from her food bowl and Tyson pounced. It did not take Lily long to realise her mistake and they ended up scrapping.

About half an hour after his daylight robbery, Tyson's owners arrived to collect him. I was at a complicated stage of the recipe and asked one of my guests to answer the door. He returned with a bottle of wine and thanks, so I didn't get the chance to say goodbye to Tyson.

Tonight, the house seems very empty again. The Germans have gone home and there is no dog snoring at my feet. Despite his attention-seeking behaviour, Tyson has made me feel more at ease in my skin. He has been the focus of the caring that I used to give to Thom and in return I became, albeit temporarily, the most important person in his life. I am no longer invisible.

Thank you Tyson and thank you Thom. Having a dog to stay, so it didn't have to go into kennels, was the sort of gesture you would have made.

Sunday 3 August

It was a warm muggy evening and Peter suggested going for a swim. However, by the time we arrived at Hove seafront, the sky had turned grey and I could almost smell rain in the air. When we stepped on to the shingle, I knew I didn't want to go in the water – normally I'd swim anywhere, any time. In fact, Thom was always complaining about my desire to jump into German canals and English ponds, and would watch perplexed while I splashed around and tried to tempt him in. Today it was me rather than Thom who guarded the towels while Peter called out how surprisingly refreshing the sea was.

On the way home, I zoned out of Peter's anecdotes about his family and friends. It was harmless but nevertheless exacerbated my tendency to detach, observe and become a bit player in my own life. I finally understood how Thom must have felt when I endlessly prattled away about nothing in particular.

The sun was metamorphosing into the deepest red. Peter suggested stopping to watch and naturally I took the turning for Devil's Dyke, a local beauty spot – exactly what Thom would have done. From the car park, we had a perfect view across the Sussex Downs and sat in silence as the red light bled into the ground. Of course, I remembered the last spectacular sunset that Thom and I had watched together. To celebrate his fortieth birthday, we made a trip to the West Coast of America and marked the actual day by flying over the Grand Canyon – rather than my black-humoured suggestion of visiting nearby Death Valley. How was I to know Thom would only celebrate three more birthdays?

Peter must have sensed my mood because his stream of inconsequential chatter stopped:

'Do you believe you will meet up with Thom in the next life?'

I wanted to tell him that, for me, sunsets have stopped being romantic. They can only be a symbol of something ending. But like Thom, the man whom I seemed to be turning into, I kept my counsel.

Back home, I took another step down the same road and criticised Peter for pouring white wine into red wine glasses. I even used the same words that Thom would have used and, for that moment, believed them with the same passion. (Previously I'd followed Thom's house rules because it made him seem more alive, but this was definitely taking it one stage further.) Over supper, I found myself taking on Thom's role as the style police and nagged Peter to get a more modern haircut. He looked a bit forlorn.

'At the beginning of the year I decided to stop seeing people who were already in a relationship with somebody else,' he explained. 'I've partially succeeded. I've stopped dating men with living boyfriends.'

But Peter it is much worse than that. If I've become Thom, you are dating a dead man. And if I'm now Thom, whatever happened to Andrew?

Perhaps I should discuss this with my counsellor but our sessions already feel like a wallow in pointless misery.

Tuesday 12 August

My next assignment for 'Revelations' involved another close brush with death. On 18 February 1996, Paris Panther was caught up with the IRA Aldwych bus bomb in London. He had taken the opposite approach to Ingrid Pitt and, rather than trying to forget, turned his experience into a one-man play.

'There was a huge piercing noise. Neither time nor space had any meaning. A million and one thoughts permeated my mind in a single moment. The world was spinning and at the centre of the storm, I felt I was being sucked into the earth; a trip into a black hole with no idea what I would find on the other side. I knew that if I passed out, I would never come back up again. My instincts were to stay alive, you don't know what's on the other side of death, so I willed myself to pick myself off that seat.

'Turning round and looking back at the twisted bus, I felt I was in another world, but untouched by the chaos. When I looked down at my clothes and hands – how could I remain the same colour when everything else was burnt? Just a few cinders from the seats and that was it. I found the driver slumped on the road, bleeding and damaged.'

Just like I'd been preoccupied with retrieving Thom's possessions from room 44c, the police had to stop Paris from returning to the bus to find his bag.

'The next day, I returned to the scene. That was the first time it dawned on me what had happened. I'd slept so well, I'd imagined that it happened to somebody else. The emotions didn't really hit me. I thought "I must be invincible." However, I started having recurring nightmares, which brought me out in cold sweats. About a month after the bombing, I started dreaming of being imprisoned in a cold clinical room with bars at the window. I felt like a criminal – guilty of something but what? I didn't contact friends, I felt that I should not be with people, and my girlfriend thought I was behaving really strangely. Paranoia gripped me and wouldn't let go.'

He went to see a psychiatrist, but felt he wasn't helpful. Unable to communicate with anybody, Paris locked himself in his bedroom. Unable to return to his normal life – and continue with his law training – he decided to keep himself busy and become a waiter. I was struck by a horrible idea – could I be keeping busy doing interviews for *The Independent* to distract myself too?

'Running around like a headless chicken, I couldn't think,' Paris continued. 'But after a few months just grew tireder and tireder, angrier and angrier until I had no energy left. I was fighting myself and maybe I should have just let go. Why not have a cocktail of antidepressants and say goodbye to the last twenty-nine years?'

I nodded at Paris, partly to encourage him to say more but mostly because I could empathise so easily. Fortunately, someone suggested to Paris that he should write about the bombing and he gradually started to acknowledge his fears and insecurities.

'Through performing the play, I feel really clean again. The bomb might have blown me apart but the tears of blood I shed on stage have helped me put the pieces back together again. It is my kind of therapy, there is no pretence at all. It was also the first time my family had truly seen the true pain because I had shielded them. In fact, it's off-stage that I act – holding my feelings in. If I was emotional all the time, I would become mad. Existence is very fragile and every day I'm walking on the edge of a very sharp knife with an abyss on both sides.'

Meeting Paris was a frightening experience. He looked so sane, it was only when I wrote up my copy that the shadow of madness leapt from the page. Instead of letting my wound heal over, I want to follow his example – to metaphorically slit my wrists to examine my anguish and watch it flow.

Wednesday 13 August

Although my days seem to last for ever, the rest of the world is on normal time. The school summer holidays will soon be over and I have still not heard from my sister. The likelihood of a visit, with my nephew (who is nine) and niece (who is seven), is receding faster than my hairline. I had hoped that after re-establishing contact with my parents, my sister would find it easier to reply to my letter. No such luck.

My mother informed me that Gayle and the children were visiting Bedford. With my nephew entering every junior tennis tournament in the Northwest, this will be the only opportunity to see them. So I told my mother that I'd think about it but felt that Gayle should have made the invitation herself.

A couple of days later, Gayle left a message on my answering machine but no apology. It seems she's going to follow the Marshall family tradition and just ignore everything. All I wanted was an explanation. It is five months since I wrote: why hasn't she replied. If she cannot do that perhaps she could give me some indication that she wants to clear the air. Instead, I got: 'Hello Andrew, it's Gayle. I tried to get you but you were out.' I couldn't face returning this call. So I didn't.

We would have been stuck in this impasse if my mother had not interceded. Although I'm tempted to remain pure to my resolve and wait for Gayle to visit me, I also want to see my niece and nephew. So tomorrow, I'm off to Bedford.

Thursday 14 August

Arriving at my parents', I was swept away by a tide of excited children. Their favourite uncle was there to play table tennis, cards, the piano and a thousand and one activities that need attention – right now. But over my shoulder, my eyes caught my sister's. What was that look? Embarrassment, regret, shame? She was impossible to read.

By the time the children were in bed, and we sat down for an evening meal, I was exhausted. All the old clutter from my child-hood home seemed to press in. The china spaniel with sad eyes, which acts as plant pot-holder on the kitchen dresser and the fruit-shaped ashtrays, which I'd bought my mother for Christmas one year – even though neither of my parents smoked. As the meal progressed, I became gloomier and gloomier. Not only had the compromise been all on my side, but I felt Gayle had totally ignored me. For once, instead of filling the silence with ever more pointless conversation gambits, my mother took control:

'You and Gayle need to talk. I'll just clear the table and then leave you alone,' she said.

A miracle! My feelings had been acknowledged and acted on; for once I was not the person putting their head over the fam-ily parapet. A flood of gratitude, relief and love for my mother coursed through my body. Perhaps people do change.

Gayle and I sat either side of the kitchen table – both waiting for the other to start. We must have shared thousands of meals here together and a million games. As small children, the plastic tablecloth would have been put over this very table so that we could paint and glue together. When did she change? When did she become so callous?

'Is there anything you want to say to me?' I finally asked.

'Just the usual condolences,' she replied. Just the usual condolences! This was the first time we had spoken since the love of my life died and that was the best she could manage. I'd had more sympathy from the village butcher!

'Why didn't you reply to my letter?'

'It was so angry, I didn't see the point.'

I tried to make her understand by sharing a few stories that offered a glimpse into my last few months. Gayle listened politely. Used to making even my counsellor cry, I was shocked how my sister's body remained rigid with disapproval. I could not reach her. I could not make her understand my pain and how she had let me down.

'I'm not good like you are with words,' she countered accusingly.

'That's why I gave you something practical to do instead and invited you to visit.'

'But it just hasn't been possible, James's tennis tournaments take up so much time and you live so far away.'

'You could have found time if you wanted to. I asked in March, so you had plenty of warning.'

Silence.

'But it's not like we've ever been close,' she replied, going back on to the offensive.

I looked at her immobile face and remembered the time that she'd returned from a shopping trip and proudly unfurled a poster of her teen idol David Cassidy. Except it wasn't a pin-up of David with his shirt off but a semi-naked woman! Without her contact lenses in, she could not tell the difference. She had certainly cried then. Although, as an adolescent boy, I was duty bound to hate David Cassidy and duty bound to love naked breasts, I still marched down to the newsagent's and got her a replacement.

Andrew Marshall

'I'd hoped that my family would be there if ever I needed them, but I can see I was wrong,' I told Gayle.

She shrugged.

If ever she was in trouble I would respond if not immediately, at least by the next day. I certainly would not wait five months! We were at an impasse. She crumbled, slightly, when we talked about the children and how our estrangement should not affect them. It was her only moment of humanity. She offered one consolation: she would try to visit next summer (other commitments permitting).

Thursday 21 August

From an interview with the theatre director Jonathan Miller, for *The Independent*, I've begun to understand why everything I've read about bereavement makes no sense. He was explaining how looking down a microscope helped him through adolescence:

'I was in a fog until I was about thirteen, unhappy and miserable at school. I didn't know who I was or what I should do. From the moment my father bought me my own microscope, I spent hours peering down this brass corridor at a brilliantly illuminated stage where I saw translucent microorganisms ferrying themselves across my microscopic disc. I was fascinated by the relationships of living creatures to one another and what determined their behaviour.

'The most interesting stuff lie in the rubbish heaps and ponds of life. It is in the negligible, the unnoticed, the overlooked that the payloads are. Looking back, if there is any rule that I have followed – and I never followed it specifically – it is the magnificence of the trivial. It is the overlooked and neglected which conceal the truth. When students come to me for an opera masterclass they expect to be given the big picture but I do the opposite. Recently we did just a short section of Act I of *La Bohème* where Rodolfo is making his first tentative flirtation with Mimi. I deal with the microscopic details of embarrassment and shyness – instead of having some great theory about love. What sort of posture does somebody stand in when they are making a suggestion that they have a faint suspicion will be misinterpreted? It is in the discovery of the truth of the minutiae that you can begin to build the ingredients of the possibly large.'

Miller is right. I don't need to have some great overarching theory about mourning, just to look down the microscope at particular moments of loss and build a way out from there. Perhaps interviewing celebrities really could be healing.

Friday 22 August

My last counselling session and I have finished the story of what happened. My counsellor believes talking to him should help get everything 'off my chest'. But my diary seems to fulfil that function. He offers no insight into how I could move forward. He cannot begin to answer the question I'm grappling with:

'What's the meaning of life?'

In my dreams, Thom is on the top deck of a bus. He's waving but before I register it's truly him, the bus has turned the corner. I stand on the pavement and stare at the space where it was. Something about the advert along the bus side looks familiar. It's the sixties campaign for Strongbow cider. Thom is on the bus that took me every morning from Bedford back to Northampton where I still had one term of infant school to complete.

Monday 25 August

My internal debate about the best way forward – head for the normal life or surrender to the berserk – took another twist by interviewing rock legend, David Coverdale (Deep Purple and Whitesnake), who told me about his mother's death:

'I slept on a recliner chair in the hospital – strangely I spent my first day on this planet with her and so it seemed appropriate that I should be there for her last. Most of the family spent the night in a type of waiting room nearby. The next morning the nurses said she was fine and that all her vital signs were stable so we went over to the hotel to get showered. No sooner had I walked in than my auntie called telling me: "You'd better get back. She's going." You see; she didn't want me there for the actual demise. She loved me so much that even at that stage she was protecting me and didn't want me to see her pass away. The nurses let me sit with her body and I thanked her for everything – not in a morose way but chatting about favourite times. I kissed her head and said my final goodbyes.'

I could not help but think about Thom's death. My experience had been the opposite. I had been woken up by his struggle for breath to witness the end but I had been too wrapped up in myself to offer Thom any comfort or say any final goodbyes.

'My driver drove me away from the hospital,' Coverdale continued, 'and I turned to him and said: "I'm an orphan." He replied: "You're never an orphan when you've known the love of your parents." It was such a magical thing to say – like having warm water poured over a cold heart.'

Perhaps if you've truly known the love of your partner you're never a widower? After the interview, I explained about my bereavement and how I felt stuck. Coverdale was insistent that I find a creative outlet to ease my pain. He has certainly used aspects of his mother's death in his songs. But how? I don't want to just howl in anguish.

Friday 29 August

As the Munchkin predicted, I have landed a job in Camden, well sort of. I sold my interview with David Coverdale to *Take a Break* magazine whose offices are in, yes, Camden. They are desperate for 'human interest' celebrity stories and pay almost three times the rate of *The Independent*.

Even better, Emma Daley, who normally does 'Revelations', is moving abroad and I've been given the column. As Live TV is only a couple of floors above *The Independent* at Canary Wharf, I dropped in one Wednesday – while Kate and Patricia were in make-up – and Emma did a handover. She had only one future interview lined up – with Carol Shields who won a Pulitzer, and had been nominated for the Booker Prize, for her novel *Stone Diaries*. Emma searched her desk and produced Shields's latest novel: *Larry's Party*.

I have never read literary fiction. I'd always thought it would be too difficult. So I planned to just leaf through *Larry's Party*. After all, I was interviewing Shields about a life-changing moment, not writing a literary profile. However, I quickly found myself engrossed. *Larry's Party* was not only easy to read but it seemed full of what I can only describe as truth.

Carol Shields had her revelation in 1983 at a women-only literary conference in Vancouver, Canada. At this point in her career, she'd written four novels but had little faith in her work: 'Talk about ordinary people, I write about them because I am one.' She returned home validated: 'At that point, the problem for women writers was that we just didn't trust our own experiences because on literature courses women and their experiences were discounted. Although my first two books were considered minor domestic novels, now they've been reprinted and taken seriously. I had a sense that people didn't know what I was writing about. I wasn't sure myself, because I was just finding my way.

'Whenever I've been away on a conference I unload to my husband but it took me about three days because it was such a rich experience and not always a comfortable one. There was a risk that any changes might unsettle my family and the life I was comfortable with. So many new ideas came at me at once that I was completely unprepared for the impact.'

Bereavement also brings change and in thrashing about trying to find a new direction, I have been exposed to new ideas too. A whole category of books – literary fiction – had just opened up to me. Instead of shying away from prize-winner authors, and thinking they are not for the likes of me, I will take the plunge.

Shields had a very enquiring mind. After the interview, she wanted to get my take on men and our overwhelming need to punch something or somebody. It was very flattering. Shields' husband returned and she settled down to sign a pile of her books. She returned my copy with the inscription: 'For Andrew – with thanks for quick questions!' I was not certain what that meant but I walked away strangely excited.

Perhaps writing could fill the void.

Sunday 31 August

I needed to get away from Hurstpierpoint and all my memories. Although Peter would have leapt at the chance of a break, I phoned my childhood friend Richard (with whom I'd spent my birthday weekend). His father had died a couple of months ago and I thought we could recover together. A long weekend of leisurely walks along the seashore and plenty of talking would be the perfect prescription – our destination the Suffolk Heritage Coast.

Southwold is perched on the edge of the world with marshes to the north, a watery inlet to the south. The remoteness of this picture postcard world is reinforced by just one road in and one road out. We arrived on a cold Saturday afternoon and the town immediately brought back memories of summer holidays from my childhood in genteel English resort hotels. I could almost picture myself building sandcastles on the empty beach in my anorak. Unlike other resorts commercialism has only tickled this community, the slot machines banished to the far end of the esplanade and the prime sites taken by dozens of brightly painted beach huts – their reds and blues a stark contrast to the almost white sand. Fishermen's cottages and grand summer residences from the last century compete for the best sea views. Right in the middle of the oldest section of the town, a lighthouse incongruously towers above the cottages. The folly of some rich Victorian or a necessary aid to the local fishing community? I was overcome with an urge to rent a cottage for the summer and write an Agatha Christie-style murder mystery.

Just like my memories of childhood holidays, it started to rain and we had to shelter in a café with a cup of tea. Spending time with Richard further underlined my nostalgia. Our friendship stretches back uninterrupted from short trousers on our first day at school all the way through double maths and doughnuts in the playground, on to first love and first jobs. His father was almost as much a fixture in my childhood as my own, so I could share his grief for this always smiling, always friendly man. Richard was one of the few people Thom was happy to see even when he was feeling ill. This was the first extended time together since our respective bereavements.

While I was haunted by my vigil, Richard found being with his father at the end very comforting and was worried about his younger sister who arrived too late. We even debated whether it is better for someone to die suddenly, so their loved ones are spared witnessing the suffering, or whether a slow death at least prepares everybody.

Early on Sunday morning, unable to sleep, I switched on the bedside radio and hoped that the music would help me drift off. Yet despite being tuned to a pop station, I was assaulted by classical music. From my years working in radio, I knew that meant a royal death but I was blown away when the solemn announcer mentioned Diana, the Princess of Wales. Sleep was impossible. I spent the next hour watching television and letting the truth slowly settle.

Around about eight o'clock, I knocked on Richard's door and broke the news to him. He switched on his TV and we watched together. When the clash of grey-suited announcers and bright cheerful flashbacks of Diana visiting children's homes became unbearable, we decided to dress for breakfast. I thought I'd reached a resting point in my recovery somewhere between intense pain and quasi normality, yet I found myself back at day one. I sat on the edge of the bath, trying to catch my breath after brushing my teeth. I felt exactly the same as the morning after Thom finally passed away, when I could only achieve basic tasks in a zombie-like trance.

'Oh, my God,' I told myself in the bathroom mirror, 'how are you ever going to escape?'

It felt like I had two small children hanging round my legs as I dragged myself up the few steps back up to my room. Exhausted, I crumpled down on the bed and surveyed my clothes in the wardrobe. In the same way that deciding what to eat seemed impossibly complicated when Thom died, I had no idea what to wear. Not up to the challenge, I picked yesterday's clothes off the floor and put them on. I was as ready, as I ever would be, to face the day.

After Thom died, I was amazed that the rest of the world continued unchanged. However, when Richard and I finally emerged from the guesthouse, normal life had been suspended by Diana's death. The flag on the sea scouts hall was at half mast, nobody was talking above a murmur and the blackboard outside the pub no longer advertised bar snacks but offered condolences to Diana's family and friends. We went to the newsagent's but

Southwold had only the early editions from before the accident. The front page of the *Sunday Sport* was particularly bizarre. It featured a scantily clad woman leaning over some scales who claimed: 'My breasts weigh more than Kylie Minogue'.

Later when we visited Somerleyton Hall, gardens and maze, Lord and Lady Somerleyton had put up a sign to explain that the house was open but that they were in mourning. We also dropped in on a friend of Richard's who had rented a cottage for the summer with her children. The TV was on and we watched more of the coverage. Her husband is an actor who gave Diana coaching to help her public speaking and the media thought he was having an affair with her. Reading between the lines, the experience was pretty traumatic. However, Richard's friend was full of praise for Diana and like everybody unable to believe that she was dead.

Everybody remembers where they were when they heard the news about President Kennedy and my generation will bore future ones with their Diana stories, but I believe the most telling detail will be the first person you phoned. Richard had spent the last twenty-four hours convincing me that his relationship with his girlfriend was over and that moving into a new house marked the beginning of a new life. Yet he called her to discuss Diana's death. I ached to phone Thom and pick over the news in just the same way we did whenever we were apart. He was endlessly entertained by the English obsession with monarchy and in a reflex action I almost asked to borrow Richard's mobile.

When I finally arrived home that evening, there were no messages on my answering machine. I even dialled 1471 in case somebody had hung up. Nothing. No calls wondering what I thought, no calls wondering how I was – just an empty house. Sadly it dawned on me: I am on the edge of many people's lives but at the centre of nobody's.

Monday 1 September

There is nothing in the newspaper this morning beyond Diana, the TV guide and the crossword. I dropped into Asda supermarket at Brighton Marina. They have set up a book of condolence and there was a queue of people waiting to sign it.

Wednesday 3 September

The outpouring of grief is so overwhelming it is impossible to believe that we are mourning just one person, however famous, beautiful or good. Although the flowers and prayers might be for her, it feels like we are witnessing something far more profound. Normally, we feel a moment of sadness and move on, shrugging off other people's pain because strong defences are the only way of coping in our busy and stressful lives. However, with Diana's death these protective layers are constantly assaulted by televised images of grief and there is still no other story in the papers.

In the make-up room at Live TV, before recording this week's episodes of *Agony*, Kate remembered her mother's death and how she felt orphaned all over again. Patricia, the hostess, told how Prince Charles returning from Paris with Diana's body had made her re-experience her flight back to England with her father's body. Although it happened ten years ago, Patricia's memories were so vivid it seemed like it happened only ten months ago. Except this time round the grief was one step removed and Patricia felt this allowed her to properly understand her feelings.

Friday 5 September

I had an early morning interview for *Take a Break* with soap star Malandra Burrows who was promoting a pop single. I knew from the press release that she had played Kathy Bates in *Emmerdale* since 1985 but I have never watched a single episode. The PR officer had suggested meeting at reception in her London hotel, so I sat in the lobby hoping to correctly identify the celebrity. There were one or two well-dressed women who could have been famous, but they were too preoccupied with checking out. So I did not challenge them. I had just got out a book to read when an attractive young woman walked straight over and asked:

'Are you Andrew Marshall?'

I obviously looked like a journalist.

Malandra talked about her dogs and how one of them nearly died. Afterwards we discussed Diana and there was a tear in Malandra's eye. I feel more comfortable in this new England of open tears. I am no longer a freak and my compulsive need to remember Thom seems less self-destructive.

As it was still early, I decided to visit Kensington Palace and the shrine to Diana. As I walked out of the tube station, I was struck by just how many people were carrying bouquets. I walked faster, there was something exhilarating about joining a crowd united in one purpose. Even before we reached the gates of the palace, I could smell the millions of flowers and hear the low murmuring of thousands of respectful people. Even though I had seen the pictures in the papers, I was not prepared for the sheer quantity of teddy bears, notes and balloons that surrounded the gates to her house, the sheer scale of the devotion or just how quiet a crowd could be. I knelt down and read some of the intensely personal notes left by well-wishers, their informality a stark contrast with the tall wrought-iron railings and the palace of long corridors and stiff protocol.

I wanted to tap into the group energy but there was something holding me back. I sat on a park bench and tried to acclimatise myself. Next to me were two sixty something women:

'I can feel my dead mother and father with me. I really can, I know they are here and I'm sure they are looking out for me,' said one to the other.

'There must be lots of spirits witnessing this, millions of them, I bet they are drawn by all the energy,' replied her friend. 'It is almost holy.'

All the mourners around me were drawing comfort from being together, but all I could feel was detached. So I moved away. Perhaps the beauty of the flowers would help me open up. I found myself wishing, though, that the mourners had taken the cellophane off the flowers. I almost chuckled and gave myself a stern talking to: don't pretend the barrier is just cellophane!

Dejected, I started to make my way home, but it was only back at the tube station that I understood. Kensington Palace had become the headquarters of the new more emotional Britain. I might be in sympathy with the idea but standing at the epicentre of unrestrained feeling, my upbringing still held me back.

There were hundreds of caring people who would have been only too happy to give me a hug but I remained strangely cold and aloof. I cannot escape generations of Marshalls.

Saturday 6 September

I did not fancy spending the day of Diana's funeral alone. As John had accompanied me to Germany for Thom's funeral and been master of ceremonies for his memorial service in England, it seemed right that I should watch the TV coverage with him. Driving over to Woking, where he was staying with friends, I'd never seen the M25 so empty. Everybody was probably in front of the TV. I braced myself; it was going to be emotional.

When I arrived at Woking, John and his friends – John Brocks (who helped sort out my computer) and his wife Nicki – were already watching the TV coverage. I got out my tissues and took a seat. As the funeral procession left Kensington Palace, I noticed that the white lilies on Diana's coffin were in exactly the same arrangement as those on Thom's.

At Westminster Abbey, the ritual of the Church of England funeral service, the faith that I was born into, was surprisingly satisfying. The glorious music seeped into my soul. Especially the final piece 'Song for Athene' by John Tavener. The choir sounded as if they have been sent down from heaven to heal our wounds as they sung: 'Alleluia. May flights of angels sing thee to thy rest.' Finally, the pallbearers from the 1st Battalion, Welsh Guards bore Diana's coffin out of the Abbey and I felt a strange sense of completion. Amazingly, I had not even opened the packet of tissues.

After watching the hearse set off towards Diana's family home in Althorpe, I needed fresh air. In keeping with the mood of the day, John suggested visiting Brookwood Cemetery, which was within walking distance and where Dodi Fayed had already been laid to rest. As we set off in the afternoon sunshine, our hosts, John and Nicki Brocks, explained that Brookwood was built by the Victorians after they had run out of plots in central London. At one point, it was the largest cemetery in the world with special funeral trains for coffins and mourners from the London Necropolis Railway Station. Because of the size of Brookwood Cemetery, we had not expected to find Dodi's grave. However, we heard some noise and stumbled across the garden of remembrance created by his father. With fewer people and flowers than at Kensington Palace, our presence felt almost like an intrusion into family grief. A simple stone with DODI in large white letters was surrounded by mature bushes and carefully clipped lawn, where a few days before there would have been only mud and weeds.

Although we were silent at the graveside, walking back to the house, the conversation returned to the events of the past week. Nicki Brocks said:

'Diana and Dodi's death was such a surprise.'

It was a harmless remark, but I almost wanted to grab her and shake some sense into her.

'Don't you know that people die,' I almost shouted aloud. Even though she was pushing her young son in his buggy, she could not connect the miracle of birth with the inevitability of death. But then our society is determined to hide the bodies away so that instead of filing past Diana's open coffin, the public queued to sign an official book of condolence. No wonder our mortality is such a surprise.

In the same way that losing Thom exposed all the fault lines in my life, Diana's death provided an opportunity to examine the cracks in our national psyche. Her life seemed to dramatise the battle between what is private and what is public. Where did the working Princess end and where did the woman who wanted to love in peace begin? She touched our lives so profoundly because on a smaller scale we are all struggling with this modern dilemma – what do we show the public and what do we keep back for our own private world? Is it acceptable for men to show their vulnerable sides? Is it unprofessional to bring your problems to work or unrealistic and almost sub-human to expect to switch off? Gays and lesbians wonder if it is safe to come out at the office and co-workers whether their office romance is anybody else's business but their own. We are all walking a tight rope.

Thursday 18 September

I am irritated that my latest piece for 'Revelations' has been held over. Instead, *The Independent* published an interview with John Tavener about how his mother's death changed his music. 'I didn't want to write at all. I went to see an eminent traditionalist who said, "Go to the nature you love most of all," and that for me was Greece… My intention was not to write but after six weeks I found, not against my will exactly, I was writing and I couldn't stop. It was pouring out and there was a connection… The music had a new humility. That was very important to me and I worked and prayed my way out of the grief I felt for my mother.' Tavener belongs to a tradition of sacred music which stretches back to the Middle Ages, before the scientific revolution, when all music was an act of worship. Tavener certainly believes that composing is a form of prayer: 'I feel that the music is far ahead of what I am and the music teaches me something. It's part of a spiritual journey, and the journey in my case takes place through writing music and it tells me things about my life. The act of writing puts me almost in a trance state, where I feel enormously close to God.' I decided to buy Tavener's album *Innocence*, which ends with 'Song for Athene'.

Monday 22 September

My next Revelation was with the actor David Haig who has written a play about Rudyard Kipling and his son Jack. With short eyesight, Jack should never have fought in the First World War but Kipling encouraged him and pulled strings to get him through the medical. Jack was promptly killed in action. I had been told by the PR that the play had a parallel with Haig's own family loss. His younger sister had died of a brain haemorrhage when she was twenty-two.

It was a balmy evening and we sat outside in a small concrete square with a tree in the middle beside Hampstead Theatre in London. Haig explained his interest in Kipling – an actor had told him he was Kipling's doppelgänger – and about his sister:

'I remember so clearly the last time I saw her. The red brown leather jacket she was wearing is fixed in my memory and she was as vivacious as ever. I was just twenty-six and it was a great shock. I was overwhelmed by a hundred different feelings among which was enormous guilt that I hadn't supported her enough and that I was lucky to still be alive.'

He broke off from the story for a second.

'There's another connection.'

I nodded.

'I also know what it is like to lose a child. My wife had a still-born daughter last year.'

'Oh good,' I replied without thinking.

There was a shocked moment of silence. We both knew that I meant: this would make a better story for the paper.

I started apologising.

Haig insisted there was no problem.

I felt terrible. Surely, after everything that has happened this year, I should be the last person to be trapped by base journalistic instinct.

'Don't worry. It's not a problem. Honestly,' said Haig.

But I felt that I had to tell him about my experiences and apologise again, so I did. Finally, I switched the tape recorder on again and he continued with his story of loss:

'Two days earlier, Julia suspected that she had lost the heart-beat. We went to hospital and they confirmed the baby was dead. We then had to sit in this labour ward at Guy's for roughly twenty-four hours. She had to go through a natural birth because it's healthier physically and psychologically. Through paper-thin walls we could hear mothers celebrating the birth of live children. It's a crippling experience – particularly for the mother. It is so barren and arid. The reverse of everything that is natural. To give birth to death is really perverse. When the baby was born, we had this perfect human being of tiny dimensions. We stayed with her for about three hours, which was a bizarre reflection of that time with a live baby. [Haig and his wife already have four children.]

Parents never recover from something like that, as Kipling's wife says in the play: "They stitch up the wound and go on."

'We called our daughter Grace. We are trying to build her a Japanese-style garden at home. You can't imagine two less Buddhist human beings than my wife and I, but we're drawn to creating somewhere we cannot only think about her loss but to contemplate what life is all about. We'll put in a couple of simple rocks maybe engraved with words that mean something to both of us.'

Listening to Haig, I was struck by a thought so powerful it almost took my breath away. Perhaps pain of this magnitude can be borne but only if we find some way to transform our suffering into something positive.

'This play, *My Boy Jack*, has extraordinary resonances from a point ten years ago when I was told that I looked like Kipling. Originally it had the most base motives, a greedy actor who wanted to play a part. Now it's become something really very deep and personal. There's even a scene between Rudyard and his wife that I have written as a direct result of a conversation I had with my wife shortly after the death of Grace.

'The people who survive these deaths, parents and other brothers and sisters, carry on. It can either destroy or mature them. Hopefully in real life and in the play, at least on a spiritual level, we have been strengthened. Kipling is not such a ranter; hopefully I'm less dogmatic than I was before these experiences. The balance between my tough and soft sides has changed; hopefully the play, in its writing, reflects that. I thought I was creating something that was cool but everybody tells me it is a gut felt emotional play. Writing can be beneficial but only if you stay honest and don't sentimentalise or hide the complexity of your feelings.'

I only hope that I can follow Haig's example. But what should I write? And can I manage anything beyond hack journalism?

Friday 26 September

On the weekend leading up to what should have been Thom's birthday, I tried to diffuse my sorrow by spending two days with Kate in Wales. As I drove over the Severn Bridge I remembered my last trip, back in January, to appear on Kate's radio phone-in. Thom had been well enough for me to leave him but sick enough for me to relish the oxygen of freedom. The show was supposedly about dating but turned into a symposium on grief after Kate's innocent question: 'Do you believe in love at first sight?'

Elderly woman after elderly man retold their wartime romances and the pain of now living alone. As they sobbed down the phone, I sipped white wine out of a plastic cup and tried to sympathise. It is amazing the details that stick: unable to find a corkscrew we had forced the cork down into the bottle. I could vividly remember mopping up the gush of wine and then watching the cork sink slowly down the bottle as we drank more and more. That cork seemed to symbolise my pain, forced down so I could release my caring side and nurture others – yet again. Andrew G Marshall forever the performer, a smile, a song, but tears in private. Sometimes I fear that my pain, like the cork, will be trapped for ever.

The day after the radio programme, I had treated the friend of a friend with whom I'd stayed to a Sunday roast. He chose one of those traditional family run hotels where Radio 2 floods out from the kitchen and seventies decor is alive and well. The other clientele were elderly couples bringing their maiden aunts for a run out. Between bites of roast beef and Yorkshire pudding, he recounted his lover's death. The shock of the car accident, the first hopes of recovery and the pits of depression when they were extinguished. So that was my weekend away: a phone-in full of depressed people followed by tales of what lay in store for me. Sometimes running away is harder than staying and facing the music.

When I arrived at Kate's house, this afternoon, I could almost taste the loss in the air. She wants a divorce but her husband is deep in denial. Yesterday, she served divorce papers but he has studiously avoided all reference to them. Kate was so pleased to see me she gave me a hug. It must have been the first act of tenderness in that house for years and her daughter dissolved into tears:

'Why do you love him more than you love Daddy,' she sobbed before disappearing upstairs.

It was an easy mistake. How can you explain to a seven and nine year old that ours is a brother and sister relationship? I'd already given the children chocolates – as if I was a new lover trying to ingratiate himself.

I felt another stab of guilt. Kate is using that support to break up the family. For her, it's either that or taking up her doctor's offer of lithium. Perhaps the children have every reason to be frightened of me.

On this visit to Wales I was staying with Kate's friend, Llewelyn, a thirty something doctor who lived round the corner in a house with exposed floorboards, a harp and more style magazines than WHSmith's. Although it was 1 a.m., when we returned from the restaurant, Llewelyn suggested another cup of coffee. While he boiled the kettle for a cafetiere, I leafed through his CD collection. He had almost as many Joni Mitchell albums as Thom. I put one on and we sat on opposite sofas in his large living room. On the table behind Llewelyn were four stems of white lilies. They were even arranged in a rectangular-shaped vase, just like the one Thom bought me on his second ever trip to England. (He had been shocked that I just threw flowers into an old jug, so we spent a beautiful day in Ditchling exploring the village at the foot of the South Downs and rummaging through the antique and gift shops. I'd understood, for the first time, why people enjoyed shopping.) The similarities were getting too much, I excused myself for a moment. In Llewelyn's toilet there was a stack of magazines. The top one was *Interiors* – I'd bought Thom a subscription the Christmas before last.

Back down stairs Llewelyn had moved to the floor and propped himself up against his sofa. I matched his posture by sitting against my sofa. Perhaps he did use the weights left lying round the living room; perhaps his skin had that velvety feel of well exercised muscles. Llewelyn offered a fresh pot of coffee. Could he want more than just my company? He talked about the pressure of the patients who'd be waiting for him in next morning's Emergency Surgery. I counted the six folds on his wrinkled forehead and guessed we both had our sorrows but the distance between our two sofas was too far physically and spiritually for either of us to reach out.

By 2 a.m. and I was too tired for anything beyond goodnight, I reached out to thank him for his hospitality. He was about to shake hands but I chose to ignore the gesture and went to kiss his smooth cheek. He mistook my intention and presented his lips, but suddenly that was too intimate.

Saturday 27 September

Next morning, I had a cup of coffee with Llewelyn. After he'd left for morning surgery, I played his CDs and leafed through his piles of magazines and books undisturbed. I was really tempted, but resisted the urge, to climb into his bed and discover if I could smell him on the sheets. On the living room mantelpiece was a snap shot of Llewelyn, Kate and other friends at a party. He looked so radiant in a bright red shirt that I wanted to steal the photograph, but again managed to stop myself. I put on another Joni Mitchell CD. How would Llewelyn and I entertain together? What hobbies would we share? What would we argue about?

For the first time since Thom's death I was fantasising about having a relationship – not just sex or a date for the cinema. Is this another step forward, the ability to imagine myself loving again, when only yesterday this felt impossible? I might not be ready for a real relationship but bring on the fantasy lovers.

Kate's daughter had thrown a tantrum about being left for the weekend. So instead of returning to my car, which I parked right outside her house, and retrieving my suitcase, we set off from Llewelyn's house. Soon the industrial strip around Cardiff was behind us and we headed over the Brecon Beacons. The scenery was breathtaking but driving through the small Welsh villages I could sense the stifling conformity seeping through the open car windows. No wonder Kate's bulimia kicks in after the train crosses the Severn Bridge and she has the urge to raid the buffet car for crisps, fruitcake and biscuits.

By early afternoon we arrived at a small grey stone Welsh chapel with the most astounding mountain views. The isolation was underlined by the unused plots in the walled graveyard. Kate's mother is buried here and last week would have been her birthday. Kate stood silently by the grave. I watched from a discreet distance. Later, while she removed dead stalks and fetched water for an iron receptacle and arranged some fresh flowers, we talked.

'My mother's death was a complete shock,' Kate said. 'We'd been for Sunday lunch in the pub, I gave her a kiss and drove off. Along the road back to my flat, I was overwhelmed by a sense of anguish and fear. I frequently did that journey, knew it like the back of my hand, and there was no reason for those feelings. I was so consumed with anxiety that I had to pull the car over. Something was wrong. I found a phone box and although I'd originally thought of phoning my parents opted for my boyfriend. What I later learned was that I pulled over at exactly the time my mother died.

'She'd felt ill, had gone into the kitchen for a glass of water and collapsed in my father's arms by the sink. She was trying to say something and she just died. Very, very sudden. I've always had the feeling she didn't want to go.'

I said nothing – as Kate's eyes were far away.

'I couldn't believe she had died. I blotted it out for three months. I acted it as if it was just the most normal thing in the world – everybody's mother dies eventually! I didn't want to see the body. I was fine, cool about it. I helped arrange the funeral. I was charming to everybody, read a blessing in my punk gear: black leather dress, studs and loads of black eyeliner. Back at work people were sympathetic but I brushed it off. I'm fine.'

Kate's reaction was the polar opposite of my obsession, so I was fascinated to discover if there is less pain from her more masculine approach of: shut up and get on with it.

'There were a few days when I would start work at nine but could only manage an hour at work and would return home to bed, but generally I carried on regardless. The grief finally came out on my birthday, nearly three months later, there was no card from her. Strange things bring it home. That night I tried to kill myself with a massive overdose of pills and Scotch. My boyfriend found me, phoned 999 and I was soon in hospital having my stomach pumped. My doctor's advice was simple: I had to stop or I was heading for a nervous breakdown. I was in a good job with a pension, but eventually had no choice. I was a wreck who used to cry all the time. I gave in my notice and spent six months lying in bed, hanging around cafés drinking strong coffee and not eating. My body had forced me to take time off.'

I gave Kate a kiss on the cheek as a gesture of sympathy and we got back in the car.

Our destination was Portmeirion: a fantasy village built by the architect Clough Williams-Ellis in the 1920s on a peninsula in north Wales. It is best known today as the setting for the cult TV series *The Prisoner*.

Portmeirion is an intriguing combination of cottages to rent and completely non-utility buildings: the colonnade, a dome, statues, fountains, belvederes and buildings, which on closer inspection are just facades. Everything is cunningly arranged so each angle affords another view or shows off an architectural treasure in a new light. Strolling round the village, I could easily imagine why it was chosen as a film set. However, the special wonder of Portmeirion is how man-made beauty is integrated into the surrounding natural beauty. The village overlooks an estuary where the sand stretches out to the horizon at low tide. On the cliffs, there are woodland walks seeded with Himalayan plants. It is a haven for birds.

I had always wanted to visit Portmeirion, even though I had never watched the TV series. It was only after we checked into our own cottage in the village, and I started reading the guidebook, that I truly understood my interest. There was an article by Clough Williams-Ellis about his inspiration:

'Throughout the years of my war service abroad I had a dream of something other than horrors, destruction and savagery – and what is *more* different than to build with whatever serenity, kindness and loveliness one could contrive on some unknown site – yet to be discovered.'

Ellis was building a village while I am trying to rebuild a life but both of us are trying to block out terrible memories. His front line was a trench and mine was a hospital bed. No wonder I felt a bond to Portmeirion even before I had arrived.

Our weekend was a bizarre combination of laughter and tears. Our quick exodus from Cardiff meant my suit was still outside Kate's house. An evening meal in the Portmeirion hotel demanded smart clothes and certainly not jeans – the only trousers I possessed. We sat on our balcony watching the incoming tide slowly swallow the sand and dreamed up wonderful excuses. Our merriment grew until we were almost hysterical.

Finally, Kate composed herself and phoned to arrange a dispensation for my jeans. From the gracious hotel dining room, we had the perfect view of the sun setting over the estuary and the stone boat forever moored at the quayside. Suddenly, I realised how much Thom would have enjoyed this setting. Portmeirion would have made a perfect birthday treat. He should have been sitting opposite me – not Kate. My eyes filled with tears and at least five minutes passed before I could speak.

Sunday 28 September

I woke up before Kate and sat on a chair watching her sleep. I found my notebook and wrote:

There are times when I feel pulled between two different futures. In the first, I'm living in some remote area with faithful Tyson taking long walks in the countryside. Although never quite clear where the money will come from to fund this lifestyle, I always feel relaxed and centred. Alternatively, my life revolves around a big city, latte coffee in pavement cafés, nights out at the theatre and living in a converted warehouse with river views. This vision is not big on peace but is much more exciting.

For someone used to forever planning his next rung on the ladder, just drifting along is so out of character that I often wonder who I am.

The journey back to Cardiff from Portmeirion suggested rural isolation was not a sensible option, after all. Endless streams cascading down hills and round rocks might look wonderful in brochures but there was a limit to how many I wanted to see. We couldn't even pick up the Top 40 singles chart in this remote corner of Wales and it seemed like weeks since my mobile phone had worked. Eventually I was forced to put coins into a conventional red telephone box. I'd always thought they were for tourists to take snap shots or to be converted into showers, but here people used them to make phone calls! I also wanted to see fewer sheep and more houses. In fact, the sheep were becoming oppressive, I was sure they had started arranging themselves into mystic patterns to communicate with higher beings.

My anxiety lessened as we hit suburbia and the approaching anonymity of the city. I could catch my breath properly. Can too much fresh air be bad for the brain? I hated to admit it but I was also keen to meet Llewelyn again. So I discretely pumped Kate for information about him.

On my return Llewelyn opened a bottle of Lindauer sparkling wine – Thom's favourite brand. However, this time I didn't feel the same passion, I'd learned too much about him to keep up the deception. It was as if I'd been replaying my old flickering home movies and Llewelyn had stepped in front of the screen. I projected the past on to my blank knowledge of him. There was no way that I was moving on, I'd just managed to find enough of Thom's personality in Llewelyn to fall for him all over again! My theme song since losing Thom, 'I'll Never Love This Way Again', swam through my mind yet again. Little did I realise that I'd find myself falling over and over with the same vision endlessly photocopied so each time it became more fuzzy and less real.

With Thom's birthday just hours away, I couldn't be alone that night. Enticing Llewelyn to share my bed, I was surprised and comforted to discover his skin had the same vibrant warmth as Thom's – who would sweat very easily and in the winter was better than an electric blanket. I wrapped my arms and legs around Llewelyn. Maybe if I held on tight enough, I could fool myself that I was really in bed with Thom.

Monday 29 September

If Thom had been alive today it would have been his forty-fourth birthday. We would have celebrated with champagne, a pile of presents from the frivolous to the seriously expensive and a night out at the theatre followed by a restaurant where pine nuts are a basic ingredient. But how do you celebrate the birthday of someone who is dead? I had not made an auspicious start. Although Llewelyn and I had spent the night like woodland creatures snuggled into our nest against the storm, I woke with the stench of adultery in my mouth. A taste which no amount of brushing my teeth could eradicate.

We shared another cafetiere of coffee, before Kate arrived to take me off for breakfast at a nearby café in a row of anonymous sixties shops. I laid into scrambled egg, bacon, beans and a mug of tea. There was just one other customer: an elderly man wearing a tatty overcoat that reeked of old bus stations, so bad that just sitting next to him your luck could take a turn for the worse.

Kate and I ordered extra toast and a young woman arrived with two immaculately turned out children: one in a push chair, the other a toddler of about three with blue ribbons and a Little Mermaid grip in her hair. It must have taken the mother boundless time and energy to make them so smart, but her only destination seemed to be this café for a solitary coffee. At least, it was an outing – a way of breaking up the long days.

'Happy Birthday Thom, wherever you are,' Kate said simply, putting into words what was hanging in the air.

Once again my napkin became a makeshift handkerchief. There is something very pitiful about tears on to Formica tabletops.

Happy Birthday Thom, wherever you are.

She held my hand, instinctively knowing not to say another word. What comfort could words possibly be?

Back home, I was pleased to find a card from my parents – perhaps they are not so bad after all! Peter phoned. Why wasn't I more grateful? Gary, my best friend, called too. Lying on the sofa too emotionally, and therefore physically, exhausted to sit up, it seemed that I was on the phone all evening talking about Thom. Walter suggested opening a bottle of champagne in his memory, but there is nothing more depressing than drinking alone and pouring most of the bottle down the sink. Next, I had the difficult task of phoning Thom's mother. I nearly always cry – even if we only discuss the weather and how my work is going. Despite the pain, I kept up the contact. She's an important link to Thom and hopefully I fulfil the same function for her. I doubt there are two people who miss him more. The conversation that evening was made doubly difficult by her total lack of English and my restricted German vocabulary.

However, I could understand enough to glean a small vignette into Thom's parents' sorrow. That morning at breakfast, Erwin had told Ursula that today would have been Thom's birthday – as if she could ever have forgotten. It was as if this intensely private man had marked Thom's special day by dropping his reserve and mentioning his son. I know that not a day will go by without them both remembering, but I guess this was one of the few days when they both talked and shared their burden. I was reminded of how lonely life can be even as one half of a couple.

The final call was from Elaine, our friend who would also clean for us. She was perhaps the person who'd seen the most of Thom. She could measure his health by whether he came downstairs to talk, and she could clean the bedroom, or whether he remained cloistered upstairs. Elaine was struggling with a double dose of birthday blues. Her sister-in-law was born on exactly the same day as Thom and died a few weeks after him. Elaine was uncertain whether to phone her brother-in-law and I explained how I'd really appreciated proof that people had not forgotten.

So she made the call and half an hour later was back on the phone thanking me for my advice.

I had this urge to remember exactly what Thom and I had done last year for his birthday, the year before that and back through every one of his birthdays. If seven birthdays together is all you have – will ever have – each one means more. However, try as I might, I could not remember. So I told Elaine about how wretched forgetting Thom's last birthday was making me. She cast her mind back.

'I think Thom was particularly poorly.'

Suddenly I could picture him opening his presents in his dressing gown and returning straight to bed. My mother had given him a subscription to a gardening magazine and I'd worried that he would not get to read every edition. Ironically, the magazine folded before he did. My next memories were of the year before – his forty-second birthday. I'd driven back through the night, from a contract in Manchester, so we could sip champagne at midnight and herald in his birthday. He'd been feeling sick and was worried he had caught a cold. Looking back, this was probably the first sign. On the day of his birthday, I'd booked to see Maggie Smith at the theatre in *Three Tall Women*. He insisted that he felt better and we'd gone up to London, but by the time the show finished he had a temperature of 40°C.

Perhaps it is just as well that I cannot remember everything.

Friday 3 October

The end of September and the beginning of October will always be difficult. Thom's birthday is quickly followed by the anniversary of the day we met. After all the emotional upheaval of Thom's birthday, I was worried about how I would survive our anniversary.

Tom Flood, who knows from personal experience just how hard these 'special' days can be, arranged for me to visit. We met down on Brighton seafront and roller-bladed along the promenade. His friend Richard Hawkes brought a bottle of wine and some glasses down to the seafront; considering that neither Tom Flood nor I were very proficient on skates, adding alcohol to the equation could have been disastrous, but we gossiped, joked and had a wonderful time.

After Richard left, Tom and I sat down and talked about our departed lovers, our eyes shining brightly with a strange combination of happier memories and bitter tears. It has now been five year's since Tom's friend, Engel, died. Tom's friendship has been comforting but tinged with sadness. From his example, I know I can survive but Tom is also proof: life might go on but you never heal over completely.

Saturday 4 October

Escaping what would have been Thom and my eighth anniversary so lightly, I thought I was getting stronger – a big mistake. The best friend of Sara – one of Tyson's owners – has been extremely ill. Sara had been supporting the wife but the news is not good. Her husband will be given one last treatment of chemotherapy but the experts hold out little hope. By lending me Tyson, Sara has been a rock. So I decided to return the favour and called. Even at a distance, Sara's helplessness leapt out and mugged me. I tried to remember what I found helpful at the same point in this journey. How do you hope for the best but prepare for the worst?

I remembered a journey back from the airport after one of Thom's stays in Herdecke. He had confessed that the doctor had scolded him for going down to the shop in the foyer: 'You don't realise how ill you are – we nearly lost you.' This had been news to me.

So I asked Thom to make a will. When we reached home, he had gone off to his office, written his wishes and then translated it into English in case there was any doubt. We'd cried and hugged each other and I sealed the document. It was painful but not as bad as worrying that he might die and I'd be left guessing what he wanted.

By sharing these experiences, I hoped to lessen Sara's pain and ever the professional agony uncle, even passed on the numbers of a self-help group. I put the phone down and took a deep breath, there was no denying it: I felt terrible; depression was rolling over me like a damp fog off the sea.

I had seriously overestimated my ability to help. An hour in the gym failed to achieve anything more than a temporary lifting of the gloom. How could I have been so stupid?

Sunday 5 October

Last night I went to the theatre with Peter, but even watching the classic play *Boys in the Band* only briefly lifted my spirits. In the morning I woke up in Peter's bed. It was the first time we had spent the whole night together, but Peter sensed that although I might be lying in his arms I was slipping out of his life.

Our relationship had been billed, by him, as a summer affair. Except, as the Indian summer gave way to the first autumn chill, he made a desperate attempt to re-write our story:

'Can't I stay on until you've found someone permanent to love,' he asked.

'Remember how well defended I am,' I replied coldly. For some time, I have suspected him of being more involved than is wise. 'I have to surround myself with armour plating' and almost added 'or be as protected as a virgin at an orgy.' But lying in his bed that seemed rather an inappropriate analogy.

Peter turned his back but I could sense a struggle to control his feelings. My natural instinct was to put out my hand to comfort him, but this only made things worse. I knew he was crying. He had witnessed my tears often enough but his emotional vulnerability made me shrink further into myself. Our relationship had reached a very delicate stage: he wants the affair to deepen, I want it to die.

Fortunately, Peter had to leave for church and his choir duties. Three days later he would be flying off to America for a holiday, so I decided to avoid the issues building between us. I kissed Peter on the lips and escaped into the autumn sunshine. I arrived home completely exhausted. The deadline on a newspaper article was fast approaching. Even though it was Sunday, I forced myself back to the computer and made myself start typing. I might just as well have been chipping words on to marble.

Wednesday 8 October

'He's draining your energy,' explained Patricia, the hostess of *Agony*, who is single and far more experienced in the dark arts of dating. Seven and a half years with Thom has left me seriously rusty. 'Break up with him,' she urged.

'Reject him?' I asked.

'So what's wrong with that?'

'It would be cruel.' Thom's death stills feels like rejection, so I can't knowingly put Peter through the same pain.

'But by allowing your relationship to drag on, all you're achieving is what you're seeking to avoid.'

My only attempt at a new start so far, dating Peter, is making me feel worse than ever before. It seems that just as there is no such thing as a free lunch, the carefree relationship is a myth too. I'm paying with angst and a cover charge of anguish. At least talking everything over with Patricia has clarified my options.

Thursday 9 October

I had a session with my supervisor at Relate. We talked about the possibility of me starting to counsel again in the new year.

Maybe I'll be over the worst by then?

Friday 10 October

Kate has decided to leave *Agony*. Her father is increasingly unwell and she cannot cope with spending so much time away from home. So there were auditions to replace her. I suggested my friend Nancy Roberts for the job but I think they found her too over the top.

'I can always tone it down,' Nancy claimed.

We left the Live TV studios together and took a taxi over to London Weekend Television where I was due to interview Cilla Black. The traffic was bad and I arrived about five minutes late. Cilla had already decided to go to lunch with the Head of Production instead.

Thursday 16 October – Germany

Strange unidentifiable feelings ran through my stomach as I checked in at Gatwick airport. I was shattered, both physically and emotionally. I might need a holiday but for some reason that I cannot explain, I've chosen to return to Germany and confront the past. The couple ahead of me in the queue were speaking German. There was something very reassuring about the famil-iarity of Thom's mother tongue. I'd forgotten what a central part of my life Germany has been. For five and a half years, I flew there at least once a month to visit Thom. Even after he moved to England, we would return together several times a year. It was only in the last few months that it became tied up with sickness, disease and death. So I'm returning for the right reasons, aren't I?

The bustling terminal was not the place for self-examination. It was only after I sat on the plane and looked out of the window, that I came face to face with my true feelings. As usual, I'd bought a copy of *Vanity Fair* to read during the journey. It was just another flight to Germany. Except my other purchase was a packet of tissues. It has been months since I had always carried an emergency supply.

Waiting for my baggage at Dortmund airport, I found myself looking for Thom the other side of the barrier. How many times had he collected me from that airport? How many times had I left customs and thrown myself into his arms?

I dug deep for some consolation. At least this time I would not be hiring a car and driving to that hospital – the heart of my hell. Instead, I took a taxi to my friend Martin's flat (where I had stayed during Thom's final weeks).

Dortmund was full of nostalgia but it was a gentle pain and the tears I'd expected were sweet rather than bitter. I was amazed at how easily I fell back into sync with Thom's friends. It was wonderful to talk about him and hear them recount their favourite stories. Back in England, it always seemed to be me who brought up his name. Even if I couldn't have Thom, I could spend time with his friends and walk the streets that he walked.

You don't stop loving someone just because they're dead. In fact, the love grows greater, as it's easier to forget their faults.

Friday 17 October – Germany

Today I even wandered past the block of flats where Thom had lived. I took a deep breath and stopped in the doorway of the baker's where we'd buy our breakfast rolls. I summoned up my courage and glanced across the street. The beauty parlour underneath the apartment block was still there, but somebody had knocked down one of the poles on the pavement by the bus stop, which stops cars parking there. In my heart, I could feel the swirl of a thousand orchestras tuning up. I looked directly at Thom's old front door. To my amazement there was just a rather dark entrance to a very normal building. My imagination was so vivid that I'd almost expected a shrine to our good times together with flowers, candles and pictures of Thom. Of course, there was nothing on the doorstep beyond a few fliers from a discount warehouse.

I felt relief and something else? Yes. A sense of freedom. I could visit the past without deifying it.

Saturday 18 October – Germany

Thom made many promises he never kept, beyond vowing to love me for twenty-five years. He often talked about us taking a boat trip down the Rhine, visiting Vienna and touring the Sauerland in autumn.

This smaller version of the Black Forest must have felt like nowhere land to someone growing up gay in the sixties. Martin and his partner, Uwe, claim that even today young gay men in small Sauerland villages routinely marry because it is impossible to be different with fewer than a thousand neighbours. Thom's instinct was to escape the prison of woods and mountains but their natural beauty must have wormed its way into his psyche. He would sigh over autumn in the Sauerland, the way that Frank Sinatra would praise autumn in Vermont. However, I'd never been over during the season when the leaves turned red, gold and amber. Thom's birthday, which he liked to celebrate in Germany was too early and a month later, when I'd next be over, would be too late. This time, I was determined to make the pilgrimage.

After two days in Dortmund, Jürgen collected me for the second leg of my journey. If I cannot see the autumn colours with Thom, I've decided to do it with another member of the Hartwig family. Our first stop was Bad Sassendorf and Thom's parents. His mother is easily the most emotional member of the family, with a bad knee, severe arthritis and plenty of time to dwell on the unnaturalness of losing a child. Walking into their neat ground-floor apartment, I immediately spotted a picture of Thom I'd never seen before on the sideboard. He had the broadest smile and round healthy cheeks. It must have been taken fairly recently because I recognised the suit, which these days I often wear on my TV show. I picked up the photo to take a closer look and tried to control the tears. My memory of how he looked is fading so quickly that I expect his photos to somehow disappear too, until Thom's footprint on our world is completely erased.

We sat on the terrace and basked in the unseasonably warm weather. There was something very comforting about being with his family. They were certainly pleased to see me again too. Of course, we had the German institution of *kaffee* and *kuchen*. The apple flan was home-made. Erwin had followed Ursula's instructions – because her arthritis made it difficult for her to hold anything heavier than a teaspoon. It was of course the same recipe that she passed onto her son and which he'd often baked for our visitors. It was wonderful to savour again something that I thought was lost for ever.

The conversation was entirely in German. So my concentration would waver and my thoughts kept returning, unbound, to the agony of my last trips to Germany. Sitting with Jürgen and the mother that Thom had tried so hard to protect, I was riding the most ferocious wave from the past. But like a practised surfer,

I was held aloft rather than submerged and drowned by the salt-water. I was facing my fears. I was surviving.

Jürgen had booked us into the Berghotel Hoher Knochen in the most mountainous part of the Sauerland. Our journey took us through small villages – full of whitewashed houses with black timbers. I felt an urge to wear a felt hat with a feather and we even spotted a couple of 'happy wanderers' wearing lederhosen and long socks with tassels; the complete picture postcard stereotype of Germany. Perhaps the tourist board had paid them to be part of the scenery and live out our fantasies. At home I have pictures of Thom as a young boy in similar lederhosen on a forest trail proudly holding his walking stick.

In the evening, we feasted on regional dishes and I tried hare for the first time. Jürgen and I did not talk much but instead enjoyed a silent companionship, both knowing that the other was thinking about the ghost at the feast. I was profoundly moved when Jürgen did talk about Thom. His eyes moistened as he recounted the little things that reminded him of his brother: the phone calls after ten in the evening, songs on the radio and CDs he'd given him.

I wish my sister felt the same way about me.

I might not have cried in front of Thom's parents or Jürgen but later, alone with my diary, the tears ran down my cheeks as I wrote down the love that was unspoken but implicit in every gesture. Why do I torture myself?

Sunday 19 October – Germany

We purchased a map at reception and set off for the highest point in the area. With the bright clear sun shining through the trees, I am transfixed by the beauty of the forest. The tree trunks stand in rows either side of the path like columns in a cathedral. Towering above me, the pale bark becomes stone and the golden leaves, stained-glass windows. For a split second I feel at one with the world and that if I stand still for long enough I can make sense of some vast greater plan. Thom might never have brought me to the Sauerland but with his brother beside me, I feel the whole world is interconnected and that somehow Thom has a hand in this perfect day.

On our arrival at the summit, I am not surprised to find that with typical German efficiency there is a car park and a short walk marked out for Sunday walkers to take ten minutes of gentle exercise and feel they have earned their *kaffee* and *kuchen*. Having trekked for one and a half hours to reach the café we had a feeling of superiority as we devour a mountain of cake. After refreshments, we consulted the map again and planned our return journey. On the map, our walk resembled a squashed circle – a shape that would return and dominate my dreams that night.

It is not surprising that my nightmares often feature the horror of Thom's last twenty-four hours: the pain etched across his face and my inability to do anything more useful than watch helplessly. Returning to Germany and spending so much time with my fellow witnesses has thrown further fuel on to the flames and everything feels more vivid. Previously, I've woken up in a sweat and escaped by opening a book and reading until I'm exhausted and fall back into dreamless sleep. However, this time I was determined to press on through the blackness of the nightmare.

'Hold on,' I tell myself. 'Be brave' and this time I step into a serene light. I am back in the wood again, but the morning's journey has taken on a very special shape. It is as if our route follows a chalk mark drawn round a body rather like the ones police mark out at a crime scene. However, among the glorious trees, there has been no struggle and the arms are by the body's side as if it's in a sarcophagus.

Suddenly, I realise that I'm walking round my own corpse but instead of a scene ripped from a horror movie the sun streams through the leaves and I'm at peace. There is nothing to fear. My life has come a full circle. I have returned to Germany, the beginning and the end of Thom's journey, but in my dream I have made the most difficult journey of all. I have come to terms with my own time span on earth.

As I lay in the darkness, now completely conscious, I resolved to read some textbooks on bereavement. Perhaps one of the most important ingredients in accepting the death of someone we love is to look at our own mortality firmly in the eye.

Tuesday 21 October

Sitting in the departure lounge of Dortmund airport, I felt far stronger than the last time I was here, two days after Thom's death. Not only do I possess more energy, but I can look further ahead. Previously, I could picture myself arriving home then nothing beyond the end of that week. Now I can think about six months ahead, which is achingly close to having a future. What's more, I seem to have managed to break out of the loop where Thom's death obliterates the memories of our life together. So I've reclaimed my past too. In addition, I believe, and hope, that I have created a bond with Jürgen that will be strong enough for me to remain part of Thom's family for ever.

Yet there was sadness mixed in with the joy. Who can I gossip with about the tangled relationships of my German friends? Thom and I would have enjoyed speculating about what was happening between Martin and Uwe. Why had Martin, who was supposed to be too ill to go to work, disappeared for so long and why wouldn't he tell Uwe where he had been? It had happened not once but twice. But without someone to dissect a dish hot, you have to eat it cold and alone.

When I arrived home, there was a message on the answering machine from Peter. I should have called but I was tired and had to prepare for *Agony* – especially as this will be the first edition without Kate. I am not looking forward to another early start, struggling with countless changes of clothes, followed by a full day of being bright, amusing and caring.

I need a proper holiday.

However, a further week away means saying 'no' to someone even more daunting than a boyfriend: a potential employer. Being freelance, I fear that if I'm not always available someone else will fill the void – after all that's how I found my best contracts. However, fresh from reconnecting with Thom's past, I feel stronger. The world might have been spinning too fast, but my head is finally clear. It is much better to step down off the merry-go-round than to be flung off and have my face ground into the concrete.

I phoned my travel agent and booked a flight and hotel in Madrid for later in the week.

Saturday 25 October – Madrid

It was a warm sunny day and I decided to relax in Madrid's Parque del Retiro. I stumbled across a monument, which is supposed to celebrate the life of King Alfonso XII but looks more like a wedding cake. The columns are topped not by a bride and groom but with mythical gods and goddesses, and proud lions poised to leap across the lake that captures their reflection. Of course, I had to have a closer look and found what I hoped was the entrance. The man at the kiosk asked for what seemed like an extraordinary amount of money but I paid and tried to find the path to the monument. The attendant called me back and beckoned to a rowing boat. Rather than an entrance fee – I have hired a boat! My Spanish phrase book has let me down, yet again, but making the most of it, I rowed across to the monument. The lake is small so I only needed a few strokes to pull up beside the monument and admire the exquisite workmanship. It seemed pointless to row round in circles, so I copied the other rowers, shipped oars and laid back to enjoy the autumn rays. The stress of the last few weeks ebbed away as I let my hand trail in the water.

Large fish crept up to surface to swallow unseen insects. The boat bobbed languorously. I had become part of the reflection of the white marble monument, rather than just an onlooker. With nowhere to go or anything to do, I let my mind skim the surface. Perhaps I spend too much time trying to make sense of why Thom had to leave. Would knowing our fate make life easier? If I'd understood Spanish, I'd never have discovered the pleasure of messing about in boats and more beauty than all the staterooms of the Royal Palace, which my guidebook had marked as 'must-see'. Maybe I should also stop reading about these places of interest. Does it increase my pleasure to know that a mural or a tapestry came from the seventeenth century rather than the sixteenth century? I certainly do not need to know anything about King Alfonso to adore the Ruritanian splendour of his statues. Would we really enjoy life, get more out of it if we understood its mysteries? Perhaps, there is no universal plan. Perhaps, it is just up to us to seize the day.

In the evening, I went to the newly restored opera house. In the interval between the ballet (*El Sombrero de Tres Picos*) and the opera (*La Vida Breve*), I explored the public rooms. They looked even more sumptuous than in the spread in this month's *Hola* (*Hello*) magazine with photos of the Royal Family's visit on gala opening night. I bought a drink and leaned against the wall like I was waiting for a friend to return from the toilet. When my glass was empty, I did another circuit. I returned to my seat and perused my programme. It was in Spanish and I did not understand a word.

Not once did I wish that Peter had been there too.

Sunday 26 October – Madrid

My last trip to Spain had been an orgy of beauty but there was no deliverance in Madrid's Prado Museum. Perhaps it is the curse of popular places – all those tour guides with groups following their rolled-up umbrellas. Perhaps I find Goya dull and El Greco too nightmarish. Like all addicts, if the fix does not work, I increased the dose and visited the El Museo de arte Thyssen-Bornemisza after lunch.

I had never heard of this gallery before but it turned out to be the most perfect collection ever. Starting at the top of building, with Italian primitives and mediaeval art, one progresses down through the Impressionists to the Expressionists until finally arriving at Pop Art on the ground floor. The collection included Miró, Van Gogh, Monet, Lichtenstein, Mondrian, Holbein and Picasso. So much perfection but this time it is just art for art's sake. There was no internal transcendence. No syringe lunged into my heart, just beautiful art.

However, standing in front of Holbein's portrait of the young Henry VIII, I felt a direct connection to someone who had changed my life. The reason that I was brought up Protestant and spared the Catholic guilt for being gay was directly down to this man and his divorce. I stood as close to the King as Holbein would have done all those years previously. I stared into Henry VIII's icily determined eyes and he held my gaze. Over four and a half centuries later, this painting still possesses immense power. Great art is immortal. I want Thom to be immortal.

That night, Thom returned in my dreams. He seemed so real that I could actually nuzzle his neck. I felt his warmth, his gentleness and that sense of complete protection. The location for our tryst was rather strange: an international peace conference. It was not a prestigious one, because we were in a small basement and sat on old stacking chairs. Thom moved his chair right next to mine, he leaned over and put his head on my shoulder, his arm round my back and snuggled against me. Even though it was a dream, I knew that Thom's return would be only temporary. However, he had no idea that he had died or that we were only allowed twenty-four hours together. Goodness knows why we were wasting our time on something as futile as a peace conference! Thom seemed so happy listening to the key note speaker, I wanted to warn him but I knew he would not understand.

My sobs woke me up. Paradise was lost.

Monday 27 October – Madrid

Music was something Thom and I shared together – our joint collection boasts almost a thousand albums. At suppertime, the right music was as important to complementing the mood as the right wine. We would play each other favourite tracks from favourite artists. He introduced me to Joni Mitchell, the depth of talent of Roberta Flack and the later work of Marianne Faithfull. In return, I'd bring back the latest CDs from Radio Mercury by artists like k.d. lang, Harry Connick Jnr and Mary Chapin Carpenter.

Several CDs have come out over the past six months that I longed to share with Thom. Like k.d. lang's *Drag*, a collection of indolent ballads about smoking, which would definitely have been A1 on our personal jukebox. I heard it at a friend's house and even walked into the music shop, held the CD in my hand but could not bring myself to buy it. k.d. lang's Brighton gig was one of the last concerts we attended together. She sung even more beautifully live than on her CDs. Another album was from an artist we discovered together. Maxwell's *Urban Hang Suite* was in a pile of CDs that I brought back from work after quickly flipping through the songs. I'd half forgotten the album until Thom started raving about Maxwell's smooth soul charm. It became the CD we were most likely to play on long car journeys and I even found it calming when I drove to visit him at Herdecke hospital in Germany. So if Thom had been alive Maxwell's *Unplugged* would have been an obvious purchase, but how could I enjoy it on my own?

It was raining in Madrid today, so I drifted into a large department store and into the music section. One of the listening posts had Maxwell's *Unplugged* so I put on the headphones and found myself bathed in his glorious voice again. Something inside clicked and I was finally ready to buy both this CD and *Drag*. I would give anything to hear Thom's opinions on Maxwell's version of the Kate Bush song: 'This Woman's Work'. But I bought albums by Finley Quaye, Erykah Badu and The Verve too.

Tuesday 28 October

I flew back from Madrid this morning. Sussex feels particularly cold but I stayed in and played my new CDs, particularly Erykah Badu. My collection is no longer frozen in March 1997 and I'm back in touch with one of my longest lasting passions: music.

Monday 3 November

The trip to Madrid felt very different from Seville; this time I was lonely. Instead of licking my wounds alone, I wanted company again. However, I cannot imagine Peter being anything more than a friend. I might protest that a) he's too good for me, b) he deserves better and c) I'm too emotionally defended for him. However, if I'm honest, he is too high maintenance. We are no longer having 'play' dates but flirting with real feelings – both his and mine. I can cope with neither.

It has been weeks since we have spoken. First, I was in Germany and Spain and then he was in China. However, he came round for coffee this morning and seemed very distant.

'I think we'd be better as friends.'

'I thought that's all we were,' he said.

'What do you mean?'

'When I did not hear from you.'

'OK. So that's official.'

'Fine.'

I drifted into this relationship, drifted through it and now have finally drifted out the other side.

Saturday 8 November

Patricia, the hostess of *Agony*, was excited. Her guru was coming to London. In the past twelve months, she has flown over to Ireland and up to Scotland for his weekend workshops.

'I really think you should go.' She pressed a leaflet into my hand about Emaho, a Native American Shaman who 'from an early age has received visions and spirit empowerments'.

'He won't force me to do something too new age, like making a circle with my own urine?'

Patricia laughed: 'Nothing like that.'

I looked at the details again. There was a special introductory offer of just £10 for a one-day course. What had I got to lose?

Following Patricia's advice, I decided to suspend all judgement and just see what happened. The venue was a bleak

youth hostel near King's Cross. My fellow searchers for spiritual enlightenment all seemed to know each other. None of the
women had a scrap of make-up. The few men present seemed
to have been marched to the barber's and made to have the
same deeply unfashionable haircut. I sat down on a chair next
to Patricia and did my best to look like I belonged. Everybody
was waving to friends or turning round to chat to someone behind them. I read my leaflet about the course for the tenth time.
Slowly hush descended, Emaho had arrived and was making individual eye contact with everybody. There must have been over a
hundred people in the half circle and I had to admire his courage
in making such a low-key start. I thought that I might giggle
when he looked at me, but I was able to return his gaze without
being too self-conscious.

Once we had all been made welcome, Emaho started to talk
in a low compelling voice. He spoke for an hour and a half – with
no notes, no overhead projectors and no exercises to draw us into
his world. Not that the woman next to me needed much help,
she had her eyes closed and rocked back and forth as she drunk in
each syllable. Emaho's total disregard for our modern attention
span was rather refreshing. By leaving spaces between the words,
I could take his ideas and try them out on my own life. His
thoughts about reincarnation and how we return as metaphor-
ical immigrants began to fix in my imagination. According to
Emaho, successful immigrants embrace their new culture while
keeping true to their own traditions. When we are reborn into a
new family, we must copy these good immigrants. It was quite
an interesting twist on modern psycho-babble which criticises
our parents for not providing what we need. Perhaps I should try
to fit in with my parents' emotional rectitude rather than forever
pushing them to embrace my culture.

Before the lunch break, Emaho told us to prepare for the fire
dance. Patricia leaned closer and whispered:

'This is something really special. I'd hoped it would be this afternoon, but you never can tell.'

'But what is it?'

'Sssh! You'll find out soon enough.'

'I like to think of the fire dance as a gift from Europe,' Emaho explained. 'It has emerged over a series of workshops over here.' We were all dismissed with the advice to: 'Eat wisely.'

We all stood up and I was surprised to discover that Emaho was quite short. I could have sworn he was taller.

When I returned from a nearby restaurant, everybody had taken off their shoes and socks and changed into jogging shorts and T-shirts. I removed my socks and shoes and joined my fellow disciples cross-legged on the floor. Emaho was already bent over a small piece of cloth, on which were two gilt candlesticks in the shape of dolphins. Their spiritual effect was lessened because they reminded me of the cheap ornaments I would bring back from our English seaside holiday for my grandmother.

'What's that?' I whispered to Patricia.

'It's known as the altar,' she replied.

Emaho was busy cutting flowers with a sharp knife, and arranging them round the edge of the altar. When the preparations were finished, he made a silent prayer and left the room. Immediately, his disciples started to come up, kiss pieces of jewellery and photos and place them among the candles, flowers and pots.

'They're asking for them to be blessed,' explained Patricia as she added one of her own treasured possessions.

My first reaction was wishing I had known and brought a picture of Thom, but as more and more trinkets were placed on the altar I became increasingly uncomfortable. It smelt too much of Catholicism. I could feel my Protestant ancestors (who had fled religious persecution in France) marching round my stomach cursing the creation of false religious icons. I remembered the visit that Thom and I had made to bonfire night in Lewes, Sussex. How we all jeered as an effigy of the Pope was carried shoulder high through the streets on its way to be burned.

'Stop it!' I told myself. 'You promised to have an open mind.'

Emaho returned and switched on a tape of rhythmic chants and drumbeats. He started to limber up. Everybody followed his example and soon I too was jogging on the spot and letting my hands shake by my sides. So far so good. After about ten minutes, Emaho suggested the newcomers sit and watch until we felt comfortable enough to join in. I found a place by the radiator with a good view of the altar.

The chants moved up a notch and everyone else began to dance with more abandonment. Suddenly Emaho grabbed a woman out of his congregation and threw her prostrate in front of the square of cloth. He shoved his hands into the candle flames until they were black with soot and pulled the chosen one, who was now almost in a trance, back up on her feet. He smeared soot across her face, bellowed at her forehead and threw her back into the dancing throng. I was shocked. In fact, shocked is an understatement. I imagined myself dancing at the back desperately hoping not to be picked.

Two of the newcomers got up and joined the throng. I pulled my knees up to my chest. Emaho had a cold and blew his nose on a black handkerchief from his back pocket. He grabbed another unlucky disciple and smeared her face with black soot and all his germs. Although I've never been particularly worried about bacteria, I could hear Thom's voice insisting that this was deeply unhealthy. I watched as more dancers were blackened and slowly it dawned: everyone would be initiated into the fire dance! Some of the more unlucky dancers even had water poured over them from a small pot on the altar. Emaho blew his nose again. I knew with every fibre of my body that I didn't want to be smeared in candle soot and shouted at.

By this time, I was the only newcomer who was still sitting cross-legged on the floor. What should I do? I wanted normal sensations: buying a can of coke or crossing a road – anything but dancing and smearing and nose blowing. So I quietly stood up and slipped out of the room. I felt an immediate sense of relief and started searching for my socks and shoes. Except they were still locked away and all the course organisers were jumping from foot to foot like whirling dervishes.

I wanted to bang on the door and demand my shoes and socks. I had never realised how attached I was to them. It was too cold to just leave the youth hostel. So I sat in the lobby and watched backpackers arrive in duffel coats and pretended that it was normal to hang around barefoot. An hour later, when the last disciple had been smeared and the candles blown out, my cold feet were reunited with those much missed shoes and socks. Patricia was still high from the whole experience:

'Are you coming back tomorrow?'

Monday 10 November

I went to see my doctor about changing the prescription for my asthma inhaler. He wanted to know how I was doing and we talked about his last home visit:

'I thought that you were angry with me because I'd told Thom that he was going to die.'

'No. I was grateful for your honesty.'

I must have looked glum.

'Have you thought of counselling?' Dr Toynbee asked.

'It wasn't a great success.' But then nothing seems to tame the black beast and the long shadows he casts.

'Perhaps you're ready now.'

I felt too exhausted to argue and at least this time I won't have to pay.

Friday 14 November

I am not certain if I am being pigheaded – and have to do every-thing differently – or just creative. However, I've decided to turn planting Thom's tree into an event. So I invited Martina, Thom's favourite nurse from Germany, over to England, partly to thank her for the extra care and partly as I know it would have pleased Thom. However, if I'm being honest – or what is the point of keeping a diary – I still feel compelled to face down my demons.

Martina is an important witness to what happened in Herdecke. She was at Thom's bedside at the very end and be-yond. After I stumbled out of that death room and drove away into the night, she prepared and washed his body for the morgue. What exactly did she do? Actually, I don't want to know that. There are limits to my courage.

Waiting for Martina at Gatwick airport, I wondered whether she would recognise me. Not only has it been eight months since the funeral, but this morning I decided to shave my beard off. Thom would not have approved, but I decided that the beard belonged to somebody I used to be – one half of a couple. So I attacked my face first with Thom's hair clippers and then foam, a fresh blade and water. A few minutes later, I found a stranger's face staring back at me from the mirror. It has been ten years since I've last been clean shaved and I look younger and surpris-ingly vulnerable.

In the event, Martina had no trouble recognising me. We greeted each other shyly. After all, we are virtual strangers and the person who brought us together is missing. Martina is in her late twenties. The sort of girl that men marry rather than fool about with – although she has never mentioned a boyfriend. She had applied the slightest touch of make-up – a line under each lid to bring out her bright clear eyes. Her new shoulder-length hair also suits her. We retired to Gatwick's self-service restaurant with a copy of *Time Out* and started to plan our first afternoon together. The more we talked, the more three dimensional Martina became: a flesh and blood person rather than the angel of mercy who tended Thom's needs and finally the angel of death who helped his passage into the ultimate unknown. I had been a little worried about how we would get on, but had put my trust in Thom's judgement. My faith had not been misplaced, it turns out that we both enjoy art. Martina's interest is modern art, so I suggested *Sensation*, an exhibition of young British artists from the Saatchi Collection currently on at the Royal Academy. It had been in the news after ink was thrown over a painting, which recreated Myra Hindley's famous police mugshot using the handprints of small children.

As Thom would have approved of my invitation to Martina, I'd been hoping for a sign that he is still with me. Walking along Piccadilly, on our way to the gallery, I smelt the familiar incense of vanilla candle. It was the first time in almost five months and I had begun, selfishly, to worry that he had other things to do beyond watch over me. Perhaps if you want something from your guardian angel you just have to ask? With embarrassing sentiments like those, perhaps it would have been more appropriate if I'd have taken Martina to the Royal Academy's other exhibition of Victorian fairy paintings!

Fortunately, we decided to stick with *Sensation* as the exhibition was one of the few places in London where death was not ignored but celebrated: a former puppet-maker had made an exact replica of his deceased father in a piece entitled *Effigy*. Marc Quinn's *No Visible Means of Escape* is a hanged corpse, which has literally been disembodied with only its skin left behind. There was a strange beauty about Damien Hirst's *Some Comfort Gained from the Acceptance of the Inherent Lies in Everything* – in which the bodies of cows had been sliced up into twelve tanks full of formaldehyde. It was possible to walk between the tanks and

look at the inner workings of the animals. According to the catalogue, the piece brings: 'The viewer one step closer to the truth of
mortality and immorality. We are urged to look at death without
the veneer of sentimentality.' It certainly made me reflect on my
obsession with understanding and writing about Thom: where
does art end and freak show begin?

The exhibition was strangely exhilarating almost like a theme
park devoted to sex and death. Of course, I found the former
easier to look at than the latter but somehow the combination
made me feel a little more human than when I walked in.

The return from London was interminable. The trains were
running late, the wrong sort of rain, and ours was formed of
just four carriages. Finally, we started to talk about Thom. I told
Martina that I was writing about him and she confessed that she
was too. I coyly suggested showing me, but she laughingly deflected the idea. I tried again – without success. I wish I could subpoe-
na her work. She was the person that Thom could have shared his
fears with – kept back from me in case they increased my burden.

However, as we get closer to home, I realise that while I want
to know more about Martina she is equally curious about me and
my home. Perhaps she is approaching the same mystery from a
different angle? She knew Thom for just nine months and passed
his friends in the hospital corridor. I was his lover and this is the
first chance for us to talk in depth.

By the time we arrived home, it was dark. So Martina couldn't
inspect the garden, which Thom loved and often talked about. I
showed her round the house, the museum to Thom's worship at
the shrine of Alessi. She looked confused.

'Isn't this what you expected?'

'I didn't know what to expect.'

That's when it dawned on me. Even when Thom was ill, he was
still making plans to renovate and transform our home. (I found
detailed drawings in the back of his Filofax.) Martina knew all

about how it could look but nothing about the mundane reality. There was something touching about imagining Thom lying in his hospital bed with no more plans for living but detailed plans for a new bathroom.

It reminded me of an article that I once proposed to a woman's magazine: 'Who knows you best, your husband or your best friend?' Thom laughed when I asked his opinion. I certainly was not allowed to know everything. Even if I could become Hercule Poirot and round up all his friends and family, I would be no further forward. I could hear all their testimonies of where they were on the night that Thom died, how they felt and their individual clues but he would always remain unsolved. Perhaps we can never truly know someone we love; maybe their mystery and our desire to uncover more is what binds lovers together.

After dinner I showed Martina my collection of photos of Thom, starting with the traditional German portrait for the first day at school. He is standing with a large cardboard horn crammed with sweets, a treat to ease any trauma, beside a small black board with 'Der erste Schultag 1960'. Already you can tell just how charming he could be. He smiles at the camera full of confidence and with no fear about the world into which he is about to step. Most of the photo collection is from our seven and a half years together, yet it was not the shots of him healthy and radiant that Martina was drawn to but those from his last Christmas. She only remembered the Thom that looked grey and drawn. Her good memories belong in my files marked: sad, complicated or poignant. It was an evening when we were both destined to cry a lot.

Saturday 15 November

I took Martina to Beachy Head today. Although the weather was generally better than when I scattered Thom's ashes, it was still a little misty. I used the same car park as last time but when I stepped out of the car, I couldn't help laughing. With better visibility, I realised that we had not been walking towards the sea – and risking falling off the cliff and being dashed on to the rocks below – but heading inland. It seemed a fitting postscript to that disastrous day.

Even though I was wearing several layers of clothing, the wind still felt chilly. We walked to approximately where we had scattered Thom's ashes. I took my coordinates from a small dip in the grass that I recognised from last time. We stood and stared across the open undulating horizon. I shivered. The wind or the memories? Having finally visited the forests where Thom grew up, I understood his fascination with Beachy Head: the emptiness of downland after the claustrophobia of tightly growing trees – the light after dark.

I took the bunch of asters that I'd bought from the village greengrocer's, and started throwing the purple blooms into the air. It was impossible not to remember my last visit and be grateful that this time it was flowers. They seemed the perfect symbol for Thom: beautiful for a moment but soon to fade and die. Martina chose to just place her bouquet on the grass. We stood drinking in the atmosphere, my mind replaying the way the flowers had danced in the wind and superimposing them over the grim picture of Thom's ashes being liberated. I felt a wonderful moment of connection between the past, the present and hopes for a better, more healed, future.

When emotionally stressed, I find nothing helps more than something to eat. So we drove to Birling Gap for coffee, buns and a marvellous vista of the Seven Sisters chalk cliffs. On days like today, I like to sit in the café and gaze out at waves beating against the coast and shudder at the danger. The sea moves closer by one metre each year. Four years ago, one of the nearby coastguard cottages had to be demolished. After one hundred and seventeen years of relentless pounding, its foundations were about to collapse into the sea. Birling Gap underlines the temporary nature of everything.

I was so wrapped up in my own feelings, I had neglected Martina. She stood erect on the metal platform that jutted out from the cliff. Her eyes never left the sea. She hardly heard when I told her I was going inside for a coffee. She just stared out to the far horizon, so I left her alone. While I dulled my heart with a layer of stodge in my stomach, she remained transfixed like a latter day *French Lieutenant's Woman*. The wind and rain soared up around her but she was impervious. Even from thirty yards and through double glazing, I knew she was crying. She had been used to helping Thom get better and sending him back to England. Obviously she knew he was dead – after all she'd washed his corpse – but visiting the spot where his ashes were scattered was the final proof that she would never see Thom again.

Finally, the rain drove Martina from her shoreline vigil. As she drunk her hot chocolate, my mind was as busy as the waves below. I tried to quiz her on why she befriended Thom, but all she could suggest is being the middle child she had no role in the family; neither the confidence of the firstborn nor the special protection of the youngest. I imagined her parents being kind and distant people; it sounded rather familiar.

Yet why choose Thom? For a second I was gripped by paranoia. Had she fallen in love with him? I'd never previously questioned her devotion, I just thought everybody was susceptible to Thom's charm. Had I welcomed an alternative widow into my house? The rain was still lashing against the windows. It seemed pointless to make a run for the car, so we sat wrapped in our private thoughts. Martina was probably remembering Thom, while I grappled with why she was so moved.

Could there be a greater power, a hand that shuffles our fates and sent Martina, against her will and reason, into Thom's orbit?

By nursing Thom with love, rather than professional detachment, Martina had made the indignity of his body's failure more bearable. Maybe life is more than a random collection of coincidences? Certainly when my time comes, I hope I find someone like her.

Finally, Martina broke the silence:

'I'm shocked at how much I've been affected – especially as so much time has lapsed since Thom's death,' she confessed.

'I know. It's tough.'

'I thought long and hard before I allowed myself to become his friend.'

'Why?'

'You just open yourself up to pain and heartache.'

'And you can't tell your colleagues or they'd think you were unprofessional.'

She did not answer.

'Would you like something to eat from the cafeteria?' I asked – guilty that I could offer no other comfort.

This time Martina shook her head, so I bought myself another plate of chips.

In the evening, so that Martina could have a proper conversation, I invited a German friend of Thom's who lives in Brighton and whose husband also speaks German for dinner. Opening my recipe books, I realised it was my first formal dinner party since Thom's death. Even when he was alive, I was banned from the kitchen – beyond peeling the potatoes. My only other responsibilities would be pouring drinks and keeping the conversation lively. This time I'd had to plan, buy the food, cook it, make certain everything was ready at the right time and stop the kitchen descending into chaos. As Martina is a vegetarian, I couldn't even cheat with a good cut of meat. After half an hour reading Thom's cookery books, I found a dish, which appealed to Martina but didn't look too complicated – although I would have preferred a more exotic name than Baked Noodles with Spinach, Mushrooms and Cheese.

Everything went to plan and my guests were all very complimentary. I even remembered that cooking can be enjoyable. If the bereavement journey is the opposite of falling in love, where you submerge part of your identity into the new relationship, I reclaimed a small part of my personality this evening.

Sunday 16 November

We arrived slightly late for the tree planting. The majority of other people dedicating trees had already left the goat farm. The BTCV (British Trust Conservation for Volunteers) staff were very welcoming. They had decided that one apple tree would be too lonely, so Martina and I had one each to plant. Due to some misunderstanding, crab apples have been ordered but there seemed little point in complaining. Anyway, I had a sneaking suspicion that Thom would have approved. The trees were already seven feet tall and he never had the patience to wait for anything to grow.

The weather was better, a warm late autumnal day. So digging a hole for the large rootball was an invigorating experience. I even managed to work up a sweat and felt truly alive. My one moment of sadness was writing a short message for Thom on the dedication tag, but it soon passed. When we'd finished, and recorded the occasion with photos, I produced a bottle of Lanson Black Label champagne out of the cool box – Thom would have expected nothing less. I handed round his best crystal glasses to the staff and the farmers and everybody drank to his memory in style.

Talking to the owners about their farm reconfirmed that this was definitely the perfect location. Thom had to always have the best of everything and his tree will not be fed to just any old goats but cashmere ones! More importantly, I have somewhere pleasant to visit and remember Thom. Sometime in the future I will bring a picnic to eat under his tree, and who knows might even make crab apple jelly.

Returning Martina to the airport on Sunday evening, I was worn out but it had been worth it. I felt closer to Thom than I had in quite a while.

Tuesday 18 November

I have decided to be reckless and spend some of Thom's life insurance policy commissioning Gary Sollars (the artist who painted a picture of his partner's death bed) to create a work of art in his memory. There is just one problem: Gary only takes on projects that interest him. I wish I had his nerve and did not spend half my time writing pointless articles for fear of not meeting the mortgage repayments.

We had a meeting in Gary's cramped paint-splattered studio. He made coffee and I tried to find enough space to lay out the photos that I'd brought of Thom. Fortunately, he works as much from photographs as from live models. We talked for about an hour. The upshot is that I'll do some research and find a list of artists and pictures that I like. He has kept some of the photographs of Thom and will let me know if he's interested. Hopefully, I will have something beautiful for my walls and I can keep taking the art drug at home.

Thursday 20 November

Being an organised person, Thom had arranged our music collection alphabetically by female artists, male artists and groups.

My new CDs have been lying beside the hi-fi since I returned from Spain and today I decided that they looked untidy. Slotting the new CDs into place, it occurred to me that there was a flaw in Thom's system. After the groups section, Thom had put duos and trios. The Everly Brothers were a duo – fine. Yet the Pet Shop Boys, also two men, had been filed under 'group'. Is Steely Dan two men or a group? I could not remember. It was all too complicated so I took control and amalgamated the duos and trios into the group section. I felt audaciously brave, I might be the curator for Thom's life but at least I can choose my own filing system!

Saturday 22 November

Without even thinking I found myself wandering through the North Laine in Brighton, browsing through designer boutiques, junk shops and strange ephemera. My feet carried me into a shop devoted to cult movies and I started flicking through the Bette Davis section for pictures that Thom didn't already own. I remembered my previous Bette successes: T-shirts, original movie posters and even a photo signed by the diva herself.

Hang on, I don't need any more Bette in my life. I've inherited a copy of nearly every Bette Davis film – in both English and German. Suddenly, it dawned on me: I had started my Christmas shopping. It might only be November but I'm responding to an ancient rhythm with its roots in my childhood. Bonfire night was the date I'd start saving my pocket money. As an adult I have continued the tradition, preferring to look for presents without being elbowed and jostled.

Even sadder than shopping for a dead man is discovering treasures that would have delighted him – a copy of an advert for one of Miss Davis's early movies and, even better, a 'wifey dearest' paperback written by her ex-husband Gary Merrill. I retreated to a café to recover but even carrot cake and a banana milkshake does little to restore my equilibrium.

I am knocked out at round one of the annual orgy of parties, decorations and goodwill. How would I ever make it to the New Year?

Sunday 23 November

Last night a friend suggested going out for a drink. It seemed better than staying at home and nursing my depression. We had a great time wandering from bar to bar in Brighton and ended up in a nightclub. After dancing and chatting with other friends, I spotted a man to whom I felt strangely drawn. He was black, short, about forty years old and had a mysterious grin. I smiled back. He walked over and introduced himself as Roy. We talked until the club was almost ready to close and then he invited me back to his flat. It was more than just sexual attraction and I felt incredibly relaxed in his company. Back at his place, he poured us both a glass of wine. We took about one sip each and disappeared into the bedroom.

When we woke up the next morning, Roy started asking the most extraordinarily perceptive questions as he ran his hands gently over my body. Within five minutes, all my defences were down. I told him all about Thom and my dread of Christmas. Instead of the usual expression of sympathy, Roy had a question:

'What have you gained from Thom's death?'

Gained! I've nobody to share a Christmas tree with.

Slowly, Roy drew me out. I confessed about the vanilla candles and my almost religious experience in Seville. Experiences that I have told nobody about – beyond Kate – in case they think I'm losing my mind.

Listening to myself talk, I realised that Roy had a point. I was no longer the same person who, almost a year earlier, had listened while the doctor delivered his terminal diagnosis. Then it was Roy's turn to be a little coy. There was something that he was not telling me. What?

With a little encouragement, Roy explained that he was a member of Brighton's Spiritualist church. Normally, he would never go out clubbing. However, last night, he felt that he was despatched on a mission. It was only this morning, when we started talking, that he finally understood.

Perhaps Roy is right. The last nine months have not all been about loss. I am more self-aware and seem able to connect with other people on a far deeper level. But if given the choice... I would immediately surrender these gifts for my old life with Thom.

Monday 24 November

Depression is lapping at the edge of my life like waves on a Mediterranean beach. The sound is so soft that I'm not always consciously aware of the sadness but I can never eradicate it completely from my internal shoreline. I have started weekly sessions with the counsellor that Thom turned down. I have very little recollection of our conversation, but he was wearing a nice jumper.

Monday 1 December

Before meeting me, Thom was not keen on Christmas. But I was not going to be defeated by such cynicism. I put up a tree, filled a stocking (which played 'Jingle Bells' when you pressed it) with pointless trinkets, gave him more presents than was really sensible and introduced him to pantomime – although it was rather difficult explaining to a German where Roland Rat fitted into the tradition. I was rewarded by a card thanking me for bringing back the magic of Christmas.

It was not all mistletoe and tinsel. Thom had campaigned long and hard not to visit his parents. He was not about to swap this freedom for spending Christmas with mine. Gracefully, I hope, I conceded but the battle taught me something: you are never really an adult until you feel comfortable having your own Christmas dinner in your own home.

I have such happy memories of the run up to our German-themed *Heiligabend*. Exotic smells would waft from the kitchen and Thom would be continually phoning his mother about some recipe. Occasionally, like a scene out of the *Golden Girls* he would become Rose worrying that his *Knödel* hadn't set, while I was Dorothy hoping it didn't include herrings! An old disc of German carols and bells from Bochum cathedral would ring out through the house. When he was a child, his parents had played this same record on Christmas Eve while they decorated the family tree. Thom would listen through the door until it was flung back and he was admitted into a wonder world. Each year, Thom would import all sorts of fascinating biscuits, sweets and decorations from the Christmas markets, which every German town holds in December. It is not surprising that the German village at Disney World's Epcot has a year round Die Weihnachts Ecke where you can buy these trinkets. Germans certainly know how to celebrate Christmas, and to my eyes their vision is bright and sparkling with genuine folk roots.

One year, the pre-dinner Christmas Eve conversation turned to the meat our guests could not eat. I desperately tried to change the topic, but rabbit became fixed as the food least likely to pass their lips. Unfortunately that was exactly what Thom was basting in the kitchen! I retreated and we had a quick counsel of war. Maybe we should pass the meat off as *Kaninchen* and hope that nobody wanted a translation? Back in the living room, everyone was discovering new reasons for refusing rabbit. When the prime mover in the 'Eat No Bunnies' campaign, Jackie (Maureen's daughter), broke off her diatribe and calmly asked:

'By the way, what's for dinner tonight?'

I couldn't help laughing and admitting the truth. It was worth it for her look of stunned surprise and everybody's desperate attempts to extract their feet out of their mouths.

Thom was a brilliant cook and either as *Kaninchen* or rabbit the meal was a great success.

Tuesday 2 December

This year my local supermarket is selling Christmas trees and just walking past the parents and children choosing one for their living room makes me catch my breath. Trying to look the other way, I almost collided with a trolley laden with Christmas fare. I snatched a few essentials and rushed out of the store.

While trying to escape from the preparation celebrations, I have become even more obsessed with writing about Thom. It is the nearest thing to living with him, so I get anxious if I'm away from home for too long. I keep checking my watch and calculating how long until I can switch on my computer again. Today I was up in London for lunch with Kate in Old Compton Street and afterwards an interview for *The Independent* with the author nominated for this year's Whitbread First Novel Award. Phil Whitaker was a doctor but his burning ambition was to be a writer:

'Two words reoccur every time anybody describes my decision to stop full-time medicine and follow my dream of writing fiction: Brave or Courageous. In *Yes Minister* speak that means it is a completely stupid thing to do.'

I was fascinated to understand what drove him on:

'As part of my medical training, I made a home follow up to an elderly man who had advanced cancer of the prostate. In hospital, it was all very medical and professional but the impact of meeting him again with his wife was quite profound. The visit is intended for students to discover how disease affects patients' lives, but I had an enormous number of feelings going round in my brain – especially watching the pair of them together trying to cope with the idea that he might be dying. They lived quite a way outside of Nottingham and I remember travelling back to the city wrestling with the dilemma of being a vulture by learning from others' misfortune. It felt an uncomfortable relationship, especially as I have a burning hatred of how some doctors don't engage on a human level with their patients.

'There was no formed decision but I came home and just switched on my computer and started writing a story. I don't know why, because I'd never done it before, it just felt like the thing to do. I didn't think that writing would help, I just had to express myself but afterwards it did feel cathartic.'

On the train home from the interview, I started making jottings about Thom. Even remembering the sickness and pain is better than the empty jollity of 'Jingle Bells', mince pies and the hokey-cokey at the office Christmas party.

Saturday 6 December

Everything is reminding me of Thom – even hobbies that I followed alone. Line dancing has been my safety-valve during Thom's illness and one of my sanctuaries since his death. It makes me feel alive and by concentrating on the steps I can shut out any problem.

At my club's Christmas party, one song was particularly painful to hear: 'All I Want for Christmas is You'. As Mariah

Carey sang and we twirled and clapped, I knew exactly what she meant. Forget the book tokens, new saucepans and boxer shorts – all I want for Christmas is Thom back again. Is that being too greedy?

The party was much less successful than last year, we were in a smaller venue and it underlined how many people have given up. The club has reached a critical size and I fear it will not survive another year.

'Everything has its time, and the line-dancing craze is over,' suggested one of my dancing friends.

I could not share his philosophical mood I've had more than enough change. I want to cling to the safety of my twice-weekly line dancing.

I cannot face the thought of yet another hole in my life.

Tuesday 9 December

Today I interviewed Jim Crace who was nominated for this year's Booker Prize and is in the running for Whitbread 'Novel of the Year' for *Quarantine*. His 'Revelation' was tied up with the funeral of his father:

'I was brought up in an atheist household. My father, an old-fashioned trade union socialist, was strongly anti-religious to the point that neither myself or my brother were even christened and that was rare in the forties. However, it was not until my father died that I realised what it really meant to be an atheist and that left a very hollow feeling.'

I nodded as Jim Crace talked and asked journalist-type questions, but my mind was struggling with something bigger. What do I believe?

Even at Thom's bedside, I never questioned where he was heading. I was buried up to my neck in 'now' with no breath for 'next'. I'd sort of consigned God, faith and mystery to some unknown date in the future. I was what? A half-believer? An agnostic? A blank?

Jim Crace's father had no such doubts.

'He was just sixty-seven, struggling against cancer, and he knew he was going to die. It was the winter of discontent, the last few years of the Labour government before Maggie Thatcher, and one of the strikes was by the gravediggers and cemetery workers. My dad's only concern about his funeral was that his body should not cross a picket line!

'He said that when he died he would not tolerate anybody saying any religious words over his grave. He didn't want any hymns, any music, any flowers and for sure he didn't want any priest. A rather difficult demand to press on your wife and children; especially as his death was long, horrible and affecting. My much-loved father dies and I am not allowed to mark it by any rite or ceremony, but it was what he wanted so that was the rule we followed. It was the biggest mistake we ever made.

'It was a monstrous day. Even though we told friends not to come, there were still about fifty people standing outside the crematorium. My father was a man with a lot of admirers; a lot of people loved him because he was a one-off. They obviously hadn't heard that nobody was supposed to show up. Totally unprepared we went into the chapel to some piped organ music. Nobody said anything, nobody did anything and then suddenly the coffin went and he was cremated. Everybody was confused – it was such an inadequate way of burying him.'

Jim Crace made believing in nothing sound worse than my muddling through. I wanted to tell him about the candle, the smell and hope.

I want to believe.

I want the comfort of certainty; but cannot bring myself to kneel in front of priests, bishops and the altar.

'Our decisions were made in ignorance of what funerals amounted to and how we felt about our father,' Jim Crace went on. 'Even though I did not want to believe in a god, I did wish the ceremonial rites associated with religions could be afforded to us. It is such a necessary emotional part of grieving. Even though the religious ways of burying somebody might seem simple minded, nevertheless they are generous spirited. They say: "Here was life well lived, a man well loved – deserving of our grief." If today I could unstitch time, I would defy his rules, cross a few picket lines and bury him properly.

'For many years, I felt that my atheism had failed me, which is an odd phrase because people normally say: "My God has failed me." Atheism was an inadequate belief, it was not a set of beliefs but an absence, a hollow, a cave. For a while I described myself as an agnostic, which is a cowardly way of avoiding the issues, but it felt more comfortable.'

So what is the alternative, I thought. There has to be an alternative?

'My father's funeral might have reduced a comfortable un-thinking atheism into a void, but it was filled and explained while I was writing *Quarantine*, which is my dramatisation of Jesus's forty days in the wilderness. Maybe I would have never come to this accommodation if I had not been addressing these very subjects in my book, which gave me good cause to think about God and the natural world.

'I now feel that atheists are the new mystics, you can enjoy great-er transcendence not believing in God. Evolutionary theory is more mind-boggling with more reason to wonder at the beauty than seven days' creation. The mysteries of the universe are deepened by a recognition that the world is an inside job with complicated explanations rather than the simple idea that it is an outside one.

'My father never went anywhere without his pockets full of acorns. On his many bird-watching walks, he was always poking acorns into the ground. He thought eternity was: oak upon oak. Today I understand more of what my father was about and I find that very moving. When I'm out walking, I carry acorns too. My atheism has changed from something sad and inadequate to where I take a great pleasure from landscapes, the natural world and science.'

In the end, I kept quiet about my experiences with the great unknown. Maybe, I thought I'd sound childish? Maybe, my thoughts are too unfinished? Maybe, I'm a coward.

So I wished Crace good luck for the competition and he admitted already knowing that he'd won. Afterwards, standing on the pavement, I almost rang his bell again. There was more that united us than divided us.

In the evening, Gary Sollars came round to borrow more photographs and take pictures of some of Thom's possessions. Out of this strange alchemy will hopefully spring a living breathing work of art, capable of speaking to future generations: Thom's small piece of immortality.

Wednesday 10 December

I have been plagued by memories of Christmas past again. Around this time, two years ago, Thom had a high fever – with hindsight the first act in our tragedy. I was concerned, but not yet really anxious. Money was tight; I had a freelance contract in Manchester. I returned home on 23 December. Thom was still in bed. Instead of worrying, I launched into a frenzy of activity: tracking down last-minute ingredients, collecting our order from the butcher's, buying and then decorating the tree. Finally, I stood in the kitchen surrounded by food, but with no idea how to cook a goose. Upstairs there was a sick boy who needed my non-existing nursing skills. I had to face reality and phone our friends to cancel. As I replaced the receiver, the depression really kicked in. Thom managed to struggle down to inspect the tree but really didn't have enough energy to even enjoy opening his presents. It was the most miserable Christmas I have ever spent.

However, I did learn one important lesson: it is always better to make the best of a bad situation than to give up altogether. It might have been difficult to entertain alone but eating frozen lasagne for Christmas lunch was far bleaker. By becoming depressed, I had not helped Thom, just added to his guilt about being ill.

For what would turn out to be our final Christmas together, we were both determined to make it a holiday to remember. Thom seemed to start on page one of the Christmas edition of *Meine Familie und Ich* (*My Family and I*) and baked his way through to the back. There were enough home-made chocolates and biscuits to feed the five thousand, so he made and decorated small boxes to fill with treats for the nurses who came to our house each day. He created dozens of edible snowmen out of cookies with liquorice for hats and big red smiles piped on with coloured icing sugar.

With the years of commuting back and forth between England and Germany, and the previous year's illness, last Christmas was the first we bought a tree together. After about half an hour of intensive searching at the garden centre, and much discussion, Thom was thrilled to find the perfect specimen: tall, straight and velvet green. (This was particularly important because Thom's father would wait until late on Christmas Eve, when the shops were about to close, to buy their family tree. In this way, he always got a bargain but also a short or misshapen tree.) Next we moved on to decorations; Thom decided that the theme would be matt blue. My bright blue baubles had already failed the style test, so I ended up carrying about £200 of new trinkets to the car.

For someone in very poor health, Thom found an incredible amount of energy that day. Although I set the tree up in its pot, Thom did all the rest. Afterwards, he looked drawn and grey but at least this colour coordinated well with the tree.

In the photo, he looks so proud of his achievement – the most beautiful Christmas tree ever.

Thursday 11 December

This is a busy time for interviewing celebrities because everyone has something to plug for Christmas. So I did my second interview of the week for 'Revelations'. This time it was novelist and politician Michael Dobbs (best known for his book *House of Cards*) and once the Deputy Leader of the Conservative Party. Just like me, he was struggling with a type of loss, but a loss all the same. He had been with Mrs Thatcher when she arrived in Downing Street (eighteen years ago) and had been with John Major (this year) when the party was kicked out of power.

'On election morning I went to Downing Street to finish clearing up. It was like a ghost city. Everybody knew a change-over was coming; you could sense it and taste it. A huge amount of shredding had been going on for days and days beforehand. I was going round, saying goodbye and learning some new things too. I had time, finally, to look in the corners and cupboards and make a few notes. I knew my life was about to change dramatically. I had a similar feeling on election night 1979. After the count, we went back to Margaret Thatcher's constituency offices to say thank you and drove to Downing Street via the Mall. I remember very vividly that as we came to the roundabout outside Buckingham Palace we were joined by police motorcycle outriders and two further security cars. It became a great convoy and I knew my life would never be the same again.

'As I looked at Number 10's familiar rooms, for the last time this May, I also remembered John Major taking me round the Cabinet Room. It was fascinating to have some of its history pointed out by him. There is a patio just outside which still has the same tiles from 250 years ago, we know because there is an oil painting in the corner of the view showing exactly those tiles.

'When the exit polls and the computer projections were coming through I was at Conservative Central Office. I was very, very angry: good friends would not just lose their jobs but also their complete way of life. I understood what was about to happen. I was not going to like it, in fact it would hurt hellishly, but it was something that just had to be. All the youthful excitement of 1979 and my naïveté had gone. I felt frightened but also strangely liberated.

'Just a couple of months before the election my wife was ordained as a Tibetan buddhist. She had suggested I should strip away the clutter and decide what is truly important to me, rather like she did when choosing her new spiritual life.

'Going through a time of great change, this advice has real meaning for me. I had to seize the opportunity of the election defeat and get back in contact with my writing and my family. I needed to become a more rounded human being rather than a political animal. In the end, it took me about thirty seconds to switch my computer on; while everybody else was watching Blair march into Downing Street, I started working on my book again. It was the beginning of the rest of my life.'

Dobbs told me he was depressed over losing the election for about two months. I sensed that he was putting a brave face on his marriage, which seemed at a turning point too.

I have to keep reminding myself that I am not the only person having to deal with unwanted change.

In the evening, I spoke to my friend Steve – who is training to become a Master in NLP (Neuro-linguistic Programming). I am still angry with him for splitting up with his partner a few months after Thom died. I know this will not sound rational, but how could they *choose* to break up? However, Steve had a useful tip for surviving difficult times. Instead of worrying about how I will cope on Christmas Eve without Thom, he suggests picturing how I will feel on 27 December when it is all over.

Saturday 13 December

I doubt I'll buy a Christmas tree this year. I couldn't bear it. Even before I met Thom, choosing a tree with my beloved was one of my favourite fantasies about falling in love. In my dreams, I could picture a handsome tall man with blond hair and we'd be holding hands as we decided which tree to place our presents under.

OK, Thom was short and dark, but reality was even better.

Sunday 14 December

I've been trying not to open the kitchen cupboard where all un-used ingredients from last Christmas are stored. Nevertheless, I cannot throw away the baking chocolate, the crème de coco, the marzipan nor the muscovado sugar. It would be such a waste, so these items mock me every time I look at them:

'We know you'll never bake anything with us.'

I shut the door quickly.

Meanwhile, every time a Christmas song comes on the car radio, I hit search. My record, so far, is three different stations in a row.

Monday 15 December

I did some client assessment interviews for Relate tonight. I was a little dubious but it only involved listening to a couple's prob-lems and deciding whether they are suitable for counselling. Still it begs the question: is someone who is mocked by the contents of his kitchen cupboard in a fit state to judge?

Wednesday 17 December

I went to *The Independent*'s Christmas party after filming another five episodes of *Agony*. Ingrid Miller, Kate's replacement, has far more conventional advice. So I've been asked to step away from always being rational and sensible. Is this a good idea?

Patricia was my 'plus one' for the party. We arrived too early and only a handful of guests were already there. The editor, Andrew Marr, was propping up the bar. I was surprised both that he knew me and that I enjoyed the party.

Tomorrow, I return to London to give advice on the *Lorraine Kelly Show* on Talk Radio about 'How to survive Christmas'.

I wish I knew the answer.

Monday 22 December

We were originally asked to record this week's *Agony* on Christmas Eve. However, I stood up to the producer and explained that day would be stressful enough for me without coming up to London with four changes of clothes, so the recording was brought forward to today.

Everything went smoothly in the studio – and mercifully there was no Christmas theme to the problems or tinsel on the set – but on the train home the man opposite wore a tie decorated with Santa, Rudolph and a chimney. Is there no escape?

Tuesday 23 December

At 8.30 this morning, I had another session with my counsellor. He really does have a good collection of jumpers. After spending an hour talking about Christmas Eve last year, I began to wonder how our guests remembered the evening. First, I phoned our friend Peter Hammond:

'Thom was very much in control of the evening and enjoyed playing the prima donna cook. Any offer of help was knocked back, but with good grace rather than like a martyr.'

Although he was aware of my concern that Thom might overextend himself, Peter was oblivious to the true state of his health.

'He didn't look ill. It was such a shock when, just a few weeks later, I was phoned and told he had died.'

Peter reminded me what we had eaten. I had made the starter and Thom had cooked venison. The other guests, Nancy Roberts and her husband, had brought a French chocolate log for dessert and we also ate Thom's home-made biscuits and chocolates.

'It was a lovely clear night and the stars were all shining,' Nancy remembered. 'The house looked absolutely beautiful – like a blue Christmas grotto. Everything was gorgeous, the tree was stunning and the table had a magnificent centrepiece with blue beads, holly and ivy draped around the blue candles. I remember thinking what a high fashion Christmas – it was so chic. Thom was scurrying in and out of the kitchen like someone who was in perfect health. I had been a little nervous coming down. Would he be up to it and would everything be difficult if he was very ill? Yet from the moment I walked into the house, I felt relaxed and happy. What I remember most is Thom's warmth and hospitality; afterwards we made him lie down because he was exhausted.'

It was also the first time ever that he had not cleared everything up before going to bed. I had finished off the next morning. I still cannot believe how well Thom did. For one evening we had pretended that there was nothing wrong – and got away with it.

Although our guests brought back lots of details, I was angry that I couldn't remember everything. Nancy thought I might have forgotten for a reason. The day before, she had been interviewed for a newspaper article about her best and worst Christmas ever.

'Until the journalist phoned me I had blocked out the Christmas my mother was dying,' Nancy said. 'Suddenly all these years later, I remembered how we all went to the hospital and I had brought her a little ready-decorated Christmas tree. I could see us sitting there exchanging presents over her bed. We all knew she was dying and she did on 8 January. The interview brought it all back but you block out the pain.'

However, you also block out the good memories too. As hard as I racked my brain I could not remember what presents Thom gave me or what I got him. Tears rolled down my cheeks as Nancy told me her story; I needed the inspiration of the happy version. So I asked her about it.

'We set out in the midst of a blinding blizzard and had to put chains on the tyres. Just as it was getting dark, we pulled up into this magnificent picture perfect Alpine town where they had had a metre of fresh snow. It was like stepping into a Christmas card. The hotel was wonderful, a converted monastery. We raced up into our rooms and changed just in time for the lighting of the candles on the Christmas tree while the children sang carols. We feasted on roast goose, changed into warm clothes and trudged down to the village church for a multilingual midnight carol service. As we all came out afterwards it had just began to snow again. It was wonderful – we were surrounded by families but not our own. The best combination!'

So those were Nancy's best and worst Christmases, but for me last year is the best and the worst of times – all rolled into one.

After putting down the phone, I looked at the photos from the evening. They were the last photos ever of Thom and me together. He is leaning in close to me, so our cheeks are touching. He seems to positively radiate happiness. The love in his eyes is strong enough to power the Christmas tree lights behind him. I turned to the first ever photo of the two of us. We are on a hill overlooking Barcelona. Thom has leaned in and rested his head on my shoulder. I'm standing with my arms crossed but his gesture turns my awkward pose into a special memory of awakening love.

Thom has always brought out the best in me.

Wednesday 24 December

There are few words that strike a stronger chord in our hearts than: 'I'm dreaming of a white Christmas'. They chime as loud as 'I love you' and perhaps sound even better than 'I was a fool to leave you, I've never found anybody half as good as you, could you possibly find it in your heart to have me back!' Just the opening chords are enough to make us feel dreamy and nostalgic for something we cannot quite put our finger on. It has such a powerful hold on our collective memories that Bing Crosby even turned up on Radio 1 this morning.

I cannot even remember a year when I actually experienced a white Christmas, and normally my reaction to snow would be absolute horror. Just think of all those blocked roads, people being trapped at motorway service stations and old-age pensioners frightened to leave their homes in case they slip and break something. A heavy snowfall would either make it impossible to drive home to my parents for Christmas or perhaps worse still trap me there. As another seasonal perennial insists snow is only acceptable to the indolent: 'Since we've no place to go, let it snow, let it snow, let it snow'. When did anybody today have nothing better to do than sit beside a fire?

These songs remind us of a simpler world where we are not working seventy-hour weeks and don't suffer holiday stress because we cannot find a wrapping paper that matches the Christmas tree baubles or feel guilty for not following Delia Smith's Christmas timetable and starting to bake in October. Our dreams of a white Christmas are a dream of an imagined time when the milk arrived on the doorstep in time for breakfast and there was always home-made cake for tea; when families stayed together and had time for each other. Thom was my family, no wonder 'White Christmas' makes me yearn for the past.

Christmas always brought out the child and the parent in Thom and I. I'd opened his eyes to the joy of Santa Claus and in turn he'd looked after me and cooked wonderful meals. When you're bereaved you have to take back all the responsibilities handed over to your partner. No wonder I feel as exhausted as I did after Thom died, no wonder I've returned to lying on the sofa flicking through my satellite channels.

It is not that I have been thrown back to the beginning of my journey, more that I have discovered a new loss. My little boy inside has lost his protector, his Santa Claus and his daddy. Thom was not only my lover but the parent we all dream of whose door is always open without questions and judgements.

I cannot do Christmas on my own, I don't know the recipe for mulled wine and I don't feel strong enough to care for that small boy myself.

However, by early evening, I had rallied. I wrapped presents and packed an overnight bag. I feel it is important to be with people who loved Thom, and my parents do not fit this category, so I'm spending Christmas Eve and Christmas Day with Maureen and her family. However, not wanting to appear too rejecting, I will drive up to Bedford for Boxing Day.

Although Maureen and I had planned a quiet evening, we were swept along by a tide of visitors. Elaine arrived with my present, a copy of *The Prophet* by Kahlil Gibran, which she had read from at Thom's memorial service. Other friends of Maureen's arrived with the dessert for tomorrow's lunch and we were invited into the home of Tyson's owners for drinks. Tyson was thrilled to see me again, Mike and Sara are going away until the New Year and I will pick him up on Christmas night. Before I knew it, we were yawning and ready to retire for the night. I was amazed at how easily I survived this crucial day without Thom. Perhaps over the past month I have done enough worrying to sop up all my distress?

Thursday 25 December

Christmas Day passed in a whirl of activity: peeling potatoes, listening to the morning service on Radio 4, Maureen's grandchildren opening their presents, roast turkey with all the trimmings and charades with a cup of tea. With two small children and eight adults in a small cottage, there was no room for Thom's ghost. But not used to being with so many people, I was exhausted by six o'clock. I collected Tyson and headed home. I had been desperate to avoid my own company, but now there was nothing I wanted more than to be sitting alone in front of the TV. With Tyson curled up by my feet, I felt relaxed and self-contained. Perhaps one day I might become used to living on my own again.

Friday 26 December

Tyson is not a good traveller – he whines and fidgets remorselessly. When I explained my plans to drive up to Bedford to Mike and Sara, they were amazed that I was taking him on a two-hour car journey. They put it down to kindness, but the truth is I cannot face my extended family without an ally, so I planned our trip like a military campaign. Before setting off, in an effort to knock some of the bounce out of Tyson, we had a long walk. On the way to my parents, I stopped at a forest just off the M25 and gave Tyson another chance to stretch his legs. Finally, as we drove into Bedford, we took a third walk in a park on the embankment of the River Ouse. I had been worried about controlling him around so many strange dogs. However, Tyson seemed to sense that he had to be on his best behaviour. Even when there was a nice boxer dog to sniff and his rather rude owner screamed at me: 'Get your dog away from mine,' Tyson came charging back immediately.

On pulling up outside my parents' home, I took a deep breath. How would I cope? There would be fifteen guests for Boxing Day lunch. My extended family is not known for their collective sensitivity or empathy. The greatest merriment, one Christmas, was reserved for my announcement that I was training to become a Relate counsellor – how they laughed and laughed at that joke.

People become counsellors to make sense of their difficult families, and of course I am no exception. However, even the most buttoned-down families have to find a way to express something, so I've found myself in the role of being the emotional one. I could ask the difficult question, show the forbidden feeling and then be rounded on for being 'oversensitive'. This time I had a new part to play: grieving widower. I stifled my backstage nerves, and rang the doorbell. Curtain up.

Tyson and I were the first to arrive. The dog bounded into my parents' home, overcome with the excitement of new places to explore. Immediately, he charged up and down the stairs and out into the garden like a small child. Every time his wagging tail brushed past the Christmas tree, he set all the bells tinkling. Fortunately, my parents, taken in by Tyson's charm, overlooked his forwardness. My mother cemented their relationship by filling up his water bowl.

Tyson made friends with everybody – beyond my cousin's smallest daughter whose face was at exactly dog height. Every time he came too near, she would rush off into her father's arms. With lots of food around, I had to keep a close eye on Tyson in case he ate lunch before we could get to it. Despite the excited children and wrapping paper being thrown about, Tyson remained on his best behaviour. However, at one point he disappeared; it was ominously quiet. I finally tracked him down in the dining room with a plate of cream crackers, which my mother – who should have known better – had left on the bottom shelf of her hostess trolley. If Tyson could mount his defence, he would claim this as dog bowl height. Fortunately, he did not disgrace himself further. (Later, my mother confessed that rather than throwing the plate of biscuits away, she had just removed a couple round the ones Tyson stole and served us the rest. No wonder Thom thought my kitchen hygiene standards were so lax.)

I was saddened that none of my family: my sister, aunts, my uncle or cousins had asked how I was coping and nobody spoke about Thom. Back in early December, when I had imagined this day, I had expected people to speak privately to me about Thom but that he would not be acknowledged publicly around the lunch table. So when my mother had enquired if there was anything that would help me through Christmas, a very thoughtful gesture, I asked for a toast in memory of Thom. At the end of the meal, over port and Stilton, my father stood up and reviewed the past year – the new babies, passed exams and for the first time ever Thom was talked about as an integral part of our family. We drunk a toast. I was very moved, he had gone further than I had even dared to hope. Thank you. I went to bed wondering if I'd been too hard on my parents and feeling guilty for dumping some of my anger at their door.

Saturday 27 December

My sister, her husband and the children left soon after breakfast and with fewer distractions I had time to contemplate my mother's relationship with Tyson. Yesterday, she had insisted on spoiling him with the lunch scraps, which were normally saved until his suppertime. She also found tasty bits of meat to add to this meal: 'Just to give it a little flavour.'

Today she talked to Tyson as if he was her third grandchild, telling him to keep his nose out of the oven because it would burn him. When I wouldn't let her feed a titbit she turned to Tyson and sympathised: 'It's a hard life for a dog.' Later we all took Tyson for a long afternoon walk. My mother would worry if he disappeared into the bushes or ran off in the opposite direction to greet another dog. Finally, I understood: she communicates with my sister through her children, so was now treating Tyson like my child and using him as a bridge to step closer. No wonder, subconsciously, I felt the need to bring him with me.

Monday 29 December

I had my weekly counselling session but I wonder if it is doing me any good. My counsellor is just too nice, too sympathetic and too willing to let me wallow in self-pity. He might provide a warm bath of empathy but the water eventually grows cold and you're left shivering. I need to be challenged.

Wednesday 31 December

I've never been keen on celebrating New Year. All the clubs are packed and I am nearly always driving. However, Thom loved the magic of watching one year end and the next begin. I always received the most passionate kiss of the year just after the clock struck midnight. Last year Thom was too easily exhausted for us to go out, but he cooked lobster with three different sauces. At midnight we raised a glass of champagne and although we wished each other a Happy New Year, I think neither of us imagined 1997 would bring much joy.

This year, I celebrated with Kate and Patricia, and some of Kate's friends. We met at the home of a gay couple where one was a chef and the other a restaurant critic. They had spent ages preparing hors-d'oeuvres and later we went to a wonderful restaurant just round the corner from their flat in Vauxhall. Patricia and one half of the gay couple were keen to watch a firework display at Tower Bridge, but that would mean rushing dessert. The two of them left straightaway, but the rest of us decided to stay.

At midnight everybody in the restaurant burst into shouts of celebration and 'Auld Lang Syne' and I suddenly noticed that the gay couple were apart. I was overcome with sadness.

'Thom would never have allowed us to be apart at midnight,' I told Kate. She squeezed my hand.

'Happy New Year,' she said. 'Happy New Year.'

Monday 5 January 1998

I had the strange experience of being counselled myself in the morning and counselling others in the evening.

My counsellor started, as always, by asking what had happened since our last session. It reminded me of the dreadful essay set at the beginning of each new school term: 'What I did in my holidays'. I had also grown to hate all the counselling standard techniques, in particular 'Reflecting back'. The counsellor repeats back what the client has just said. In the jargon, 'this makes people feel heard'. I've used it plenty of times myself but now the tables are turned and I feel trapped in a bizarre comedy sketch.

'It's been tough.'

'So, it's been tough.'

'I'm glad it's over.'

'You're glad it's over.'

'Yes.'

'I see.'

Worse still, I am struggling with questions like:

Was Thom destined to die or just unlucky?

Is there a purpose to all my struggling?

What happens when we die?

But all my counsellor can offer is: 'How do you feel?'

I saw only one couple at Relate, in the evening. My supervisor thought it best to break me in gently. They arrived full of hope but I felt a bit of a fraud. For over ten years, I have seen counselling as the salvation for my clients. Oh dear.

Tuesday 13 January

Kathy Reichs has a professional interest in death. She is a forensic anthropologist and spends her life minutely examining corpses to expose any foul play. She also has a book to promote – a thriller called *Déjà Dead* – based on her fifteen years working for the Laboratoire de sciences judiciaires et de médecine légale in the Canadian province of Quebec (North America's oldest forensic science laboratory). My interest in death is purely personal, although I do have an article to write for *The Independent*.

Death is not a topic that most people are willing to discuss. Although none of my friends have said it directly, I sense their uneasiness about my need to talk and still talk about Thom. So in a strange way I was looking forward to meeting Ms Reichs.

I hoped that with somebody who performs eighty autopsies a year, I would no longer feel a pariah. If I was being scrupulously honest, I also confess the wish that I had not left so quickly after Thom's death.

The morning after Thom died, when Walter and I returned to the hospital, we were invited to view the body. He accepted but I stayed behind to collect up Thom's belongings. At the time, I reasoned: why torture yourself? Today, however, I am not so sure. Walter reported that they had put a flower into Thom's hands and that he looked calm. I found that hard to believe. So I left without viewing the body and subsequently have all these questions: what kind of flower? Do corpses really look peaceful? What happens to a body after the person to whom it belonged no longer needs it? Kathy Reichs might just have some answers.

We met in the lobby of a hotel near Victoria Station. Her PR ordered tea and Reichs started passing on some tricks of her trade. To clean away rotting flesh and allow a closer examination of a skeleton, she recommends immersing it in Spic and Span – a brand of US household cleaner. Apparently you should not use hot water. The process works best at a slightly lower temperature.

'I am normally quite clinical,' she said. 'I have observations and measurements to make. There is a report to be written too. Although I never want to dehumanise and become totally detached.'

I found it hard to understand how she could be so cool but decided to be professional and try to keep focused on the interview.

'You need to know the context of a find,' she explained. 'Was it on the surface, was it buried? Was it in the water, how acidic was the soil? Did you have scavenging animals? If I have information along those lines I can date the body. However, once all the tissues are gone it is harder to tell whether it is ten years or thirty years old.' Her tone was always that of a scientist. 'I have a case at the moment. We know who it is, when she died and how.

There are six bullet holes in her head. She was dismembered and thrown in a lake. The question here is what kind of tool was used. I will be focusing on the traces left by the knife or the saw.'

Try as I might, I couldn't keep my questions away from spiritual matters. I was surprised to discover that Ms Reichs has not yet decided whether there is life after death. Amazingly enough, someone who has to take all her street clothes off and wears surgical scrubs so as not to reek of her most decayed customers, had never given the topic even passing consideration. When I asked if she thought the previous owners of the bodies she is piecing back together might be looking down and watching as she works, Reichs looked at me if as if I had arrived from another planet. I hope I had not given her nightmares.

We found something in common after I told her I could not take A-level Biology because it involved dissecting rats. She confessed that at her school they worked on frogs but unable to kill hers, she liberated it into her back garden. So what drives her to do her job? She thought for a moment:

'I get a lot of satisfaction out of contributing to giving somebody an identity. To giving a family closure. To be able to say: "Your missing daughter is here, we've identified her." I hate to ever let anybody be buried as a Jane Doe. I also like going to court and testifying so a murderer can be got off the streets. I worked on a serial case, which gave me a theme for the book. The killer, who is now serving three life sentences, was arrested for one murder and admitted killing another woman two years earlier. He dismembered her body and buried it in plastic sacks at five different locations.'

I wondered how she felt meeting someone after hours and hours sifting through their gruesome handiwork.

'I usually feel totally underwhelmed. You look at these nondescript little guys who could be your uncle.'

Kathy Reichs and I might not have seen eye to eye but meeting her did help me to heal. Her biological approach allowed me to finally detach Thom's spirit from the body that I dared not view. Although I had intellectually known this before, by metaphorically looking over Ms Reich's shoulder I was able to make an important internal shift. Her book has already been to the top of the American and Canadian book charts and her PR expects a similar trick in the UK. I would like to think this a sign that we are becoming more honest and able to look death straight in the eye. But I doubt it.

Friday 23 January

The producers of Channel Four's *The Big Breakfast* are looking for an agony uncle for a slot with their host Denise Van Outen. I had my screen test today. It was just a researcher with a hand-held camera asking what advice I'd give for certain problems. I think it went well. I hope it went well. This could be the moment that my career finally takes off and I can stop worrying that my latest commission to write an article could be my last.

Sunday 25 January

One of my regular partners at line dancing claims to be psychic. In the break, he asked what I'd been up to this week and I let slip about my audition. I was sort of hoping that he might give me a clue as to the outcome. Immediately, I hated myself. First, for believing that he might know. Second, for wanting the job so badly. I needn't have worried because he was completely blank on the audition.

'It doesn't matter,' I lied.

'Don't worry about my plant. The rain has fixed it.'

It was my turn to look blank. Fortunately, the pause was over and the DJ had announced a Sixteen Step.

'Shall we?' I asked.

When I told the story to Maureen, expecting her to laugh at my stupidity, she went very quiet.

'What's the matter?'

'It's Thom's plant. At least that's what I call it.'

'Sorry?'

'You gave it to me to say thank you for my help with his memorial service. It's in a tub on my patio but I thought it was going to die.'

'When was this?'

'Remember I couldn't come to the scattering of his ashes because I was ill?'

'The weather turned bad and we thought we were going to drop off the edge.'

'Like the psychic said all that rain "fixed" Thom's plant. It's flourishing now.'

Wednesday 28 January

Ingrid Miller, Kate's replacement on the TV show, has decided that she cannot cope with *Agony* any longer. She already has a comment column in the *Star* and an agony column in a weekly magazine, so today was her last show. I found it strange that there were no auditions arranged for her replacement, but I had an appointment with the boss of Live TV after our recordings – perhaps he would explain. At the last minute, he asked Patricia to join us.

He calmly thanked us for all our hard work and told us that they were using the opportunity to replace the whole team. We were effectively fired. The whole meeting took less than five minutes. I tried to be philosophical. We'd had a long run but as a freelancer, I need my regular slots.

Patricia and I were meeting Kate for cocktails at the Savoy. It seemed like a hopeless indulgence for someone who had lost almost half his regular income but we needed a drink. Kate's response to the news was typical:

'Don't worry. Something will turn up.'

I do love her.

Thursday 29 January

Every time the phone rang, I thought: this time it must be the producers of *The Big Breakfast*. I really need that job. In the middle of the afternoon, I let the phone ring a couple of extra times – this was it, I told myself, 'Don't be too keen.'

It was the library informing me that the book that I'd ordered had arrived. Finally, I cracked and phoned the researcher. From the tone of her voice, I could tell she had already lost interest in the project.

'I don't know if we're going to do that segment now.'

Goodbye career breakthrough.

After yesterday, goodbye career.

Monday 9 February

I told my counsellor that I don't think I want any further sessions.

'So you feel you have come to an accommodation with your feelings and have no further problems,' he suggested.

I nodded. The reality is that I have a million problems, I just don't think counselling will help. But I kept quiet. It did not seem fair to vent my frustration on my counsellor. I could have just as easily directed it at myself. I've always thought counselling was the magic cure.

Walking back from the health centre, I have a flashback. One of the private rooms off the hospital corridor in Herdecke is wide open and I glance in as I stride past on my way to seeing Thom. For just a second, my eyes meet those of two men inside. One is in the bed and the other sitting on a chair. Patient and visitor. Except neither looked particularly healthy, almost as if the roles could be reversed by a day, a month or an opportunist infection. It is amazing what you can know in a second. Something about my steps on the linoleum had made them look up. Both gay, but friends rather than lovers. An everyday hospital tableau. Except for their hungry eyes that registered even five steps past the door. Almost as if we'd met in a gay bar on the way to the toilets or to get another drink. Eyes that said I'm available. I want you. Except these were jealous eyes. Maybe envious that Thom and I had each other while they were essentially alone. Although now when I look back, I cannot help wondering if they were jealous of my health, my luck, my ability to walk past the door. There are times when I'm so ashamed, so guilty, so grateful.

Tuesday 10 February

I interviewed the actress Annette Crosbie (best known for playing Margaret Meldrew in the sitcom *One Foot in the Grave*) for 'Revelations'. She turned out to be a very private person and only agreed to be interviewed to highlight how greyhound racing abuses dogs.

'When I'm in a play I don't even put up good luck cards in my dressing room in case they reveal too much about me,' she explained.

Her campaign had given her life a raison d'être that acting had never provided.

'I will most probably go to my grave being angry,' she said. 'Sometimes I think it must be wonderful to go through life without constantly having adrenaline pumping through your veins. It keeps me alive and vibrant but it's also very wearing. I can get very, very upset. But I feel I have no choice, this is the way I am made. At least now with the greyhounds I've finally found somewhere to channel my energy.'

After the interview, I told her about my constant need to write about Thom.

'But someone might read it.' She looked at me with incredulity.

Later, I saw the copy of *She* with my article about Thom's death was on the newsstands. It was titled: 'Why I Want to Die Alone' and featured a black and white picture of a woman taken in a Berlin clinic that 'captured the moment just after death'. I quickly turned the page and then turned back again. She did look peaceful but so very young.

Thursday 12 February

A couple of weeks ago, I interviewed the playwright Mark Ravenhill and was amused to discover that he came from Haywards Heath – just a couple of stops up the line from my station. The PR offered tickets for his play *Shopping and F***ing* at the Queen's Theatre in the West End.

Today, Tom Flood and I went to see the play which has a reputation for being so 'in yer face' that one of the cast of the Welsh production walked out in protest. Although there was plenty of violence, I found the play uplifting. An urban fairytale with a message: if you keep on telling the story sometimes the ending can change.

Saturday 14 February

Valentine's Day was suffocating. All the newspapers and radio stations were full of love messages: 'Fluffy Rabbit loves the Big

Hunter, Sweetpea loves Daddy Bear, Cuddlepuss cannot live without Dog's Breath' – OK I made up the last one, but there were more code names than MI5's annual convention. I tried to pretend that I didn't care about receiving a Valentine – the day is not as commercial in Germany and beyond a card we didn't bother – but who am I fooling.

Today the world was divided into the haves and the have-nots and this year I belong firmly to the second category. A journalist phoned me up for a quote and I tried to be detached and funny:

'If love was a car, we certainly would refuse a ride; look at the accident rate, almost fifty per cent of all relationships end in divorce. But oblivious to all the pile-ups we drive past on the other side of the road our hearts full of flowers, cuddly toys and chocolates.'

I want to preach the gospel of self-reliance, stand on my own two feet, enjoy my independence – but the truth is, independence is grossly overestimated.

Richard, my childhood friend, and I had agreed to go out tonight and he suggested *Amy's View* – the David Hare play at the Aldwych Theatre with Judi Dench and Samantha Bond. Once again, there was something liberating about watching people on stage struggling to change and grow. Especially when I feel so stuck myself. I had no idea that the character Amy died in the play, or I would probably not have agreed to go, but the play had an important message about carrying on after loss, and more about mother and child relationships than was entirely comfortable. In the programme, David Hare wrote about his first experience of art with a capital A and his belief in its power to give shape and purpose to our lives.

After the theatre, we went for something to eat. All the restaurants were themed for Valentine's night and it took us a while to find somewhere with a table:

'Restaurant owners must love tonight.'

'Surprisingly, the profits are down.' Richard runs a catering business, so he should know. 'Instead of jolly tables of four or six, which would probably drink four plus bottles of wine, you have all these tables for two with a glass of champagne each and if you're lucky sharing a bottle of wine.'

We opened up the special 'Lover's menu' where everything had been themed red and pink.

'I doubt the food will be much good either.'

He was right. The salmon d'amour – bits of smoked salmon forced into a heart shape – had too much mayonnaise.

'They'll probably think that we're lovers,' I whispered.

'I doubt it,' replied Richard. 'We're talking to each other.'

I laughed. It was not just that he was right, I still felt high on the promise that people – at least on stage – can change.

Even better, a night at the theatre is cheaper than an hour of counselling.

Monday 16 February

One of the advantages of being a journalist is being sent random bits of information. In my pile of 'possibly interesting' press releases was one from the London New Play Festival about their writing school. So I hooked it out and phoned my friend Elaine to ask if she fancied coming too. (She has been writing a sitcom based in a Welsh funeral directors'.) Unfortunately, Elaine cried off but I felt strongly enough to phone the number provided and ask about the first day: Introduction to Playwriting.

I explained my background but that I had done no creative writing. Would I be able to cope? The director of the London New Play Festival was so encouraging, I signed up for the full five days.

If watching plays is therapeutic, it might be even better to put my demons on stage, stand back and see what happens.

Wednesday 18 February

I met Kate at the Savoy. She had just been for another reading with the Munchkin and once again had a message from Thom. I was not certain whether to laugh or cry. During Kate's many visits to mediums and clairvoyants, it was almost impossible for her to discover anything without Thom bursting into the conversation.

If there is a heaven, I picture it with lots of telephone kiosks where you can put your twenty pence in the slot and talk to your loved ones down on earth. Thom seems to be forever barging to the front of the queue and knocking on the glass to signal his impatience. When Kate's relatives open the door to explain they won't be long, Thom pushes in and grabs the receiver.

'He says there's no need to go to Beachy Head, if you don't want to. He's with you all the time,' Kate relayed from the Munchkin.

I was quite astounded she could actually name the place where I have scattered Thom's ashes; the old familiar pain swelled up and I began to cry. Knowing he is watching seemed such scant comfort, I wanted to be able to touch him, hold conversations with him and have a jolly good row for dying on me!

'He also tells you not to worry about the party, it will be fine,' Kate continued.

This was more comforting news. I had thought long and hard about how to mark the anniversary of his death. I toyed with going abroad but I've learned that wherever I go the memory of Thom comes with me – the clairvoyant was certainly right about him never being far away. It would be better, and certainly cheaper, to stay home. At least I'd have the comfort of familiar surroundings – the opposite of when Thom died. However, a large party was not very appealing either. I would be under too much stress to stuff vol-au-vents and worry how well everybody was mixing.

So I have settled on a compromise: a small dinner party with close friends. In what felt a very grown-up idea, I booked caterers. But I suppose at thirty-eight, I finally qualify as an adult.

I sent out the following:

— ❧❧ —

Invitation

To........................

The time: Monday 9 March 1998 at 7.30 p.m.
The place: xxxxxxxxxxxxxxxxxx
The occasion: Dinner Party

We will be marking the passing of one year since Thom's death by raising a glass and a full fork in his memory. I would also like everybody to bring something appropriate for the occasion. It could be a poem or a short excerpt from a book, a piece of music, a picture, a memory to share, a clip of video or even a piece of performance art! The choice is yours.

RSVP

— ❧❧ —

That should get my friends talking about Thom. I'm fed up with them shying away whenever his name is mentioned.

Saturday 21 February

Before Thom's anniversary dinner party, I invited round two sets of neighbours for a meal and managed to use up some of the ingredients that had been mocking me from the storecupboard.

For Spezzatini di Vitello, I needed funghi porcini and a jar of gourmet beef stock all of which were almost at their use-by dates.

Our conversation was full of village tittle-tattle but one topic leapt out and encapsulated my mood. Michael Smith told a story about a village that he, and his wife, Jackie, had visited in Spain where instead of burying their dead they cemented the bodies into a wall. On the first anniversary of the death, relatives retrieve their loved one and take them home for the day. I could picture the villagers with the dead body as guest of honour propped up in a chair. There would be singing and dancing – perhaps even with the body. All in all, it seemed a wonderful way to celebrate surviving a year without someone you loved.

Perhaps I have not heard from my friends about Thom's first anniversary dinner party because they had also heard this story and fear I am secretly Spanish. The village might be apocryphal, but I could picture the olive trees and the simple stone buildings. I know the inhabitants laugh more than they cry.

Unthinkingly, I had followed Thom's strategies for throwing a successful evening: loading the dishwasher after the main course; clearing the table rather than going to bed when the guests left. Whether the clairvoyants are correct and Thom has become my guardian spirit is not important, he is always with me. I have integrated his personality into mine and in that way he lives on through me.

Wednesday 25 February

The twenty strong congregation was much younger than I expected with only a few old ladies and lots of men. The room was long and narrow, half meeting hall and half church.

Obsessed with the idea that Thom might want to say something on the first anniversary of his death, I had called Roy and asked him to take me to a Spiritualist service. I took my coat off; it was far warmer than any Anglican church I'd ever sat in. The service was led by an elderly woman and a man around forty who Roy informed me was making his debut as a platform medium. I wonder who was the most anxious, him or me.

After hymns, prayers and a sermon, it was time for a demonstration of powers. Unfortunately our inexperienced medium was extremely nervous and seemed unable to make connections, although the people he singled out almost turned somersaults in their attempts to make sense of his messages. By this point I had relaxed, Thom was never somebody to wait in queues – he would either have been first on or not bothered at all. Slightly embarrassed the trainee medium sat down and his mentor took over, her first message was for a lady at the front – apparently her mother was there. After reassuring the daughter there will be a new man, eventually, the medium announced there was time for one final message for the man at the back. I turned round to look at him and realised: I was the man at the back!

Of course I expected Thom, but she had a man in his fifties. (Thom was only forty-three and often taken for younger!)

'It's somebody who is family,' the medium explained.

I was desperately trying to remember how old my uncle had been when he died.

'Do the names Jeremy and James mean anything?' My confusion increased (later I remembered that Jeremy was a mutual friend of both Roy and I. My nephew is called James.) My natural scepticism was growing stronger.

'He loved white lilies, there were white lilies on his coffin,' she said. Thom had indeed loved lilies and his coffin was covered with one huge arrangement; tears start pouring down my face. It was as if every one of my senses had been plugged into a larger universe. Everybody else seemed to fly out of the room and I became so connected to this elderly woman I could almost touch

Andrew Marshall

every colour around us more vibrant.

'He really loved you,' she explained. 'You're being messed
around at work?'

I nodded.

'Don't worry – that will soon sort itself out.'

As she spoke, she tilted her head in just the way that Thom
would have done and her voice took on the same rhythm as his.
The energy I could sense was Thom's love, a warm ray beaming
from his heart to mine.

It was an incredibly beautiful moment.

I no longer felt like a motherless child.

I was so close to Thom I could reach out and touch the hem
of his coat.

Yet, he also appeared far away – the long meeting room had
been stretched until it became a corridor into infinity.

Suddenly my time with Thom was over, the medium asked
us to pray and I was snapped back in a rather ordinary room
behind a parade of shops in Brighton. I shuddered, understanding just how addictive visiting mediums could be. Whether it
was self-deception or something close to a miracle – I had felt
reunited with Thom. He has spoken to me and I'd basked in his
love again, but immediately I wanted more, more, more. Yet even
sitting in the Spiritualist Meeting Rooms some rational part of
my personality understood that, in the long term, I would receive
far more happiness moving forward rather than forever trying to
recapture that nirvana. But it was so, so tempting.

We returned to Roy's flat and telephoned for an Indian take-
away. Over tandoori chicken pasanda our conversation took
some very bizarre turns. During our general chit-chat, Roy suddenly broke off and started addressing spirits he claimed had followed me into his seaview flat.

'Hello,' he said to something standing over my left shoulder.

'I can't tell him that!' he told another unseen creature.

After supper, Ray allowed me to curl up in his arms on the sofa. He ran his hand through my hair and I felt more connected to the world than I had in months.

'You always think that your task was to look after Thom and help him through his last few weeks,' said Roy.

I nodded.

'Have you ever considered it might be the other way round? Perhaps the two of you fell in love and created your strong bond so that when he died he would have the power to look after and guide you.'

If true, Thom was the perfect guardian angel. He never did anything by halves; in fact he was such a compulsive shopper I've only just finished using up all his skin creams.

I wanted to believe Roy, but he interrupted my thoughts.

'The ceiling has gone all spongy, I think that means it's time for you to leave.'

Friday 27 February

Kate, Patricia and I had lunch at the Bluebird Café on the King's Road in London on a special deal thanks to collecting vouchers from *The Independent*. Apparently, Princess Anne and her bodyguards took advantage of the same scheme. Afterwards, I interviewed the actress Samantha Bond for 'Revelations'.

Kate hopes to make Thom's anniversary dinner but might be doing the breakfast show on Talk Radio that week. Although we started making the television show two and a half months before he died, Kate never met Thom. He didn't even answer the phone when she called me, and therefore never had the opportunity to exchange a few words with her before passing her over to me. Certainly he watched the video of our show, so saw the two of us work together and I've shown Kate pictures of him. I don't know why but the thought that they had no direct contact is very painful.

No replies yet to my invitation; I was worried that they had got lost in the post. So I made some calls, one friend seemed particularly uncomfortable.

'I don't know if I can cope.'

'What do you think it is like for me?' I wanted to demand, 'I have no choice – I have to attend the first anniversary, I can't do it alone.'

But I just muttered how I understood and how I hoped that she would come.

Tom Flood was more sympathetic:

'Friendships that made sense when you are one half of a couple fall to pieces when somebody is missing.'

When two couples are together the conversation flows effortlessly, but when one member of the group steps into the kitchen the conversation sometimes flounders. Everybody smiles and ignores the difficulty but take an inward sigh when the fourth person returns. Sometimes I feel that all my friendships have been fractured and can never be the same again. Surprisingly, the people most willing to talk about Thom are my new friends.

Thursday 5 March

There has been feedback from my article in *She* about bereavement. Rosalind, the deputy editor, forwarded some of the letters.

'I was travelling to Birmingham on the train and purchased the latest SHE for one and a half hours of unadulterated "reading heaven". Halfway through this article, I had tears streaming down my face and was hastily trying to wipe them away before anyone noticed. I've always been both fixated and scared with death and dying but this article really demystified it as well as being totally honest.'

'My husband died of cancer two months ago and I was with him throughout his illness and I was beside him in our own bed when he died. However, I felt that I let him down at the very end because I fell asleep. When I woke up, I found that he had died. I felt that I had missed my chance to say goodbye or even hold his hand. Reading your article has made me realise that my husband, who was a very private person, would not have wanted it that way but rather to have gone as he did, quietly with me at his side.'

'How refreshing to read an article about death which was sensitive about the many issues raised. It was remarkably honest about the feelings involved. My mother died when I was sixteen. Her death was not discussed in the family. The result for me was a struggle with years of depression. I have discussed death openly with my own children and find that they have a natural acceptance of death. I believe that we need to be more open and honest about death. It is, after all, the only thing that we can all be sure of facing one day.'

Not every letter was so positive:

'The article was very potent and one could choose whether or not to read it - but the photograph was presented starkly and with no escape for anyone who did not want to have such an image thrust upon them with no warning. I have, in recent years, chosen to look upon people very close to me in death. I would not choose to look at photographs. I am quite put off SHE for what I consider a real error of judgement.'

Friday 6 March

The build up to the anniversary of the worst day of my life has been less fraught than I expected. By a stroke of good luck, Tyson's owners are away for the weekend so he's been staying again. Maybe his companionship has helped calm me down.

Originally, I had planned to unveil the painting of Thom as my contribution for Monday's anniversary dinner. Unfortunately, the artistic muse does not work to a timetable, so I asked Gary Sollars if I could borrow one of his other works. He was not keen, after all these canvases are his 'Little Treasures'. However, I agreed to use his regular transporters and his latest painting, *Sundreamin*, was delivered this afternoon and features two young men, one clothed and one naked, lying on the grass. It is bold, beautiful and full of life. So I have great hopes for my painting of Thom. I spent half an hour looking at *Sundreamin* but then covered it up, in case I become too attached.

Monday 9 March 1998

I read my diary entry for last year. Although I re-experienced the pain and wept yet again, I had the comfort of knowing how far I have come. After breakfast, I phoned Thom's parents. Of course both his mother and I cried. I had forgotten about the gift of the daffodils from Thom's room, but Erwin had planted the bulbs in a container on their patio. To mark Thom's first anniversary, Ursula told me, they had re-sprouted and their beautiful yellow crowns were a source of great solace.

If Thom did have to die, perhaps spring was a good time to go – as Kate suggested. It is a time of renewal after the bleak winter. I hoped that Thom, wherever he is, feels reborn – at least he is released from his swollen and painful body.

After calling Germany, I played Mary Chapin Carpenter's 'Stones in the Road' for the first time since Herdecke. I found my pressed daffodil bloom and ran my finger gently over it. Inspired, I walked up to the village greengrocer's and bought their complete stock of daffodils and filled every vase, bucket and wine cooler in the house. Just looking at the flowers, I felt full of hope.

Tyson was restless and although I had already walked him across the fields behind the house, he was keen to be outdoors again. After days of rain and hailstones, the clouds had cleared. The sky was a wonderful shade of blue, if I was a decorator I would instantly want to paint it across every room in the house. It was a perfect spring morning.

Despite my message from Kate, via the Munchkin, I knew the best place to remember Thom would be Beachy Head. As soon as we arrived, I let Tyson off the lead. He bounded across the expanse of green and I indulged myself by stopping to stare. I had never seen Beachy Head look more beautiful. A cool breeze danced across my face and the birdsong swelled my heart. I took deep breaths of fresh air, both my lungs and my whole body soared. Thom had chosen well.

I had saved a couple of bunches of daffodils to scatter at the spot where we released Thom's ashes to the four strong winds. I threw a bloom in the breeze. Tyson, thinking we were playing a game, ran after the daffodil, grabbed it and came running back with the flower jiggling up and down in his mouth. He was so pleased with himself and so like a demented Latin lover trying to woo his lady, that I could not help laughing.

There was no rush to return home, so I put the dog on the lead and crossed over the road for a brisk walk along the coast path. However, I did not get far. Instead, I found myself transfixed at the lookout point, staring into the horizon, just as Thom would have done. Coming from the centre of Germany, many miles away from the sea, he had really enjoyed living in Sussex and would often drive down to the coast just to watch the waves pound the cliff defences. Tyson, however, was impatient to be let off the lead and explore. As cliffs descended steeply along this section of Beachy Head, rather than a straight drop, I decided it would be safe. Tyson shot off to explore a thicket at the bottom of the cliff face. The angle of the hill was close to eighty degrees, so he must have picked up an incredible pace. Soon he was just a speck on the horizon. For a moment I wondered if I would have to climb down and fetch him. Fortunately, he soon became bored with chasing rabbits and started back up the cliff at his usual sprint, but after a few yards he slowed down to a trot and by the time he reached me again was panting heavily. I had to admire his courage at just throwing himself into life, bounding up to every dog even though they often rebuffed him. Dogs live 100 per cent in the moment, I wish I could learn the trick.

By contrast, I was thinking of previous trips to Beachy Head with Thom and, in particular, when his parents visited England. His father had stood at the same spot and looked over at the Seven Sisters:

'The last time I saw those white cliffs, I was in an army trying to invade your country.'

I tried to find out more but Erwin just smiled. He did not want to take the conversation any further. What would he have thought if some Munchkin had predicted that one day he'd walk over the cliffs with his son's gay lover? What would he say, if he knew that his son's ashes would be scattered there too. It is just as well that we cannot see into our future.

The pub at the top of Beachy Head is part of a chain. Doubting Tyson would be welcome, I decided to lunch at Birling Gap. It had been a pleasant morning but I still had one regret: there had been no connection with Thom. I could have tried talking to him, but feared any words would just be blown out to sea and be wasted.

However, sitting in the bar at Birling Gap waiting for my food, Tyson lying quietly under the table and my mind in neutral, suddenly above the smell of cigarettes and stale beer, there was a burst of vanilla. Thom was with me and watching me. My eyes watered but I was supremely grateful. I might not be able to touch him, or speak to him but we are truly together for ever.

With the spring sunshine warming my face, I relaxed with a walk along the beach while Tyson chased seagulls. Afterwards I drove to the goats' farm to look at Thom's memorial tree. It had survived the winter and the buds showed the first signs of exploding new life. I was feeling mellow by the time I arrived home and was thrilled to find a bouquet of flowers had been delivered. Tearing open the attached card, I discovered they were from Jackie, Maureen's daughter, to let me know that she was thinking of Thom. The second post had also brought a card from the receptionist who used to be on duty when I counselled. She had perhaps only met Thom on a half dozen occasions. There was something very touching about such unexpected people remembering and being affected by his life. Not surprisingly, I wept yet again.

Unfortunately, there were also two messages on my answering machine from friends apologising that work would stop them coming. Quite unreasonably, I felt rejected. Bereavement is still making me sensitive to any possible slight. Just as I think I'm coasting, I'm reminded just how far I really have to travel.

There was little time for self-flagellation because the caterer arrived and I had to show her where everything is kept. The menu was fan of avocado pear with fresh crab and lobster meat accompanied by a salad and raspberry coulis; venison ragout with dried fruit served with mashed potato and green beans and, finally, winter pudding made from cranberries and blueberries. Once the caterer had started, I picked up Joan Crawford's book of advice for gracious living: *My Way of Life*. I'd recently bought it from a secondhand store because it would have appealed to Thom's sense of humour. I turned to her section on entertaining:

'You may hire a maid to help with serving and clearing away, but don't pretend she's permanent help.'

I made a mental note to remember that gem, but drew the line at Joan's other advice:

'If you can spare a few extra dollars, there should be a bartender for the first part of your party. No man can enjoy himself if he's glued to the bar mixing drinks.'

Such good advice, it was a shame Thom never had a chance to read it. He certainly agreed with Joan's hatred of wire coat hangers. In the film *Mommie Dearest,* based on Christina Crawford's memoir of her mother, there is a famous scene where the actress playing Joan wakes her up her daughter and screams: 'No wire hangers ever.' She then beats her with an offending hanger. Whenever Thom would give me grief for sneaking any into our cupboard. I would taunt him:

'You're probably the only child that could have grown up in Joan Crawford's household without getting a slapping.'

The first guest to arrive was Kate, who decided at the last minute to drive down from London. She was followed closely by everyone else. It seemed strange to have all my closest friends together round the dinner table again, if I closed my eyes I could imagine we were celebrating Thom's birthday. The noises in the kitchen was not the caterer but Thom putting the finishing touches to a special dish.

During the past year I'd entertained, individually, everybody round the table but shied away from this combination. Although Maureen, rather than Thom, was sitting at the other end of my great great grandmother's table, I found that I could bear the anguish. Perhaps this is the reality of mourning: you never get over the loss but reassemble the daily minutiae into a new life. At the beginning it feels like a box of flat-pack furniture with the instructions in Swedish, but finally you discover that tab A can slide into slot B. Eventually you own something quite functional – even though there are always a few screws left over and it never looks as good as it does in the catalogue.

Between each course, somebody marked the year in their chosen way. Elaine sung in cod Latin and Maureen read a poem about forget-me-nots. Tom Flood chose a poem about friendship. As he reached the final line, I realise his brow was furrowed. It is the same poem that he'd read at his partner's funeral, six years ago. I was very touched.

Finally, it was my turn and I unveiled Gary's canvas. At 5ft by 4ft, it made quite an impact. Maureen was particularly impressed by the naked man. The painting's energy filled my living room. The fine brushwork on the legs delineated every hair on the thighs; I longed to run my hands down them and for the day when I can finally hang Thom on my walls.

The conversation naturally moved onto shared memories of Thom, I learned just how much everybody misses him and how each friend is commemorating him. Maureen has filled her courtyard garden with bags and bags of daffodils so that every pot is crammed full of yellow crowns, ensuring that her spring showing will always be dedicated to Thom.

However, the most extraordinary story is from Steve. With Thom being a keep fit fanatic, Steve finds it inspirational to talk to his photo as he works out each day on his cross-country ski machine. However, this morning, Steve felt Thom spoke back and asked him to bring 'his song' to the dinner party. I immediately know what his song should be – Mama Cass and 'Dream a Little Dream of Me'.

Thom learned English partly by singing along to her songs so perhaps his first words were: 'Stars shining bright above you'. I'm sure he believed the stars were bigger and brighter in the Californian night sky. When his dream of visiting America finally came true and we drove together down the Pacific Coast Highway from San Francisco to Los Angeles, our soundtrack was a cassette he'd specially recorded of the Beach Boys, Cass Elliot and the Mamas and Papas. With his Ray-Bans on, tapping the wheel of our LeBaron hire car, Thom sung along at the top of his voice to every song. The scenery was stunning; being British I often wanted to stop and admire, but Thom had inherited the love of eight-lane highways and wanted us to just keep moving on. He understood: the journey is more important than where we are going; the joy of travelling matters more than our final destination.

Steve had not been able to attend either Thom's funeral or the scattering of his ashes, so he was not aware that the song was played on both occasions. So what would Steve believe Thom asked him to play? Rather than revealing the track's name, Steve just put on the CD and let the song introduce itself. I held my breath. From the first gentle strum of the guitar, I recognised 'Dream a Little Dream of Me'.

We sat in silence and listened and I imagined Thom hearing this song for the first time. The Mamas and Papas and their songs like 'California Dreaming' would offer the promise of open-top sports cars, ice-cream sundaes and endless beaches. What a Technicolor world it must have been for a boy born into monochrome Germany just eight years after the war ended, a country where rabbits were not kept as pets but for meat and gardens were full of vegetables rather than flowers.

There are many rational ways to explain Steve's choice. For example, he could have spoken to another friend who told him about the memorial service and logged the information away in his subconscious. However, it is far more interesting, far more beautiful, if Thom really had whispered the title into Steve's ear.

I hadn't thought of playing Cass, but Thom was right; his first anniversary would not be complete without her. Up to this moment, I'd needed scientific proof to truly believe in life after death and that everything on earth has a purpose. However, listening to 'Dream a Little Dream of Me', I chose to be a believer.

Thom had received one of my invitations and decided to attend.

Until the final bars faded away, Thom felt among us – a beautiful gift.

Next, my guests asked to hear Judy Collins sing 'Four Strong Winds' from the memorial service. The song is about two lovers parting, but the singer promises: 'I'll look for you, if I'm ever back this way.' I had to smile, it seems that Thom is always looking us up.

Being a weeknight, most of my guests left early but Steve stayed to chat. I had not seen much of him since he parted from his long-term lover. He was keen to tell me he has fallen in love again, this time with an Internet buddy. They had exchanged emails, liked what they read and eventually decided to meet as friends – with no pressure for anything else. However, the chemistry was too strong and they hung a 'Do not disturb' on their hotel room door for most of the weekend. I was pleased, partly because I want the best for my friends, but more importantly Steve has given me hope that someday I will love again.

Tuesday 10 March

I come downstairs to the washing up but with contentment still singing in my heart. The warmth of the central heating has brought the remaining daffodils into full glorious bloom. The air is heavy with their heady aroma. I feel that I have opened up too. My blood is coursing right round my body even into areas that Thom's death closed down. It might sound strange, but until you've lost part of yourself, you cannot recognise what it feels like to be whole again.

AFTER

Twenty years on, I am surprised by how many ingredients for my recovery were already in place. I did the playwriting course and, for the next twelve months, wrote about nothing but death and loss – but it helped get something out of my system. I decided to get a dog of my own and first Flash and then Pumpkin have brought life and joy into the house. Most important, I have a new partner: Ignacio (and the garage is now home to his motorbike rather than Thom's boxes). We met in late 2001, had a civil partnership in 2008 and then got married in 2015.

Recently, Ignacio and I were invited to the wedding of Jürgen's younger son and I saw all of Thom's family again. I've also visited his best friend Walter on a couple of occasions. Thom's name will sometimes come up but I no longer feel the need to cross-examine his family and friends. I also still exchange Christmas cards with Martina, Thom's favourite nurse.

My relationship with my parents continued to get stronger and deeper. They welcomed Ignacio into our family with an open heart and not only attended both our civil partnership and our marriage but helped pay for it. My sister came to both ceremonies and my nephew and niece (and their partners) helped celebrate our wedding.

So what has been the lasting impact of Thom on my life? I think the best way to sum it up is an extract from my diary from December 2007:

Our friend David phoned, while we were in Germany, to say he was back in hospital. On our return, I went to visit. His deterioration had been rapid and at only forty-two, like Thom, he looked like an old man. I stroked his hand while we talked.

'Is there anything you would like from my house?' he asked.

On the spot, I could think of nothing: 'I won't need something to remember you.'

David nodded: 'You remember everything. You're a writer.'

Whether being a writer is a blessing or a curse, I am still not certain. However, I know it would never have happened without having loved and lost Thom.

THIS BOOK ALSO REMEMBERS

James Tait
22 August 1948 to 7 July 2007

Adam Tennant
6 March 1965 to 20 October 2007

David Waghorn
3 February 1965 to 20 December 2007

David Rees
7 August 1915 to 30 May 2011

Frances Esposito
28 May 1954 to 6 December 2012

DRAMATIS PERSONAE

Andreas *German minister.* A friend of Thom's. A guest at the dinner party Thom threw to celebrate his imminent departure for England.

David (Waghorn) *Friend.* A conversation on his deathbed helped me understand Thom's importance in my life. This book is also dedicated to his memory.

Derek (Mason) *My cousin Sue's husband.* His wedding was the first time that Thom met the majority of my extended family.

Elaine (Forster) *Friend and former work colleague.* Elaine worked first on the Action Desk (a community project) and then booking guests for my chat show on Radio Mercury. When the Berlin wall came down, she arranged for Thom to be interviewed about why he was against a swift reunification of Germany.

Erwin (Hartwig) *Thom's father.* He fought for Germany in France and Russia in the Second World War.

Gabi (Hartwig) *Thom's sister-in-law.* A brilliant chef who would inspire some of Thom's best cooking.

Gary (Grant) *Friend.* We met at University when we were both lodgers in the same cold house in Leamington Spa. We have known each other for so long that we were both officially 'straight' when we first met.

Gary (Sollars) *Artist.* He trained at Middlesex University. His exhibitions include *BP Portrait Award* National Portrait Gallery in 1995, 1998 and 2014. *Sussex Open* (winner) Brighton Museum and Art Gallery 1998. His work has been seen in group exhibitions at the Whitworth Art Gallery in Manchester and the Walker Art Gallery in Liverpool.

Gayle *My sister.* She is married with two children and lives two hundred and fifty miles away. I am two and a half years older than her.

Jackie (Ellis) *Friend.* Maureen's daughter.

Jackie (Smith) Neighbour who lives opposite from me.

James *My nephew.* In 1997, he was ten.

Jill (Marshall) *My mother.* A retired teacher.

John (Wellington) *Friend.* He was Programme Controller at Radio Mercury and gave me my first big break in radio. I returned the favour and employed him as a consultant when I had worked for Talk Radio.

John (Brocks) *Friend and former work colleague.* We cooperated on several applications for radio licences.

Jürgen (Hartwig) *Thom's brother.* Four years older than Thom and, at the time of this memoir, a senior manager in the German equivalent of the Civil Aviation Authority.

Heidi (Müller) *One of Thom's best friends.* A psychologist who had lived in Dortmund but had moved to Berlin – hence our trips there – where she had a slot on Breakfast TV.

Ingrid (Miller) *Agony aunt.* Kate's replacement on *Agony*.

Kate (Lloyd-Richardson) *Agony aunt and friend.* Co-advisor on *Agony* TV Show on cable channel Live TV.

Martina (Hahn) *Thom's nurse and subsequently friend.* We still correspond and her relationship with Thom became the inspiration for my first play.

Maureen (Wheeler) *Friend.* Maureen worked on the Action Desk and in many subsequent roles at Radio Mercury.

Martin (Kleinmayer) *Friend.* After Thom moved to England, we would stay in his apartment when we were in Dortmund. His partner, Uwe, lived round the corner.

Michael (Fay) *Next-door neighbour and friend.* A graphic designer, married to Valerie.

Michael (Smith) *Neighbour.* Married to Jackie.

Mike (Atkinson) *Friend.* A builder, husband of Sara Atkinson and owner of Tyson.

Nancy (Roberts) *Friend.* I had employed her when I worked at Talk Radio in the mid-nineties when she hosted a phone-in of medical advice. Originally from America, she moved to Europe when she married her German husband.

Nicki (Brocks) *John Brock's wife.*

Nicola *My niece.* In 1997, she was eight.

Patricia *Hostess of* Agony. The TV show where I recorded five shows a week over an eighteen-month period.

Peter *Subsequent boyfriend after Thom.* A former BT employee who, although only in his fifties, had taken early retirement.

Peter (Hammond) *Friend.* Mainly a friend of mine, we would go out for a drink in Brighton whenever Thom was away, but invited to Thom's last Christmas.

Richard (Groves) *Childhood friend.* We were at school together from the age of seven to eighteen and have remained close ever since. He runs a catering company specialising in large parties, corporate events and weddings.

Richard (Hawkes) *Friend of Tom Flood.* Richard was a neighbour of Tom Flood's. We subsequently became very close friends and this book is also dedicated to his late partner James Tait.

Roy *Spiritualist.* I met him at a Brighton nightclub.

Sara (Atkinson) *Friend.* Neighbour of Maureen and best friend of John Wellington. She worked at Radio Mercury but only after I left. Owner of Tyson.

Sue (Mason) *My cousin.* I lived with Sue and her husband for about three months while I was working at a radio station in London. We were born the same year.

Steve (Blower) *Friend.* He and his lover Andy lived in the next village and almost bought the house next door but Michael and Valerie decided to stay.

Tom (Flood) *Friend.* His partner had died in 1994 and he was the first person to whom I admitted that Thom was seriously ill. He worked in London but also had a flat in Brighton. He would often call in and visit Thom to break this journey. They would listen to opera and talk about everything beyond 'sickness and disease'.

Thom (Hartwig) *Partner.* We met in 1989. He moved to the UK in 1995 and he died in 1997.

Tony (Marshall) *My Father.* A retired accountant.

Ursula (Hartwig) Thom's mother. She had always been very welcoming and on my first visit to Germany invited me to a family celebration (St Martin's Day) at the beginning of December.

Uwe (Kress) *Friend.* He was the lover of Martin whose flat I stayed in while Thom was dying in hospital.

Valerie (Fay) *Friend and next-door neighbour.* A dog lover, married to Michael.

Walter (Führ) *Thom's best friend and a former lover.* A teacher, then in his forties, who had been Thom's boyfriend in the early eighties. I had met Walter on my first trip with Thom to Germany; right from the beginning he was supportive of our relationship, and he and his lover had often been to stay with me and Thom in the UK.

APOLOGIES

To Ignacio, thank you for putting up with my obsessions and bringing so much happiness into my life.

My family will find this book hard to read. To their credit, they have accepted Ignacio and made him extremely welcome. My sister did keep her promise and brought the children to visit, in 1998, and we have a much closer relationship today.

I know my cousin by marriage, Derek Mason, will be upset about upsetting me with his comment about 'new life' at Thom's memorial service. It is impossible to know the right thing to say and personally, I think it is better to risk upset than say nothing. (So good on you, Derek.) The baby in his arms was Lucy. She and her elder sister, Kate, came to Ignacio and my civil partnership ceremony in 2008.

I would also like to apologise to everybody else who has found themselves in this memoir. I must stress this is very much one person's partial opinion and therefore biased, subjective and probably very different from theirs. It is equally important to stress that there were many friends who helped with my recovery who I did not name for fear of overwhelming readers. Your contributions were no less valuable.

Andrew Marshall

BOOK CLUB NOTES

1. How well does our society support people who are bereaved?
2. Why do you think we are not comfortable talking about death?
3. Andrew wrote the book partly to 'stop people making the same mistakes as me'. What do you think he should have done differently?
4. What helped the most in his recovery?
5. If you could have given him some advice, based on your own experiences of bereavement, what would you say?
6. How had Andrew's parents changed from the beginning to the end of the book?
7. How has Andrew been changed?
8. Andrew contacted various mediums. Do you think this is helpful or a hindrance to bereaved people?
9. There is tension in the book between remembering and talking about someone you lost and putting the pain behind you and moving on. Which side of the divide do you favour and why?
10. If you keep a diary, how has writing it changed the way you approach day-to-day life? Would you ever publish it and who do you think would be most upset if he or she read it?

You can see more pictures of Thom and read blogs from Andrew about bereavement by going to his website dedicated to this book. You can also post your thoughts and responses to his journey through bereavement. Please spread the word about this book and if you've found it helpful tell other people who are currently in mourning.

www.mymourningyear.com

TITLES BY ANDREW G. MARSHALL

ANDREW G. MARSHALL

ARE YOU RIGHT FOR ME?

Seven steps to getting clarity and commitment in your relationship

ANDREW G. MARSHALL

BUILD A LIFE-LONG LOVE AFFAIR

Seven steps to revitalising your relationship

ANDREW G. MARSHALL

HEAL AND MOVE ON

Seven steps to recovering from a break-up

ANDREW G. MARSHALL

RESOLVE YOUR DIFFERENCES

Seven steps to dealing with conflict in your relationship

ANDREW G. MARSHALL

LEARN TO LOVE YOURSELF ENOUGH

Seven steps to improving your self-esteem and your relationships

ANDREW G. MARSHALL

HELP YOUR PARTNER SAY 'YES'

Seven steps to achieving better cooperation and communication

ANDREW G. MARSHALL

I LOVE YOU BUT YOU ALWAYS PUT ME LAST

How to childproof your marriage

ANDREW G. MARSHALL

I LOVE YOU BUT I'M NOT IN LOVE WITH YOU

Seven Steps to Saving Your Relationship

ANDREW G. MARSHALL

How Can I Ever Trust You Again?

INFIDELITY:
From Discovery to Recovery in Seven Steps

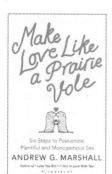

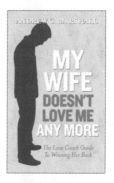

ABOUT THE AUTHOR

Writing as Andrew G. Marshall, Andrew has written eighteen self-help books about relationships – including the international best seller *I Love You but I'm Not in Love with You*. His writing has been translated into twenty different languages. He still writes for newspapers like the *Mail on Sunday* and works as a marital therapist in London and Sussex. There is more information about his work as a marital therapist at www.andrewgmarshall.com